THE SHEELA-NA-GIGS OF IRELAND & BRITAIN
The Divine Hag of the Christian Celts

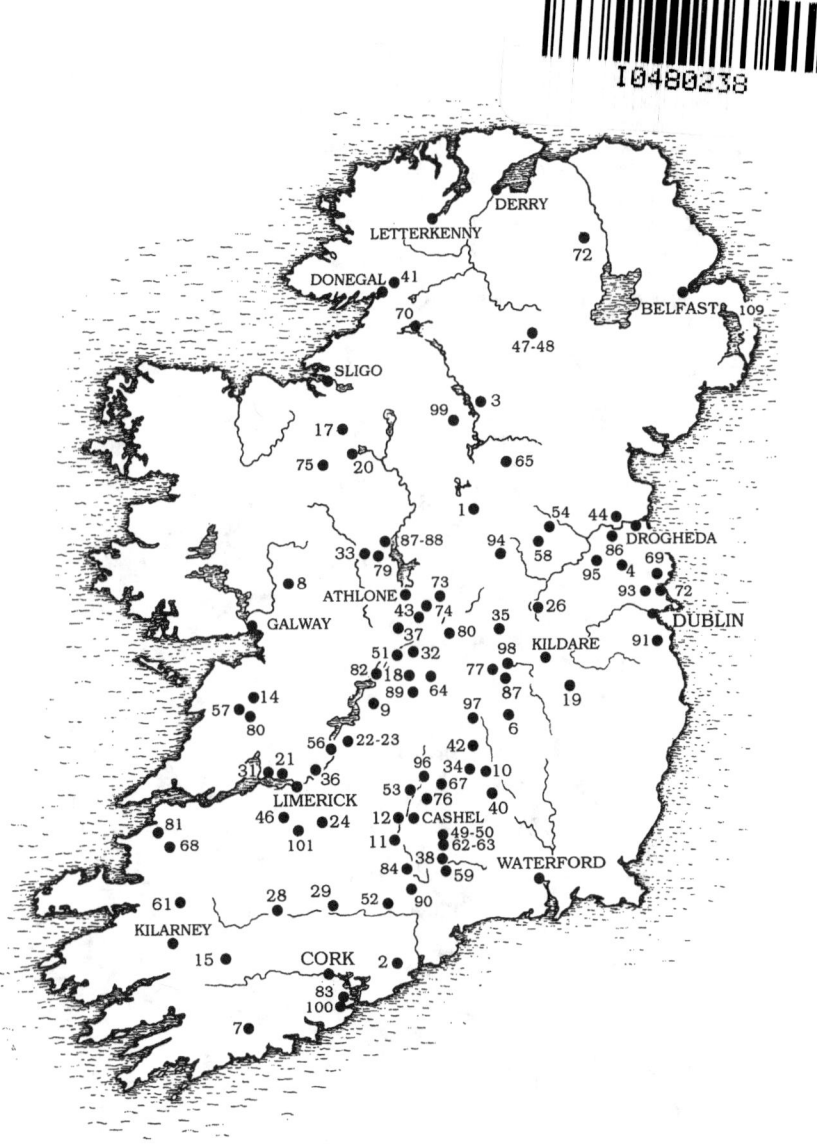

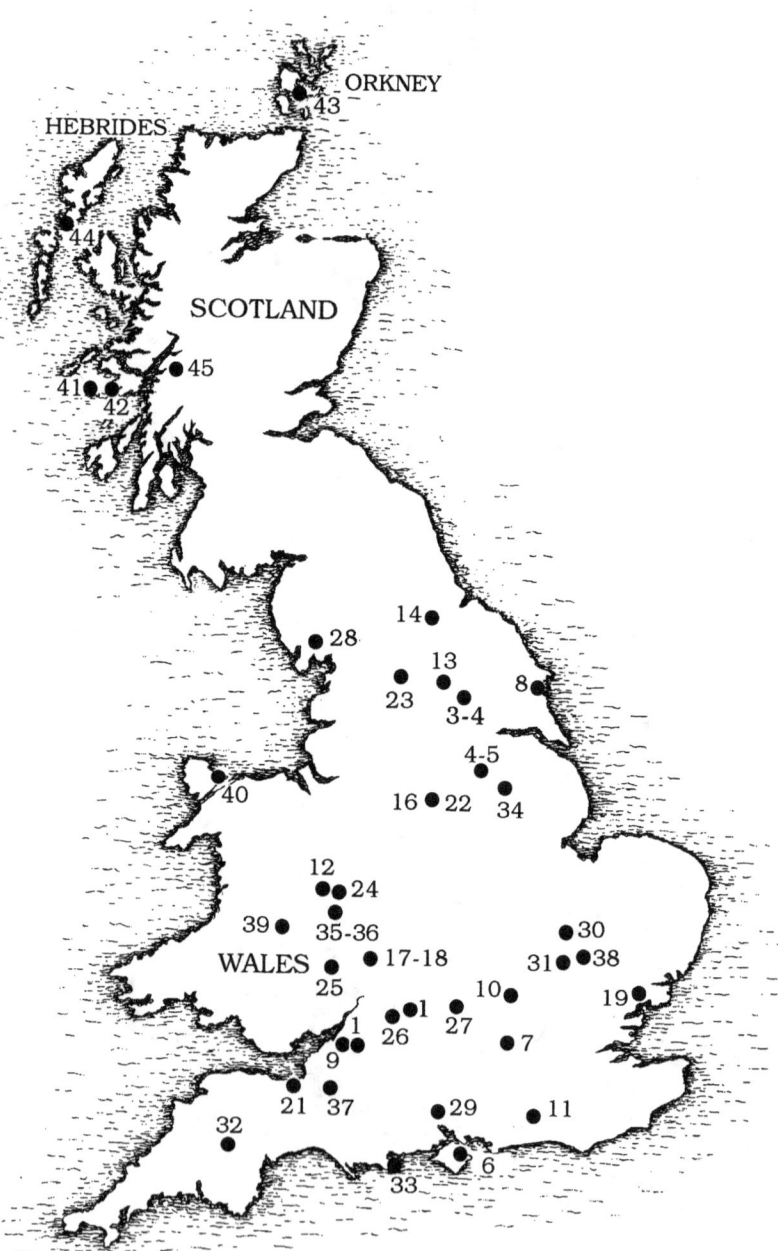

ORKNEY
●43

HEBRIDES

SCOTLAND

●44

41 ●
●42 ●45

14 ●
28 ●
13
●
23 ● 3-4 ● 8 ●
●
4-5 ●
16 ● 22 34
●
12
●
● 24
39 ● 35-36 30
● 31 ●
WALES ● 17-18 ● 38
25 ● 10
19
1 ● ●
9 26 27 7
●
21 37 29 11
32 ●
33 6

THE SHEELA-NA-GIGS
OF
IRELAND & BRITAIN
The Divine Hag of the Christian Celts

An Illustrated Guide

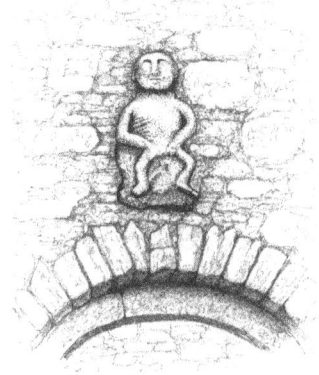

Researched, Written and Illustrated
by
JOANNE MCMAHON
AND
JACK ROBERTS

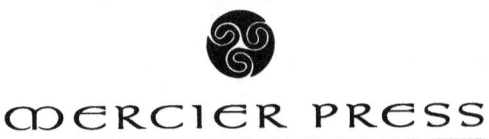

MERCIER PRESS

Mercier Press
www.mercierpress.ie

First published in 2001

© Joanne McMahon and Jack Roberts 2000

ISBN 978 1 85635 249 9

Transferred to digital print on demand in 2023.

*In memory of all those researchers whose work has been the
main inspiration and in memory of Kathleen Basford,
pioneer researcher who brought us the 'Green Men'.*

CONTENTS

ACKNOWLEDGEMENTS

Thanks to everyone who has given encouragement, help and advice in the development of this book and especially in tracking down some of the lost or forgotten figures. It is not possible to remember everyone who has assisted this work and we would like to apologise to anyone whom we may have omitted.

Thanks to: John Kirwan, Andy Halpin, Stella Cherry, Albert Siggins, Conleth Manning, David Taylor, Judith Tripos, Martin Byrne, Niamh O'Connor, Brigit O'Connor, Diedre and Toby Hall, Cary Meehan, Caroline Bechert, Claire Legeune, and John Harding whose website of on-going research is a constant inspiration. Special thanks to Keith and Gillian Jones who offered information very generously especially on two figures that were new to us as well as pictures of another five for which we had no previous illustrations.

During the research and production of this book a number of new figures have been brought to our attention. Indeed the whole project has been an on-going study from the moment of its inception and right up to the time when it was being made ready for publication. The study of the Sheela-na-Gigs is still very much in its infancy and the fact that 'new' figures are being brought to light illuminates an underlying lack of research into the subject.

The full story of how and why they came to be erected on the churches and castles of the medieval period is far from being revealed and any further developments which might enlighten us on the mystery have been, and will be, dependent upon them being released from the darkness of obscurity.

It is hoped that the spirit of enquiry into these enigmatic figures will be further engendered by the publication of this book and that it will go on to inspire further research into this as yet largely ignored area of study.

FOREWORD

An Appeal on Behalf of the Once Sacred Sheela-na-Gigs

There is something odd about the subject of Sheela-na-Gigs; unlike almost any other historical subject they are defined by their
incomprehensibility – why are these so-called provocative figures
located in religious surroundings? Historians have been reticent
to address them and it certainly is difficult to reconcile them within an historical framework. As one museum curator said after the
figure on the old church at Kiltinan was stolen, 'The Sheela-na-Gig
hinted at feelings and thoughts not normally evoked by academic
study.'[1]

Many of the examples in this book were discovered after they
were removed from churches and other religious structures in Britain and Ireland. Many were buried, some burnt or just banished
from our view because they offended the sensibilities of piously
motivated people. Fortunately some are now in the relative safety
of museums and the finest collection of Sheela-na-Gigs in the world
is currently under the protection of the National Museum of Ireland. In July 1990 there was a minor flurry of indignation when
The Irish Times published an article entitled, 'Please Can I See the
Sheela-na-Gigs', giving details of an American visitor asking to
see some of the examples stored deep in the crypts of the National
Museum. The museum said 'Sheela-na-Gigs are ugly and unflat-
tering to women', and the suggestion was made that the public
should, '... focus on Cistercian Abbeys instead.'[2] This is an intriguing comment when you consider how many Sheelas have been
found in Cistercian foundations!

In 1994, the National Museum of Ireland displayed some of
its collection of Sheela-na-Gigs as part of an exhibition of Contemporary Modern Art in the Irish Museum of Modern Art. Whilst
this was to be greatly welcomed no one has sufficiently explained
how they can be construed as falling into the category of 'Modern

Art' let alone 'Contemporary Art'! Thankfully attitudes have been slowly changing and the National Museum have placed two Sheela-na-Gigs permanently on display. They are still causing a stir as one Sheela-na-Gig, previously on display in the Cork Fitzgerald Museum, has now been hidden away in the storeroom, apparently because the figure 'attracted the wrong sort of people'.

These enigmatic figures were, and in some instances still are, a primary element of many churches and castles. They were often the only iconographic feature of those buildings and their presence was obviously important. Any ambivalence in our attitude reflects the confusion some people feel towards them. It is vital that we accept them as valid and valuable artefacts rather than treating them as inconvenient historical oddities. Only then will the Sheela-na-Gigs be freed of the many misconceptions surrounding them since their discovery over 150 years ago.

This book has been produced in the hope that we may once again be able to accept and fully appreciate the Sheela-na-Gigs, and that we will begin to respect these once highly-esteemed aspects of our heritage. One of our main aims has been to compile a comprehensive catalogue of the figures with a particular emphasis on presenting illustrations of the Sheelas. We present these images of medieval mystery in the hope that it will encourage a more open and innovative style of research.

1

Sheela-na-Gigs – an Introduction

Sheela-na-Gigs are figurative stone carvings of naked females, typically depicted as standing or squatting in a position generally described as an 'act of display'. Sometimes they are shown with thighs widely splayed and often one or both hands are shown pointing to, or touching, the genitalia – deliberately accentuating the focus upon this part of the anatomy. To further emphasise this aspect of the carving, the vulva or genitals are often over-exaggerated in startling detail. It is extraordinary that Sheela-na-Gigs are most commonly found as a form of church ornament. They are often built into the fabric of medieval churches, in some cases being placed over the main doorway.

Sheela-na-Gigs are enigmas, historical oddities – no one expects to see a naked female on a church wall – especially one displaying the vulva. The scholarly world has been discussing who put them on the old country churches, and why they were put there, for over a century and a half. Many archaeologists and historians have been intrigued by these obscenities as they appear so out of place in centres of Christian worship. Numerous theories have been proposed about their existence but they still remain a mystery, and their function and purpose is still as much of a controversy as it was back in the Victorian era. Various theoretical arguments seeking to explain their origin and purpose will be discussed in this work but no single theory can hope to answer all the questions relating to such a wide diversity of carvings.

In keeping with the symbolic style familiar to the world of Celtic art Sheela-na-Gigs are usually quite disproportionate. Their heads are large in relation to their bodies. Were it not for the sexual organs it would often be impossible to distinguish the gender of many carvings. They are seldom vested with any of the usual feminine attributes; the breasts are often barely indicated and it is sometimes questionable if they are breasts. The variety and style of these carvings is diverse – some of the figures are roughly hewn as if the work was carried out by an untrained hand, others have been finely carved and appear to be produced by skilled stonemasons. Regardless of whether they are well made or rudely carved there is a sense of determination in their multifarious designs. This indicates that the people who carved them were well-versed in that long forgotten symbolic language which probably determined their extraordinary and sometimes bizarre forms.

It is not certain precisely when the tradition of carving Sheela-na-Gigs began, or the actual age of some of the earliest examples. It seems that the motif was first commonly used on churches or other ecclesiastic sites in Ireland and Britain between the eleventh and thirteenth centuries. Almost all of the British Sheelas originate from the earlier period. In Ireland enthusiasm for the image continued up until the late sixteenth century and Sheelas were placed on castles and occasionally on other important structures such as town walls and holy wells. This practice is unknown in Britain. Out of one hundred and forty-seven Sheela-na-Gigs listed in the present catalogue only forty-two are located in Britain. One hundred and five originate from Ireland and over half are associated with castles. The greater number of Sheelas in Ireland means that they must have been fairly common, especially in the midlands which has the greatest concentration of surviving figures, and they are now often regarded as an purely Irish phenomenon.

Sheela-na-Gigs are often referred to as erotic but it appears very unlikely they were ever meant to arouse desire. Many appear quite hideous, even malformed, and the overall impression is that they represent an arcane symbolism, rather than being representational images of the human form. Sometimes they are thought of as fertility figures, but this is only an additional function that may have been applied to them because of their association with early saints. They are also regarded as apotropaic, which is probably true of those found on castles as they may have been placed there as talismanic images. Usually Sheelas can be found in very prominent positions, such as close by or immediately over a door or window. Sometimes they were employed as a corner stone, or quoin stone, often located near the main entrance.

Our ancestors regarded the Sheela-na-Gigs with considerable respect. Some figures were given names that related to their importance and there is evidence to show that at least a few of the figures played an important role in religious beliefs. However records show that religious beliefs and folk practices connected with the Sheelas came under the attack from the clergy and there was a campaign to eradicate them along with other heathen worship. In Ireland the carving of Sheela-na-Gigs appears to have ended abruptly at the beginning of the seventeenth century with the advent of the Reformation, and the final disappearance of almost all vestiges of the traditional Celtic Church. Attitudes towards the Sheelas drastically altered in keeping with the new order of the post-Reformation Church. They were repeatedly castigated from the pulpit until they were nearly all removed from their places of former glory. Weir and Jerman give some examples of the persecution authorised by the papal authorities against the figures:

> In 1631, provincial statutes for Tuam (County Galway) order parish priests to hide away, and to note where they are hidden away, what are described in the veiled obscurity of Latin as *imagines obesae et aspectui ingratae*, which translates as 'fat figures of unpleasant features', and which is believed to be referring to the Sheela-na-Gigs. It is also noted that in 1676 there was a Diocesan order commanding the burning of 'Sheela-na-Gigs' and that, 'Bishop Brehan in Waterford was ordering exactly the same thing in that year ...[1]

During the following centuries untold damage was done. Many figures were deliberately buried, destroyed, burnt or sabotaged in some way. At Glanworth Castle in County Cork a figure was found buried under a layer of rubble in a vaulted ground floor chamber during an archaeological dig and its incarceration can be dated to the 1600s. Some Sheelas, such as the figure from Llandrindod in Wales, were found concealed and built into the north wall of churches, face downwards, with an added cross crosslet carved on to the side of the thick slab. A Sheela retrieved from the river meadow near St Ives Priory, Huntingdonshire, has traces of burning. It is possible that in Britain, where the change in attitude may have been even more dramatic, removing the Sheelas from public view may have been even more thorough.

Just how many Sheela-na-Gigs existed in medieval times is open to speculation. In some instances the ancient traditions associated with them ensured them some security. Figures high up on the walls of castles or churches were safe while the building remained intact, but many fell along with the crumbling masonry. It is likely that many still lie hidden in various places throughout Ireland and Britain. It is fortunate that a substantial quantity of Sheelas have survived into the present day for they are an aspect of the medieval world that would otherwise be totally unknown to us. They are the only remaining evidence we have of a link between religion and folk belief before the collapse of the old Celtic Christian system.

As the old churches and castles began to fall down only a vague memory of what the Sheelas originally represented remained among the people. Destruction of historical and archaeological monuments was commonplace as age did not confer any sense of value, and superstition was about the only insurance a monument could rely on for survival. As people became more aware of their historical past Sheela-na-Gigs arose from their rural obscurity in the middle of the nineteenth century.

During the early years of their discovery the Sheelas caught the interest of the more adventurous antiquarian researchers. However, an element of prudery typical of the Victorian age, pervades many descriptions of the figures. George R. Lewis [1840] saw a very different figure. Amongst a long line of other carvings that adorn the corbels of Kilpeck church in Herefordshire is 'a dog, a rabbit, two wrestlers, many heads', and a Sheela with her vulva pulled up above the stomach and arms modestly hanging down her side. Despite making a drawing of it, Lewis depicted what was described by himself as, 'a fool – the cut in his chest, the way to his heart, denotes it is always open and to all alike.'[2]

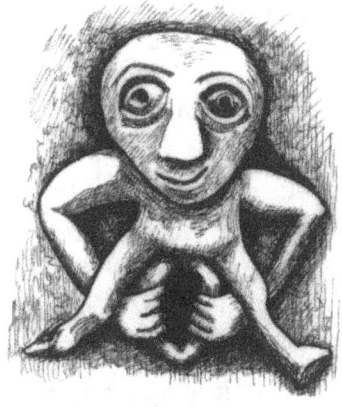 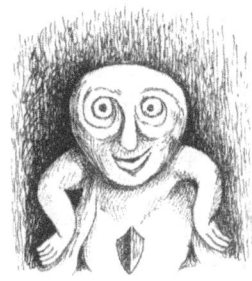

Other researchers, such as John O'Donovan, who first described the Sheela-na-Gig on Kiltinan church in 1840, were at a loss to explain the incongruous placement of the Sheelas. It simply did not fit in with the general corpus of church decoration. The stone was not the normal alternating-size pattern of the quoins and this suggested it was probably not an original part of the church. O'Donovan's suggested that the stone was carved in recent times as some lewd joke, its origin due to '... the wantonness of some loose mind', or that the Sheela came from a castle and was placed on the church by 'someone who delighted in inconsistencies'.[3]

The majority of antiquarians in the last century were convinced that Sheelas had been erected on churches and castles in a process of assimilation of pagan artefacts, perhaps to placate a superstitious populace. They felt the figures had a time-worn look and a certain 'crudeness' of execution that belied their true age. One of the most renowned archaeologists of the day, R. A. S. Macalister, said that Sheela-na-Gigs 'seem to be survivals into Christianity of a perverted representation of one of the most important gods of paganism'.[4] It was generally agreed that the figures were remnants of a past pagan age as they were evidently not coeval with the buildings on which they were found, but thought to have been re-used from earlier buildings.

Towards the end of the nineteenth century interest in the Sheela-na-Gigs was heightened after a full list of the then known figures was published in the 1894 edition of the *Journal of the Royal Society of Antiquaries*.[5] In the following years as many leading antiquarians voiced their observations and speculations, Sheela-na-Gigs were regarded from a negative or derogatory viewpoint. Terms such as 'repulsive', 'grotesque', 'hideous', 'ugly' and 'obscene' came into common usage and this expressed a general attitude towards them. In reality of course these words can only be applied to a relatively small proportion of the figures. Some are depicted as quite benign and otherworldly looking, while others have a fierce and only occasionally hideous countenance. It is apparent that the nineteenth-century scholars were describing not so much the facial or other bodily features of the Sheelas but their own feelings at the sight of the female genitalia so expressively portrayed.

By the 1930s the Sheela-na-Gigs received the attention of some serious-minded women who began to challenge these views. Edith Guest together with her colleague Helen M. Roe brought to the light a number of previously unknown examples of Sheelas; these together with the others discovered in the intervening years were subsequently published in the *Journal of the Royal Society of Antiquaries of Ireland* in 1935. Guest was no stranger to the debate surrounding the figures and remarked on how their unusually crude realism has been a hindrance rather than a help in their elucidation.[6] Guest concentrated her efforts on the investigation of the cultural context within which the figures are found, establishing a connection with the living folk tradition and mythologies surrounding the Sheelas. Unfortunately by this time the old folk traditions were on the verge of dying out and the memory of what the Sheela-na-Gigs represented had, along with so much else, been forgotten.

The widely-held belief that Sheelas were pagan artefacts, which dated from a much earlier period than the churches and castles on which they were discovered, persisted unchallenged until Edith Guest began a reassessment of the dating of the carvings. This was difficult as the old churches and castles were often in a ruined state and many of the figures were found dislodged from their original position. The majority of the churches and castles had been rebuilt from the fabric of an earlier building that stood on the same site so that it is impossible to state with certainty the age or origination of the greater bulk of the figures.

Given such limitations, the figures Guest selected for scrutiny were on quoins which fitted the alternate size pattern, keystones (forming part of the arch of a doorway or window) or those that appeared to form an integral part of the original fabric of the building. Guest found that although the evidence was scanty, '... where it can be found it is surprisingly uniform ... indicating that the figures are actually contemporary in execution with the buildings in which they are found.'' She felt that the Irish figures date to the period from around the eleventh or twelfth century until the sixteenth or seventeenth century This placed most of the known carvings within the medieval Christian period. Jorgen Andersen, author of the most erudite work so far on the subject, was also 'inclined to conclude that the Sheela was a product of the twelfth century.'[8]

Guest and Roe had set out to shed some clear light on the subject of dating and cultural context. In doing so they dragged the Sheelas out of the darkness of pre-history and placed them firmly into the Christian world. This confirmed the worst fears of the old Victorian prudes. Now the Sheelas had to be accepted as Christian icons, as Christian as the Madonna and Child, and often found in exactly the same position on a church that the later more acceptable form of the Sacred Female would occupy. As a pagan relic the Sheela can be easily justified, for as such she is merely an impotent antiquity harmlessly contained within the confines of the sacred grounds and erected upon the church, perhaps, as a confirmation of the superior powers of Christianity. But as a product of the Christian world, or possibly even as an icon of the Church, the 'crude realism' of the Sheela-na-Gig represents a terrible inconsistency which raised questions that few scholars wished to answer.

Interest in the figures in Britain received even less attention and it was not until 1970 that a list of the English, Welsh and Scottish figures, with a number of illustrations and a distribution map was compiled and published.[9] However, this list was accompanied by words of warning and 'pronouncements of disbelief as to the possibility of further scholarly advance on the subject'. Fortunately, Jorgen Andersen chose the Sheela-na-Gigs as the subject for a doctoral thesis published in 1977 under the title of *The Witch on the Wall*. It is the most thorough investigation of the Sheelas carried out so far and the book has, justifiably, come to be regarded as the definitive work on the subject.[10]

A decade later two researchers, Weir and Jerman, followed the quest for a continental origin for the Sheelas with a thorough investigation of the Romanesque art of the churches of western France. The purpose of this research was to establish a factual basis for Andersen's suggestion of a continental origin for Sheela-na-Gigs. But, as the title of their book, *Images of Lust*, suggests, the linking of this image with the theology of Romanesque Christianity implies that the Sheelas had a negative function to serve as warnings against sin and lust.

The theories promoted by Weir and Jerman have generally been accepted unopposed in modern thinking on the subject. Yet the argument that Sheelas were created originally as a warning against sin and lust just does not hold with the figures as we find them in the Irish landscape. It also falls far short of answering a great many of the questions surrounding the native British figures. Tradition does not support their view, for many references to the Sheelas indicate they were highly regarded images and evidently held an exalted position within the religious iconography of the earlier Church. It is also a widely-held belief that their purpose was to ward off evil and as such they served a talismanic or apotropaic function. However present evidence is not sufficient to prove any of these hypotheses conclusively. The origin or inspiration for the

Sheelas and the reason why the tradition was so widely embraced for over 500 years in Ireland are best appreciated through a variety of standpoints.

Unfortunately, the current academic trend towards interpreting the Sheelas in purely pragmatic terms, especially the view that they developed out of the Romanesque art of the continent, has forced a narrow view on this subject which, we feel, stultifies the study rather than moving it towards any tenable conclusions. Although the Sheelas may have arisen alongside the Romanesque, classifying those of the Celtic lands along with the continental figures has failed to account for their insular setting and, instead, separates them from the very influences that have helped to shape and create their unique individuality. In this book we hope to reinstate the native Sheelas of Britain and Ireland as an insular phenomenon in which such cultural influences as the Romanesque form a part of the background from which they may be seen to have emerged, and within which these unique figures held a valid place with an appreciable purpose and function.

2

TRADITION, FOLKLORE AND POPULAR BELIEF

From the veiled allusions recorded by the early researchers it appears that there was a great deal of folklore attached to the Sheela-na-Gigs. The snippets of local lore recorded by the early investigators show that had they delved a little deeper, they would have gained a great deal more information. One researcher has suggested that these Victorian researchers were 'gripped with near apoplexy at the sight of them'[1] and Andersen voiced his disappointment that the folklorists did not direct more research towards the subject, especially as Sheelas constituted an important, if not vital, element of the rural tradition in many areas. Whatever prevented their further enquiries their silence left the Sheela-na-Gigs hanging in a cultural void, detached from the traditions and lore that would give them any real meaning.

Often all that was recorded were the various names of the figures and that the name 'Sheela-na-Gig', now the recognised term for the whole genre of figures, has fascinated and perplexed scholars since it was first used. The earliest written record of the name Sheela-na-Gig appeared in a description of the figure on Kiltinan church, County Tipperary, by the antiquarian John O'Donovan in his *Ordnance Survey Letters* of 1840. O'Donovan reported this name was used by locals for the figure and wrote over 1,500 words trying to explain or, as James O'Connor suggests, excuse the outrageous carving the likes of which he had never encountered before. Although O'Donovan was a native Irish speaker he did not attempt to translate the

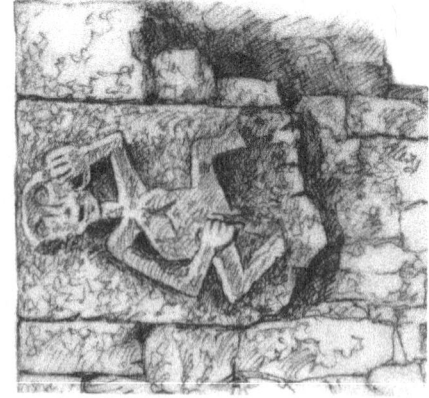

name and he also failed to elaborate on the 'incidents connected with her life', as related to him by the locals.[2] A short while later the name 'Sheela-na-Gig' was also given to R. P. Coles when he asked about a similar figure on the falling masonry of the old church at Rochestown, about twenty miles south of Kiltinan.

On many occasions it has been suggested that the name Sheela-na-Gig was either a very localised nickname, an 'unfortunate linguistic error' or a phrase of little specific relevance.[3] One critic even suggested it was a 'trifling and accidental circumstance' that Coles happened to meet an uninformed man who trotted out the name from ignorance when questioned about the figure.[4] However Edith Guest and her colleagues enquired into the origin and validity of the name and, having questioned country people from different areas, found that although it was not commonly known in all areas of Ireland it was certainly recognised outside the confines of Tipperary or the south midlands. It appears that the name may have been more widely known in earlier times for in 1781 it was recorded that there was a British royal navy ship, *HMS Sheilah-nagig* – meaning an 'Irish Female Sprite.'[5]

Although 'Sheela-na-Gig' can be considered a bona-fide name for the figures its meaning has remained obscure, partially due to the fact that O'Donovan spelt the name in three different ways in his *Ordnance Survey Letters, Co. Tipperary.*[6] One of the earliest translations of the name was by Thomas Wright who said the name 'Shelah-na-Gig' means 'Julian the Giddy', which was 'simply a term for an immodest woman.'[7] His interpretation reflects some understanding of the term in Irish, as *Síle*, which according to Dinneen's *Irish Dictionary* (1927)[8] means Julia, rather than Julian, and Giddy must be a translation of the word *giob* also spelt as *gogaide* which means 'a giddy person, a feeble old woman; a midwife; the hunkers ... Giddy is also said to have originated from the Old English words *gidig, gydig* which meant 'insane, possessed by a God' and sounds very much like our original Ghig or Gigg.[9]

Although *Síle* might refer to a woman's personal name, it has equally been translated as a name for an old woman or a hag. The most commonly favoured interpretations of the name are *Sighle na gCioch* meaning 'the old hag of the paps or breasts' or *Síle-ina-Giob* meaning 'Sheela (the name of an old woman) on her hunkers'.[10] The first interpretation appears to be of little relevance since most of the figures have very small breasts, if any at all. The second interpretation, tentatively suggested by Andersen, makes sense for the majority of the Sheelas that are often on their hunkers or squatting. But it is not an accurate description for many others, either standing or in reclining positions, such as the one at Kiltinan church to which the name was first given. In view of the fact that the figures were regarded as 'occult images' or as having 'special powers' it is also plausible to relate 'Sheela' to the word *Sithlach* meaning Holy Lady, and 'Gig' to such words as *Gui*, to pray and *Giod*, meaning God.[11] Both Michael Harrison and Tom Lethbridge further suggest it is related to *Gog* as in *Ma Gog*, the ancient Mother Goddess of Britain.[12]

A small but often overlooked aspect in the Irish rendering of the name is the use of *na*, the genitive plural of the definite article. In the first two forms of its spelling O'Donovan uses *Síle ní Ghig* which suggests a person's title. *Ní* means 'daughter or descendant of' and is most commonly used in surnames of females beginning with Ó. For example Nuala O'Brian would be Nuala Ní Bhriain. This interpretation of the name is confirmed by the Sheela from Cullahill Castle in County Laois. It was known locally as *Sheela na Guira*, or Gillian O'Dwyer, who was head of the clan and said to have been 'a bit of a tyrant'. Gillian is derived from Julia and the name should properly be spelt 'Síle Ní Ghuira'.[13] This use of the name also suggests that the Sheelas represent a local ancestor who may have had an important territorial function.

It may be the case that 'Sheela-na-Gig' actually refers to a certain class of women and was used to describe their likeness on the wall. According to the account of an observant German traveller Johann Kohl who travelled around Ireland in the 1840s:

> ... the figures of displayed women on churches had something to do with an ancient custom of averting ill-luck. A man afflicted by that

might turn for help to a certain class of females, who would display themselves, in order to avert evil and bring about good luck ...[14]

His source is a man acquainted with Irish customs and antiquities, and suggests a survival of the use of the name amongst the country people. This is also corroborated by Guest – when she was inquiring in the Macroom district about the Sheela-na-Gigs, a middle-aged woman did not understand the sense in which she was using the word. Guest states that the woman 'derived some puzzled comment from it, wondering why I should desire to seek out old women of the type which I may for brevity describe as a "hag".'[15] Apparently the woman's family had been farmers in the district for many years and from her earliest childhood she had been familiar with the word used with this inference.

The 'living Sheela-na-gigs', according to Johann Kohl used the display of genitals as a means of opposing evil. They were probably the same as the gierador, who according to the seventeenth-century Kilmore Diocesan Synod were banned from receiving the sacraments.[16] The gierador refers to women who turned the evil eye, the fortune teller or diviner, the local hag or witch. The ancient practice of displaying the genitalia as a means of opposing evil or of slighting enemies is well-attested to in Ireland. In a letter to *The Irish Times* of 23 September 1977, Walter Mahon-Smith tells of how in 1913 a bloody faction fight was averted:

> In a townland near where I lived, a deadly feud had continued for generations between the families of two small farmers. One day, before the First World War, when the men of one of the families, armed with pitchforks and heavy blackthorn sticks, attacked the home of their enemy, the woman-of-the-house came to the door of her cottage, and in full sight of all (including my father and myself who happened to be passing by) lifted her skirt and underclothes high above her head, displaying her naked genitals. The enemy of her and her family fled in terror.[17]

It is hardly surprising that many Sheelas were, and in some instances still are, considered to have the ability to protect and ward off evil. Windele noted in relation to a Sheela on Castle Warren at Barnahealy in Cork that when placed above the keystone of the door arch they were supposed to possess a tutelary or protective power.[18] A few of the figures such as the Sheela from Carrick and the cross-legged Cat Goddess (once regarded as a Sheela) on the Rock of Cashel were actually called the 'Evil Eye stone'. Another Sheela originally from Ballynamona Castle was regarded as a talisman but she was 'somewhat injured on account of her characteristics' and a later search for the figure around the turn of the century found her some distance away 'but so smashed up that she was beyond repair'. At the end of the report the author states, '... it is certain that once she left her place in the castle, the Nagles (who built the castle) did not long survive her.'[19]

Sheelas were also referred to under a variety of other names which may give a clue to their origin or purpose. In both Britain and Ireland, the name 'the Idol' appears to have been synonymous with the Sheela-na-Gigs and it is recorded as early as 1781 in a book about the Isle of Wight in relation to the figure at Binstead. According to Chambers dictionary an idol can be defined as 'an image of God: an object of worship; an object of love, admiration, or honour in an extreme degree' and this appears to be the manner in which the local people regarded the Sheela at Binstead. When the church was being repaired around 1770, the figure was removed; but the inhabitants were displeased at its removal, and procured its restoration.[20] This much weathered figure, with its hands reaching down towards a deep cavity representing its vulva, is currently residing over the gateway to the church, having been moved from its place on the wall of the church. At Lusk in County Dublin another Sheela described as being 'fancifully hideous' but called 'the Idol' was not so fortunate as it is recorded that it 'was buried by the late Rev. Mr Tyrrell.'[21] The Sheela from Clonmel was known as the 'Idol of Blue Anchor Lane' but this is a more recent title referring to the place where she was discovered.

A parish priest remembers the reaffixed Sheela on the parapet of an old canal bridge at Clonlara in the early years of this century being called Peadar Taigdhe Bhuide or Óg Peadar Táill Bhuidhe. Peadar means Peter or St Peter; Taigdhe is a more ambiguous

24

term, which may have derogatory connotations; and Bhuide means yellow or sunny.[22] A recent local name for this badly defaced Sheela is 'the witches stone'. Another Sheela once located on Cloghan Castle in County Offaly was known as 'the Witch'. Unfortunately it is now missing but according to one account it was said to represent, 'a Hermaphrodite, one of the breasts being like the sun and the other a crescent, like the moon.'[23]

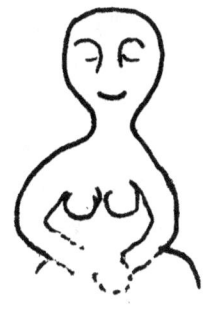

The south wall of the castle at Moycarkey was adorned with a Sheela-na-Gig that is now known only from a sketch in the Royal Irish Academy which has the caption, 'the country people have a legend and call it Cathleen Owen'.[24] It is a pity that the artist left only a brief reference to the local legends attached to the figure. The only other snippet of local lore that has been passed down is that it is said to have been 'procured from the ruins of a nearby

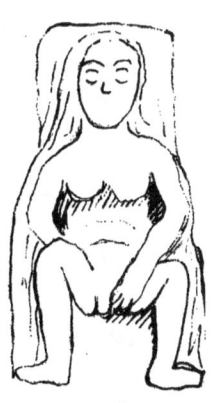

church and was placed on the castle to bring "luck about the house".'[25]

The Pennington Sheela with her remarkably pointed ears is identified by local people as the Goddess Freya, the Viking earth mother – probably due to the strong Nordic influence in the area. An unusual pot-bellied Sheela by the door of an old mill at Rosnaree in County Meath was also believed to be an original goddess. It is not known where she came from but it seems that folk belief accounted for her reuse as she has been moved to the door of the old mill and presumably assigned a protective purpose.

The few fragments of recorded folklore indicate that Sheelas were very highly revered and often regarded as being invested with great power. Traditionally this power is thought to reside in the sacred centre, the vulva which was, and in a few instances still is, rubbed to release its power. Rubbing the Sheela confers a wide variety of magical benefits, primarily the ability to cure illnesses. It is also widely believed that it had some sort of fertility power, but this may only be a secondary function applied to them because of their association with the old saints who, as will be seen further on, were believed to have this beneficent power. A number of Sheelas are believed to be images of ancient fertility goddesses and according to local knowledge, the two Sheelas at Kiltinan were said to represent an ancient fertility goddess. Barren women would scrape the figure on the church for its 'healing dust'.[26] James O'Connor, when he was carving a replica of the figure, was convinced that the triangular area just below the genitals could not have been the work of the original stone cutter and felt that it must have been scraped out over time.

It appears that at Kiltinan this practice had probably died out

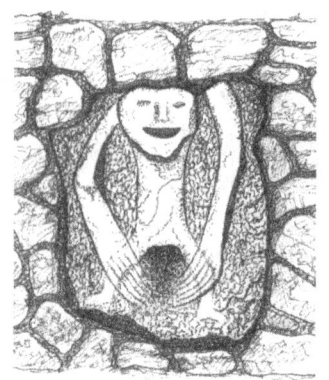

before O'Donovan's time but evidence of rubbing can be seen on a widely distributed range of figures in both Ireland and Britain. At Buckland the Sheela has received constant rubbing of her vulva leaving a deep hollow where it looks as if the fingers have had to be re-incised. At Clenagh Castle, carved on a quoin stone set close to the ground is a later, spindly figure. The pudendum is indicated by an oblong, diamond shaped depression which also shows some signs of rubbing.

The practice of rubbing Sheela-na-Gigs is perhaps one of the oldest and most persistent traditional modes of veneration accorded to many of the figures. One Sheela-na-Gig that is still being rubbed as part of a surviving Christian ritual is the figure which can be seen on the old church of St Gobnait at Ballyvourney in County Cork. This now-ruined church stands on the site of a monastery founded by St Gobnait and even today many people still travel long distances to visit the holy site on her feast day, 11 February, to 'do the rounds' at her shrine. To the pilgrims this small, benign-looking Sheela-na-Gig is St Gobnait or rather it is one of two figures that are regarded as actual images of the saint.

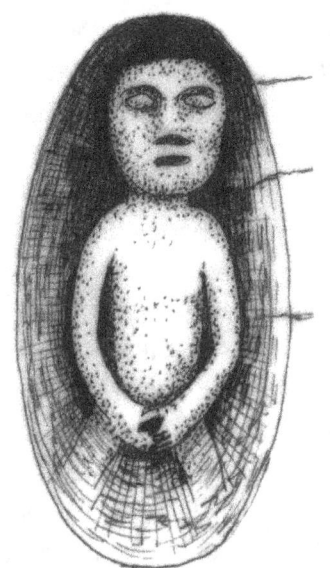
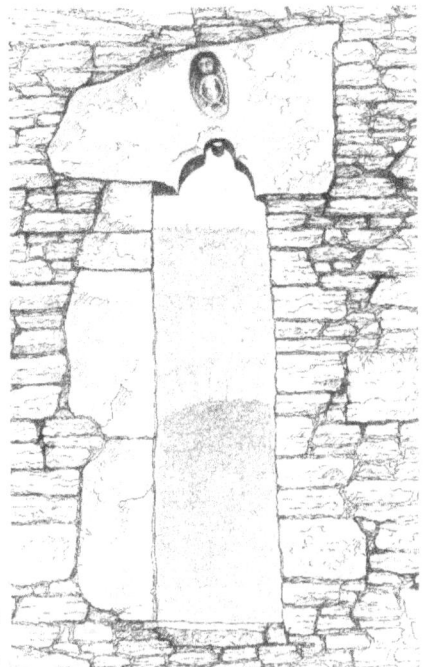

The Ballyvourney Sheela-na-Gig has been carved in relief in an oval recess which is set at an odd slant in a re-employed window lintel. The top half of the figure is in a relatively good state of preservation, with the hands clearly pointing towards the lower abdomen or genital area. However the lower half is unclear and although the legs are missing it appears as if the figure is standing. The tradition recorded by Guest was that pilgrims circled the old church, walking sun-wise and pausing at three spots of special virtue, the first of which is 'the little image of Saint Gobonet', the Sheela-na-Gig which people rub with a handkerchief while standing on a rock before climbing through the window into the church.[27]

The next special place is located in a small square niche in the west wall of the church into which the devotees put their arms almost to full length. 'At the extremity one feels a smooth round object and touches it three times: it is "Saint Gobnait's Bowl"', and its virtue is transferred to the pilgrims by crossing themselves with the same hand that felt it.[28] The 'bowl' is really a round, black stone ball, made of agate supposed to be efficacious for the cure of contusions and was originally handed about for its virtues but the priest imprisoned it where it is now. The legend attached to Gobnait's ball is that the saint objected to a local chief building a castle near her abbey. She threw her ball at the walls each night and what had been built during the day fell down.[29] The other figure from Ballyvourney, was also regarded as an image of the saint, is a thirteenth-century wooden statuette which may have a close connection to the Sheela-na-Gigs. This is a slender, graceful figure made of oak, about twenty-seven inches tall, which used to be carried around 'dressed up in rags', in the same way as the corn-dollies

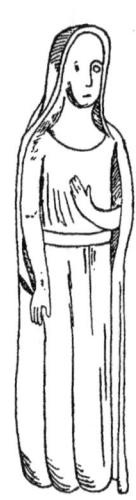

made on Brigit's Day. Windele reported that on several occasions the wooden image was attacked by the local priest because it was leading to undesirable practices but the people hid it. In the 1840s a representative of the traditional keepers of the shrine, the O'Herlihys, known as 'Gobnait's Clergy', handed it over to the parish priest and it is now located in a 'drawer' inside the parish church, and brought out only on Gobnait's feast day. A traditional ritual attached to the wooden statue is that it is measured 'with ribbons and Rosary beads' and like the Sheela-na-Gig, the figure is then rubbed lengthwise along the body.[30] This measuring and rubbing transfers the power of the statue to the ribbon which then becomes a *Tomhas Gobnatan* (Gobnait's Measure), and is thereby imbued with the power of the statue and the ability to effect cures. Pilgrims also rubbed their afflicted limbs on the statue and in contrast to the fertilising power of the Sheelas a handkerchief rubbed around the neck of the wooden image would then be worn as a prophylactic.

At Ballyvourney we can still see devotees following ancient customs that have all the hallmarks of having changed little over countless generations. If there were no folklore attached to other Sheela-na-Gigs then it could be regarded as purely coincidental that the Ballyvourney figure became connected to the figure of St Gobnait but this does not seem to be an isolated case.

Flanking the doorway of St Brigit's Well at Castlemagner is a figure, believed to be a late Sheela, that has been rubbed with a pebble or stone in a cross pattern on her head, belly and thighs. The rubbing of the Sheela is part of the continuing devotion at this holy well – the water is regarded as a cure for all kind of illness. Andersen published two photographs of this figure taken thirty-five years apart, the most recent shows wear of the area suggesting the figures being rubbed is a recent custom. Similarly in the medieval parish church of Kilsarkan a Sheela-na-Gig is carved into the lintel of the south window, and an important part of the traditional rounds is to rub the figure with a stone or pebble. Here the practice includes rubbing, in a cross pattern, on several places around the window frame and on the stone sill.

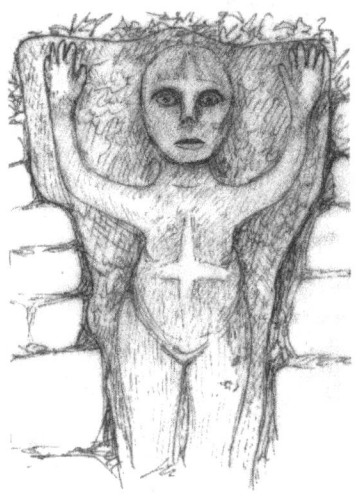

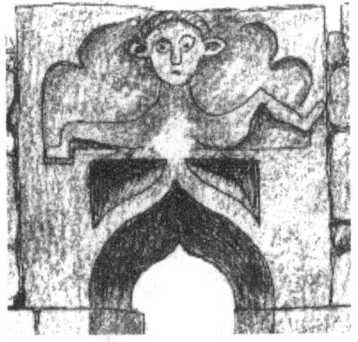

Rubbing or touching objects of veneration is a tradition probably as old as religion itself. It is impossible to tell when the practice began being applied to the Sheela-na-Gigs. Perhaps it did not happen until the carvings took on the venerability of age and began to be accredited with fertility and healing functions – a belief which could have originated from an initial function of repelling evil. In Castle Widenham a Sheela, which had become detached from its original position, was found lying beside St Patrick's

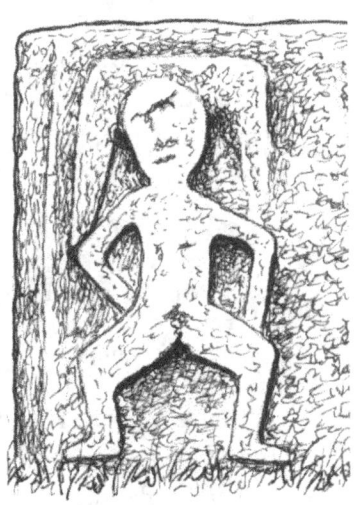

holy well. According to a report made during the last century it was frequently touched for help in childbirth but this was a recent custom.[31] A fertility association is also found in relation to the figure at Oxford where the custom was for brides, as they entered St Michael's church, to look upon the Sheela which was originally set high up on the tower.

The remarkable figure which was once built into the church at Seir Kieran is probably the most important and fascinating Sheela-na-Gig yet discovered. The figure is carved in deep relief 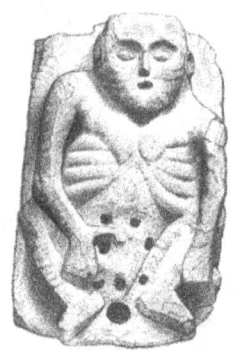 and is depicted as seated, touching its genitals with one hand and holding a cylindrical object in the other. However, a number of deep holes are drilled into the figure; there are seven in its abdomen, a large one between its feet that may represent the vulva, one located in its throat and two more holes drilled deep into the top of its head. Evidence of rubbing can be seen in the smoothness of some of the holes, especially the lowest, and perhaps they are the result of a tradition or ritualistic function that has long been forgotten.

Allusions have been made to the possible connection between these holes and the cup-marks found on megalithic stones. Many of these are the focus of traditional devotion at ancient sites around the country and may reflect an age-old belief in the cup-mark as a symbol of fertility. The importance of this figure is acknowledged by Andersen:

> Occult beliefs evoking memories of a past age, may have coloured an image like the Seir Kieran Sheela, the only absolutely convincing fertility image around the Irish carvings (a Scottish example from Taynuilt may be another instance) and ... a figure from near Birr, in Offaly ... rich in early traditions.[32]

Occult beliefs may have also influenced a group of very odd carvings found inside an ancient rock-cut chamber, known as Royston Cave in England. Amongst them is a female figure, set between a horse and a big sword, with hands hanging loosely by her side and clearly marked genitals. The first scholar to visit this site in 1742 was the renowned antiquarian Rev. Dr William Stukley. He disputed the meaning of the carvings in this subterranean oratory with the Rev. Charles Parkinson. The carvings, which are said to include depictions of several saints, look ancient but are presumed to be of a late medieval date some time in the 1400s. Andersen states: '... folk belief seems heavily involved in the decoration of the walls.'[33] It is suspected that the cave at some stage served as a secret place of superstitious worship. Whether this carving of a female figure should really be regarded as a Sheela in the sense of her medieval contemporaries is somewhat dubious, but according to Andersen:

> Memories of whatever power that kind of image may have had apparently secured her admission into this setting, which one strongly suspects is a world of witchcraft.[34]

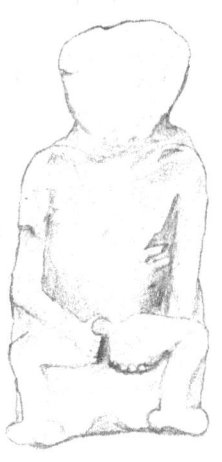

It has also been suggested that Royston Cave was a sanctum of the Knights Templar. Clonoulty in County Tipperary was the site of a former temple of the Knights Templar and a Sheela-na-Gig was found buried here up to her neck at the foot of a yew tree. The Templars, a military order formed at the time of the Crusades, apparently learnt about the mystery of the female divine in the east and on their return promoted the cult of the Virgin – hence possibly also the Sheelas. At the time of their disbandment by the Church in the early fourteenth century, Clonoulty was the wealthiest of their Irish foundations.

When some modern scholars assert that there is no folklore directly associated with the Sheelas, they are aware that folk practices connected to them are still being carried out in the present day. Unfortunately there is only a minimum knowledge of the tradition attached to them, as most of the old lore of the country is lost. It has been argued that any surviving practices that might be connected to the Sheela-na-Gigs are deemed to be unrelated to their original function. Names given to them are a later invention to make up for the unknown origin of who or what they represented.

Folk practices, especially where they have been allowed a relatively uninterrupted continuity, are seldom entirely invented. They constitute the remnants of old traditions which, even though they have often been carried over from ancient times, still retain the essence of the original theme. In the traditions related to the Sheelas there are references to goddess figures, hags or saints and a widely held belief that they hold certain apotropaic, fertility or healing powers.

In a traditional society, which Ireland was until the earlier years of the twentieth century, perception is not random and conveys something of the history connected to the object or the place. The figures called Cathleen Owen or Peadar Taigdhe Bhuide retain in those names a memory of whom those figures originally represented rather than just being titles added on at some later date. The names themselves, just like the title or term Sheela-na-Gig, by which the whole genre is now known add to their mystique but do not explain their presence. Although exploring the remnants of folklore may not lead to a reconciling of many of the questions surrounding the Sheelas, examining their role within such situations is a valuable illustration of how this imagery was perceived by a traditional society.

3

THE ROMANESQUE CONNECTION

Sheela-na-Gigs have been regarded as an Irish phenomenon. Not only is the name itself Irish but the rich tradition and large number of Sheela-na-Gigs appearing on the churches and castles here led to the assumption that the figures originated from Ireland. This belief remained relatively unquestioned until Andersen, following up Guest's inclination, published details of eleven Sheela-like figures on Romanesque churches in France, where they are classed amongst a vast array of decorative art as female exhibitionists, and suggested that the idea could well have originated on the continent.[1]

Scholars saw the possibility of an answer to the origin of the Sheelas in this idea. Some believed that by incorporating them within the framework of that particular cultural development on the continent, known as the Romanesque, the inconsistencies that had for so long surrounded the figures could be neatly resolved. A decade after Andersen's work was published Anthony Weir and James Jerman, in *Images of Lust*, sought to expand on his hypothesis through an examination of the great corpus of Romanesque art found on the churches of Western France, Normandy and Spain. As its name implies the main aim of the study was to concentrate on the many carvings of an explicit, and occasionally obscene, sexual nature that are common on European churches of that period. The purpose was to substantiate the theory that the Sheela-na-Gigs of Britain and Ireland originated from a continental prototype of a female exhibitionist occurring occasionally among the decorations found on these churches. Jerman and Weir also proposed that since so much of the artwork produced during this period illustrated the pitfalls of sin, then the original meaning of the Sheelas was to illustrate a negative attitude to sexuality – warnings to the illiterate against the sin of lust.

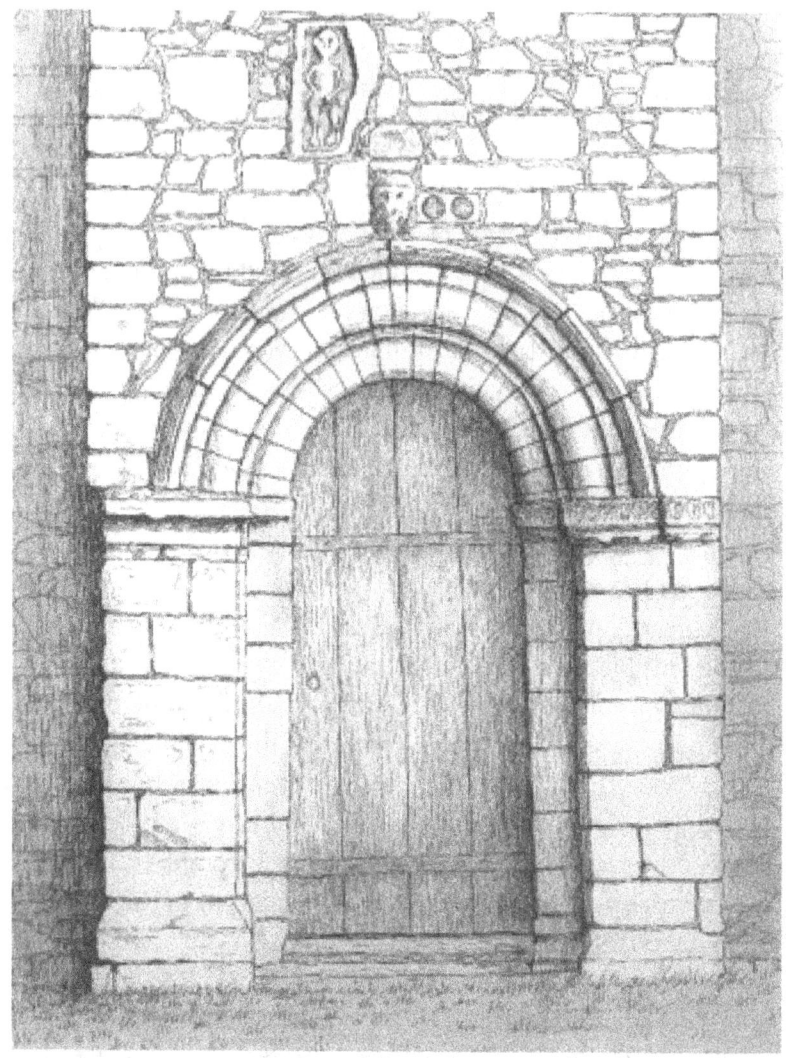

The term Romanesque refers to a style of religious architecture prevailing in continental Europe from the middle of the tenth century to the middle of the twelfth century. Many churches and cathedrals were built during this period, and the restoration of monasteries began in earnest under the direction of architects and masons who drew heavily on what was known of the classic techniques formulated in the days of the Roman civilisation. Characteristic of the Romanesque style is its use of ornate semicircular archways for doorways and windows, and decorative carving on capitals and corbels. The classic Roman techniques of decoration were then overlaid with a matrix of symbolism reflecting all those cultures associated with the Roman empire. There seemed to be no end to the stone-carvers' sources of inspiration, and it seems as if their chief objective in this crusade of visualisation was to use as broad a range of symbolic motifs as possible.

'Thou that enter gaze upon these divine things', is the inscription in Latin over the entrance to one church but the message seems to be one of damnation and hell rather than divine salvation. The compositions of the Romanesque often appear to obtain their animation from the writhing and screaming of sinners suffering the torments of hell, and it is clear that the aim of these religious artists was to promote a sense of apprehension. High on their agenda was the depiction of acts of sin – not murder, torture, acts of rape and pillage being carried out under the order of Rome – but sex in as many various forms as it was possible for those medieval carvers to illustrate.

Continental exhibitionist figures are not Sheela-na-Gigs; rather they are what their name suggests, female forms that happen to be showing off their genitalia as part of the general display. Most of these are commonly shown contorted, with acrobatic feet to ear type postures on corbels or capitals or hidden amongst the design of large compositions. Female exhibitionists occur infrequently in Romanesque art and are very often nearly lost amongst a wide range of other motifs, such as coital couples, acrobatic penis swallowers, anus exposers, females clutching serpents and beard pullers – a great many of these are in some way also baring their private parts.

Within that huge unbridled range of many thousands of carvings used by the Romanesque artists, Weir and Jerman list only seventy female exhibitionists in France and forty in Spain. None, aside from one or two exceptions, are really close contemporaries of the standing or squatting Sheelas, which were normally carved on a single slab of stone and used in prominent positions on the native churches and castles of Britain and Ireland. Far from being fond of showing females of the exhibitionist type, the continental artists deliberately depicted phallic males in abundance. In Britain and Ireland there are correspondingly few male exhibitionist figures. Weir and Jerman's list shows none in England, only one in Wales, and two in Ireland.

Understandably the precise significance of many of the carvings on the continent have long been the subject of debate amongst religious historians but they have been commonly interpreted as, 'iconographic images whose purpose was to give visual support to the Church's moral teachings.'[2] The appearance of the Romanesque sexual motifs in France and Spain occurred in a context of reforms in clerical life in which stricter standards, such as the outlawing of secular marriages and intensified safeguards around the spiritual life of the Church, were being imposed. These carvings have been interpreted as a reminder for both priests and lay people to keep their thoughts on higher things than the earthiness of the body which was regarded as a subversive territory of danger and sin.

During the eleventh and twelfth centuries examples of Romanesque architecture appeared in Ireland and the British Isles and remained an influence into the thirteenth century when it was replaced by an English Gothic style. In Ireland the introduction of the Romanesque style was heralded by the completion of Cormac's Chapel on the Rock of Cashel in 1134, and although relatively few other buildings were built in the style, its influence was retained in the later Gothic style. There was a greater fear of hell and damnation amongst the people of medieval Europe than amongst the Saxons and Celts of Ireland and the British Isles. The disturbing proportions of the continental Romanesque decoration are tamed down and the presentation of the Romanesque in Ireland is even distinctly Celtic in influence. It consists of arched doorways surrounded by heads but with very few of the erotic scenes of the continent.

Weir and Jerman list seven figures in Ireland that are found in association with Romanesque buildings: Grey Abbey, Aghalurcher, Toomregan, White Island, Rathblamac, Liathmore and Clonmacnoise. It is argued that these figures are of Romanesque origination and are amongst the earliest examples of Sheela-na-Gigs, following the importation of the exhibitionist motif into Ireland. However, there does not seem to be any direct relationship between many of these figures and the Irish Sheelas. For instance, the figure whose face is embraced by legs on the arched doorway of the Nun's Chapel at Clonmacnoise is undoubtedly set within a typical Romanesque ornament but the carving is part of the overall decorative scheme in which it does not appear to have been given any additional importance. Andersen also cast doubt on it being a Sheela. 'Can she be described as a Sheela when she does not conform to the usual pattern ... her display, after all, is due to her acroatics, and not to deliberate gesture'.[3]

At Rath Blathmac a figure is found alongside an ornamental carving on a late Romanesque window lintel that has been re-employed upside down and although it is not a typical Irish Sheela it is probably a genuinely early example. The Aghalurcher Sheela is probably of the Romanesque acrobatic style whilst the figure from Grey Abbey is thought to be male. The Toomregan figure is clearly separate from the mainstream Sheela tradition and its gender is rather ambiguous. The figure from White Island is another very curious inclusion, for although it was re-employed horizontally on a Romanesque church, it is widely regarded as a pre-Romanesque tenth century carving and does not constitute a true Sheela; it is likely to be an early predecessor of the genre. The round tower at Ratoo is also thought to be influenced by the Romanesque because of its elaborate doorway but one can hardly extend this to the figure in question. Round towers are unique to Ireland and this Sheela occurs as a singular piece of decoration beside a window, facing inward. Though a building has been influenced in part by the Romanesque style it does not necessarily follow that a carving of a Sheela is an extension of that style.

It is argued that the female exhibitionist motif, as a supposed warning against lust, arrived in Ireland with the Romanesque architectural style as part of the same drive towards celibacy and Church reform occurring on the continent. Possibly the motif was directly introduced by the European religious orders, such as the Cistercians, Cluniacs, Benedictines and Augustinians, implanted in Ireland between the tenth and twelfth centuries.

The late eleventh and twelfth centuries were a time of great changes and transition. The practices of the Irish Church with its unique blend of paganism and Christianity came under powerful pressure to conform to the European Church. At the Synod of Cashel in 1101 Irish law was partially reformed, by forbidding marriage between close kin, but it fell short of the requirements of Rome by failing to address the practices of concubinage and divorce. Such efforts at reform were regarded as too little, too late, with Irish clerics refusing to relinquish their traditional rights and celibacy remained an issue into the seventeenth century. Irish civilisation, with its powerful roots in Celtic pre-history and a strong pagan tradition of mythology and folklore underlying its Christianity, was very different from the Romanesque civilisation of Western Europe. It cannot be assumed that a motif from one country retained any semblance of its original meaning when imposed on another. The fundamental question remains: if the originators were simply concerned about depicting lust why did they not portray or copy the whole repertoire of carvings in which the female exhibitionists played only a minor role – a far more efficient means of depicting the sins of lust, fornication and avarice.

In Britain, the strong influence of the Romanesque style resulted in quite a number of Sheelas being found in typical Romanesque settings, primarily on corbels, chancel arches, capitals and roof bosses. Even these Sheelas, occurring in more typical Romanesque settings, are rarely acrobatic and appear more similar in style to the Irish Sheelas than to the continental exhibitionists. There are a few notable exceptions to this – the Sheelas from the highly decorated cathedrals in Bristol and Wells, and the unique figure at Whittlesford which is the only Sheela depicted with a

phallic male. More prevalent are the isolated figures placed in prominent positions such as the Sheelas found at Oaksey, Fiddington, Church Stretton, Buckland, Crofton-on-Tees,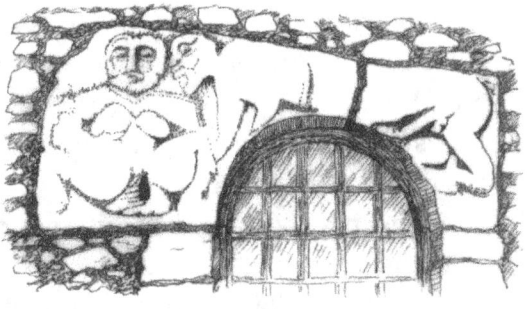
Easthorpe, Pennington and Llandrindod in Wales.

It is likely that the Romanesque influence spread first from the continent to Britain and from there to Ireland and this may account for an even more bewildering mix of carvings. It is possible that in Britain the image was freed from its context with other Romanesque images and perhaps first took on its form as the Sheela-na-Gig as we know the image today. At Penmon, on the island of Anglesey in Wales, and Iona, the Scottish outpost of an early Irish foundation, we find the insular type of Sheela, a figure that is a long way from the exhibitionist of the continent.

What is clear is that once the Sheela arrived on Irish soil it was not long before it was adapted and enveloped in a native tradition which did not necessarily view it as having a negative function. The meaning associated with the symbolism of the Romanesque cannot be transposed into the Irish context. Indications, such as their talismanic and apotropaic powers, suggest that this does not seems to be the case. A separate classification for the Irish figures is necessary and although they may have been influenced by the Romanesque, they are very much an indigenous product.

The powerful apotropaic function that the Irish Sheelas are traditionally regarded as having, is at variance with the negative function ascribed by proponents of the lusty Romanesque origin. In the continental examples, there is a lack of attachment and tradition of a talismanic or apotropaic function attributable to the figures. How and why this shift in function came about between the early insular anti-lust figures of the eleventh or twelfth centuries and the latter apotropaic figures leads to yet another area of interpretation. According to Weir and Jerman the motif was first introduced on churches as an image of lust and continued to be respected due to the importance formerly attached to the figures.[4] This is thought to have led to the later development of the Sheela as a protective or apotropaic motif.

Eamonn Kelly argues that this function is really an extension of its original purpose which sought to protect people from eternal damnation.[5] While this is possibly quite valid it stills falls short of explaining such a shift in function and purpose. An explanation for such an extraordinary shift in meaning is only necessary if we accept the premise that the Sheelas' original function was one of illustrating a negative sexuality. Many factors suggest that the Sheelas were regarded as having protective functions; yet it is only academic speculation which presupposes that the motif was brought over from the continent in order to warn the faithful of the sin of sexuality.

The notion that the Sheelas were originally erected as warnings against the sin of lust to an illiterate populace is also fraught with inconsistencies and does not make much sense unless the carvings were fully visible. While the majority of the continental examples were carved on exterior corbels, in both England and Ireland a number of Sheelas are found on the inside of churches. They are often located in positions where it would have been impossible for them to be seen. An example of this is at South Taunton where a Sheela is carved on a roof boss on the inside of the main chapel. She is almost certainly in her original position and would have been virtually invisible from below to the congregation. Likewise the two Sheelas from the twelfth-century church at

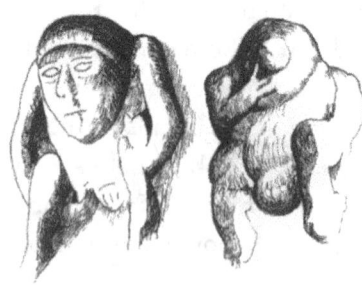

Tugford are carved on the inside of the entrance door and would have been passed unnoticed by anyone coming into or out of the church, unless it was known they were there. It is also thought that the Sheela at Romsey was erected on what would have originally been the inside of the church and according to a source of Andersen, Professor Zarnecki, the Sheela is 'in a place where it had no chance of being seen.'[6] In light of these examples we may well ask why any of the early Sheelas were located in virtually invisible positions if their purpose was to warn against the sin of lust? It seems clear then that they had a deeper significance.

Although the limbs of many Romanesque female exhibitionists may be contorted or exaggerated, the figures are pictorial representations of women. Romanesque art represents a fusion between the well-proportioned, naturalistic, clear-cut forms imported from the Mediterranean art and the asymmetrical, convoluted and zoomorphic compositions of the northern traditions. In contrast, the majority of insular Sheelas are often highly exaggerated and asymmetrical, in keeping with the northern Celtic tradition and often unrecognisable as females were it not for their sexual organs. The benign otherworldly expression of the Sheela with her two pairs of breasts in the thirteenth century parish church at

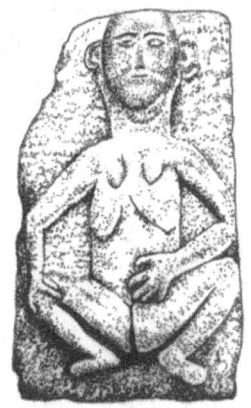

Ballylarkin and the peaceful-looking Sheela that formerly adorned Rochestown church do not give the impression that the carver was trying to depict a grotesque woman in order to portray evil, let alone an image which was to convey the possibility of damnation. Their symbolism will be examined in more detail later but for the moment it is sufficient to note that if they cannot even be recognised as representing women, then there seems little basis for assuming that they seek to convey an anti-woman or anti-lust type image.

It is evident that the carvers of the numerous figures which cover the highly decorative edifices of the Romanesque churches were skilled stonemasons whose level of expertise was of a very high standard. However, in Ireland, although there were many skilled masons around, the standard of carving the Sheelas shows great variation with some very skilfully carved and others crude or simplistic in their execution. As well as the workmanship being quite uneven, the style of the figures differs very much. It is obvious that the Sheelas are not mere copies of original Romanesque examples as, 'it is in their nature to be idiosyncratic and individual, and it is only with a few Romanesque figures that similarities can be traced'.[7] It seems probable that people were chosen perhaps for their magical rather than their sculptural skill and they evidently had some other purpose in mind than to depict an image of lust.

The theory that the Sheelas originated as Romanesque anti-lust figures does not explain the origin and prominence of the Sheelas in Ireland; it merely raises even more questions and contradictions. For instance from the enormous range of Romanesque motifs why did the Irish only import the female exhibitionist figure and not the male figures, let alone all the other erotic figures which the original carvers of the Romanesque clearly preferred? Why are Irish Sheelas often virtually the only form of decoration on a church, typically placed in prominent positions and not as part of a larger decorative scheme as with the continental examples? Why are the majority of Romanesque figures in an acrobatic posture while the majority of the insular Sheelas are standing or squatting? Why should the meaning of the continental exhibitionists as representing lust be imposed upon the early Irish Sheelas when all the evidence suggest that they were regarded as apotropaic figures? Above all, that such a minor and obscure theme in Romanesque iconography should take a strong root in Ireland as to continue to produce an even greater number of figures in the following centuries is perhaps the greatest mystery. All of this is remarkable given that the Romanesque had such a minor influence on architecture in Ireland. Despite these observations, the Romanesque is an integral factor that should be taken into account as it appears to mark a stage in the development of the Sheelas in which their proliferation on the walls of churches becomes an acceptable phenomenon. This is not to say there were no earlier native Irish prototypes or even pre-Romanesque Sheelas, but the Romanesque propensity for decoration, especially of carved figures, probably encouraged the depiction and development of a separate motif that had nothing to do with the moral message carried by its figures. The use of the motif in Britain in what appears to be more typical and consistently earlier Romanesque settings suggests that the Sheela motif may have entered Ireland via Britain, where it had already begun to be used alone and to be carved in a much more idiosyncratic manner.

It has been suggested that the Irish merely adapted their traditional images, influenced by both folklore and mythology, to the newly introduced exhibitionist motif. Having been encouraged into self-expression by the new symbolic art of the Romanesque artists they 'forged ahead with renewed enthusiasm and gusto, producing more and better Sheela-na-gigs than anyone else'.[8] If this was the case it would also explain why the insular Sheelas are so different in both their appearance and context from the continental examples. It is further proof that they are a separate group, regardless of whether their inspiration was from an insular or an outside source. It would also answer the crucial question of why only this very minor motif of Romanesque art, the female exhibitionist, was imported out of the range of alternative carvings. Even if their development is partially due to the influence of the Romanesque, a separate identification for the natively inspired Sheela-na-Gigs is necessary. In essence they are an expression of the old Celtic Church and not one of anti-lust invented by the Roman Church.

4

IRISH PROTOTYPES

There are a few earlier, pre-Romanesque, figures from the Celtic/ Irish past in which we can trace some sort of similarities and possible lineage to the medieval Sheelas. Those most likely to be established as pre-Romanesque are the few examples found on pillar stones. Whilst the majority of Sheelas are nearly always carved on slabs, which could be incorporated into the masonry of a building, the occurrence of a figure on a pillar stone is of special significance, whether or not they are ultimately proven to be older than the general run of Sheelas.

One of the most important examples, and certainly the most controversial, is the small, rather worn figure with a crooked stance, that is carved in relief on a standing stone in the church-

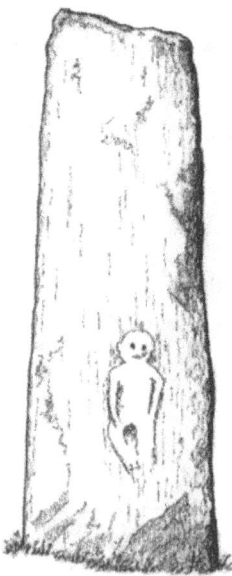

yard at Tara. Standing as it does on the most important sacred ceremonial centre of Ireland, the place where the ancient kings entered into sacral marriage with the goddess of the land, the existence of a Sheela-na-Gig here has far-reaching implications. The stone is known as St Adamnán's Pillar and is one of a pair of pillar stones, the other being much smaller and rounder, quite unlike anything erected during the medieval period. It has been suggested that St Adamnán's Pillar was originally a caryatid, a pillar with a figure carved on it that was used as a support in an earlier church. It has even been suggested that both of these stones may have originally flanked the entrance of a thirteenth-century church which was demolished without trace in 1823 and replaced by the present church.[1]

It seems very odd that not just the stone with the Sheela carved on it but the smaller, squatter stone as well, should have been erected when the church was being demolished. It seems more likely that they were erected as part of a site of an even earlier Christian or perhaps pre-Christian foundation. The yard of the present church, in which the stones are currently situated, is on the perimeter of one of the more important pre-historic earthworks at Tara, an enclosure known as the 'Rath of the Synods' which, as its name implies, is connected to the early foundation of Christianity in Ireland. Nearby is the *Teach Midchuarta*, the 'House of the Women', which in pre-Christian times, was probably a foundation or college of women residing at the site. The Sheela-na-Gig here may illustrate how the use of this image was sacred and revered as a special symbol at places dedicated to women.

Even more revealing is the fact that these two stones are regarded by some authorities as being the pair of mythological stones known as 'Blocc' and 'Bluigne' which played an integral role in the sovereignty or coronation ceremonies that were carried out at Tara. Apparently the stones were said to open wide enough to give passage to the chariot of the rightful king.[2] A careful excavation around these stones might ultimately establish their age but for the time being St Adamnán's Pillar and its evocative Sheela-na-Gig stands uncertainly between the Christian Church and the ancient earthworks of a former era.

Another Sheela found carved in relief on a pillar stone, was being used as a gate post for Drynam House near Swords until recognised and removed to the National Museum. It is not dissimilar to the Tara figure with its right leg raised as if doing a jig and may well be contemporary with it. It is suggested that it may have originally been built into the doorway of a medieval building and it is likely that it originated from a church built during the early Christian period (c. 6–12 century) as they were constructed from huge stone blocks which often flanked their doorways – a feature which is rarely seen on the churches built during the medieval period (c. 12–15 century).

What is possibly an even earlier and more significant figure can be found carved in relief on a cross-shaped stone erected beside an ancient holy well near the site of an early Christian foundation at Stepaside. It has a carving of a circle and other symbols too

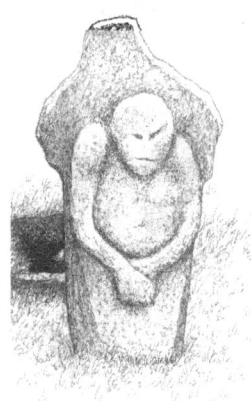 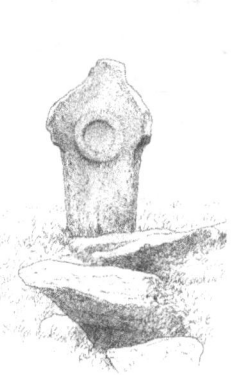 worn to decipher on its reverse side. Little mention has been made of this figure and despite its close proximity to the capital, few researchers appear to have visited it. We must rely on earlier scholars like Guest in discussing its possible date. Being carved on a type of cross usually ascribed to the early Christian period, it might date to the seventh or eighth century. Even if it proves to be as late as the tenth century it is still a figure which throws some doubt on the theory of a Romanesque origin.

The so-called Venus figure from Knockarley is extraordinarily difficult to classify though clear indications of a vulva show that it is closely related to the Sheela tradition.[3] It is a free-standing sculpture carved of local sandstone and it appears as if the stone

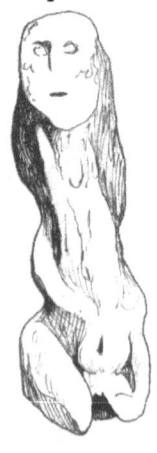 was specifically chosen as it required only minor modifications. The most distinctive feature is its elongated neck topped by a face that is inclined towards the right. The right hand lies across the belly and the left hand is laid on the thigh, while the vulva is clearly marked by a small incision surrounded by a very thick raised oval rim. John Feehan considers this figure might be of an early Christian date but the fact that it is a unique free-standing sculpture, makes it particularly difficult

to date.[4]

The likelihood of an early date for the origins of the figures from Tara, Swords, Stepaside and Knockarley illustrates the possibility that the Sheela motif was known before the twelfth century. Of these four figures, two are on pillar stones, one is on a cross-slab and another is on a free-standing sculpture, suggesting that they may have originated in the wooden churches that pre-dated the stone. Each of them is clearly carved in the Sheela tradition and they appear to be the earliest native Irish examples of Sheela-na-Gigs. It would seem, however, that it was a rare motif that was used sparingly and was probably regarded as having a particular potency. Apart from these more definite Sheelas there are also many other stone images that may be considered to be prototypes of the medieval Sheela-na-Gigs. Many of these images are deceptively similar to their medieval successors and it is still debatable as to whether some of these figures fall into the borderline class of actual Sheelas or are ancestral precursors to the later ones.

On White Island in Lower Lough Erne, in County Fermanagh, six extraordinary figures, dated ninth to eleventh century, were found on the site of an old church. One of these, a figure depicted as cross-legged with the hands and arms resting across the thighs was originally believed to be a Sheela, but since there is no clear indication of a vulva it cannot truly be classed amongst the genre. The large head is typical of many other Sheelas, but the broad grinning mouth with its upturned corners is a unique feature and one workman employed to clean up the church site 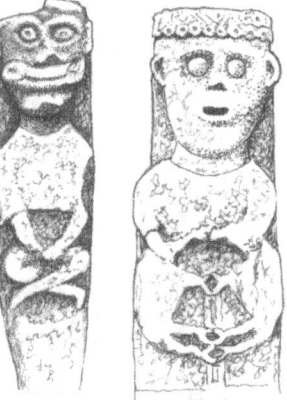 took such a dislike to it that he knocked the corner off one side of it. The White Island figure is also unusual in that she is nude apart from a short cloak-like mantle, '... which Du Noyer supposes to be a rheno, or secular dress.'[5] This suggests she is a female ecclesiastic, a feature paralleled in a few other Sheelas revered as the actual image of female saints.

This figure from White Island shares many other important similarities with the Sheelas, including the fact that it was inserted horizontally into the south wall of the old church beside a late Romanesque style doorway, which follows the tradition of using Sheelas on their side. Another effigy was also reused horizontally in the eastern gable of the twelfth–thirteenth-century church which appears to have been built on the site of an earlier monastic foundation. There are historical records of monasteries (probably consisting entirely of wooden buildings) that existed during an earlier period in this part of Lough Erne, and it is possible that the White Island figure which was a forerunner of, or at least strongly related to, the medieval Sheelas, originated from one of these early Christian monasteries.[6]

On Boa Island, at the northern end of Lower Lough Erne, can be found two figures that have been erected inside the graveyard of the old church of Caldragh. One of these is the well known

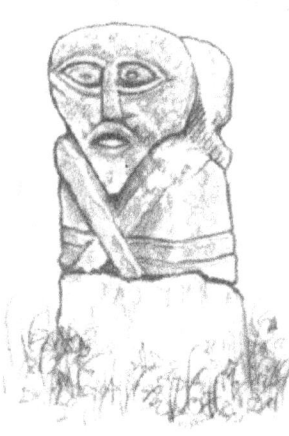

'Janus Figure', a double headed cult figure believed to have originated on a site on the island and is currently dated to around the ninth century. The arms are crossed over and the lower half of the figure is missing but there is no mistaking the sullen look characteristic of the Celtic expression. A chevron type pattern of tattooing extending from the side of its head to the cheeks is nearly identical to the markings which begin at the base of the head and extend on to the left cheek of the fearsome looking Sheela from Fethard Wall. Several other features such as a large head, the tongue poking out, a waist band and striation marks extending across the arms are reminiscent of markings found on numerous other Sheelas, that will be discussed in greater detail in the chapter eight.

Close by is the less well-known and seldom recognised Sheela-

na-Gig which originates from nearby Lustymore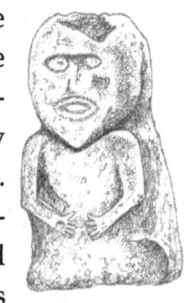
Island, the site of an early monastery. The legs are
very hard to make out but the hands are clearly gesturing towards the vulva although the figure is now
so worn that the actual vulva is not clearly indicated.
The style of this figure suggests that it is of similar tradition to the Janus Figure although it has been dated
to a few centuries later. Several other features such as
the broad-lipped mouth are shared not only by the Janus Figure
but also with the Sheela from Cavan. Stone figures such as the
ones from Boa Island, White Island and Lustymore, all precede
the medieval Sheela and must be taken into account in the search
for the development of the motif.

Nearby in Killadeas graveyard, in County Fermanagh, is another unusual figure known as the 'Bishop's Stone'. It is similar in
style to the White Island figures and is believed to belong to the
ninth, tenth or possibly eleventh century. On the west side of the
stone is what looks like a pagan idol carved in deep relief with an
interlaced pattern, and on the south side a bishop or abbot is
carved in low relief and shown in profile walking westward holding a bell and crozier. The figure of the pagan idol has been compared to the Sheelas, for as well as the large head and abbreviat-
ed body it has a vertically sloping scar or tattoo on its left cheek
imitated faithfully on the Kiltinan church Sheela.[7]

A very similar stone can be found at Carndonagh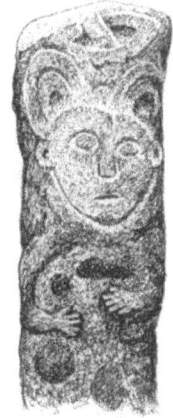
which forms one of two 'guardian' stones standing
alongside one of the earliest of the seventh century
high crosses in Ireland. The two guardian stones are
thought to date to the ninth century and are said to
originate from the monastic site nearby which is
dedicated to St Patrick. The outside surface of the
stones is carved with a mixture of symbols but on
one side is a figure carved in low relief. Its main features are very prominent round ears placed on the
top of the head (sometimes likened to horns), the

hands held across the stomach, a clearly outlined round ball or disc below the right elbow and an indentation where the genitals would be. Lawlor[8] has suggested that it may be a Sheela-na-Gig but the figure is now so badly weathered (and was half-hidden when Lawlor identified it) that this interpretation must be considered dubious. The possibility of this figure playing a role as a guardian to the high cross may have some bearing on the apotropaic function attributed to many Sheelas.

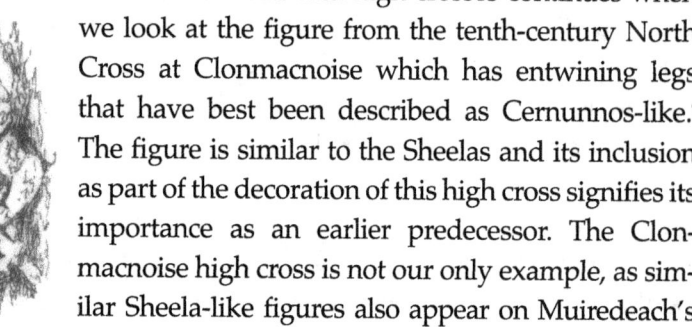

The association of Sheelas and high crosses continues when we look at the figure from the tenth-century North Cross at Clonmacnoise which has entwining legs that have best been described as Cernunnos-like.[9] The figure is similar to the Sheelas and its inclusion as part of the decoration of this high cross signifies its importance as an earlier predecessor. The Clonmacnoise high cross is not our only example, as similar Sheela-like figures also appear on Muiredeach's Cross at Monasterboice[10] which is dated AD 924 and the eleventh-century high cross at Drumcliff, County Sligo on which are two standing figures with one hand pointing towards their lower abdomen. There are instances in which a Sheela-like motif was used in relation to certain stone figures carved either singularly, or as part of a greater ornamental composition on high crosses, prior to the Romanesque and during the early Christian period.

Professor Etienne Rynne suggests that the forerunners of the motif (for both the Romanesque and medieval Irish Sheelas) were associated with a fertility cult which merged with Cernunnos, the

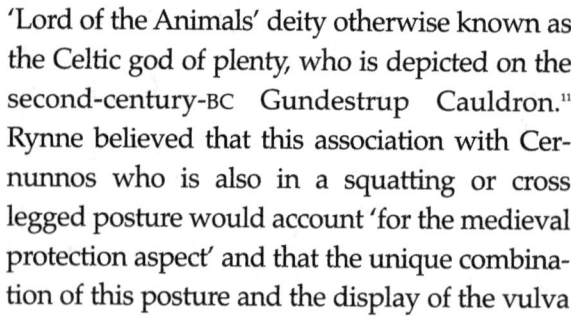

'Lord of the Animals' deity otherwise known as the Celtic god of plenty, who is depicted on the second-century-BC Gundestrup Cauldron.[11] Rynne believed that this association with Cernunnos who is also in a squatting or cross legged posture would account 'for the medieval protection aspect' and that the unique combination of this posture and the display of the vulva

50

have 'antecedents back into pagan Celtic times'.[12]

Several fascinating examples have been brought to light which appear to show a certain association of a pagan Celtic background with the Sheelas. One of the earliest examples occurs on the terminals of a fine gold armlet where the hands of a small figure are grasping or touching what appears to be her vulva, much in the manner of many Sheelas. She also has an owl-like bird perched on her head and fittingly invokes Rynne's concept of who is associated with fertility. The amulet was discovered in the late fourth or fifth century BC princely grave in Reinheim, Germany. Rynne also note that an even earlier figure on a stele from a Roman fort at Hofheim Germany, could be 'comfortably placed alongside the medieval Sheela-na-Gigs as a related carving'.[13]

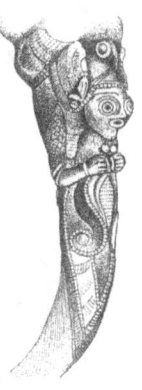

In Ireland pagan belief continued well into Christian times and it is suggested by Rynne that 'it is possible to find in an Irish context the presence of apparent descendants of the pagan Celtic cult figures.'[14] An example he gives of this is a figure grasping tightly up-drawn and bent legs which is delicately carved on the head of a bone pin found near Newbridge, County Kildare. It is believed to date from late eighth or early ninth century. Another bone pin was included in the original 1894 list of Sheela-na-Gigs and was described as, 'an ancient ivory carving of the class popularly called Sheela-na-Gigs, measuring 1.5 inches high and forming apparently the top of a pin, found close to Annagh Castle on the edge of Lough Derg, County Tipperary.'[15]

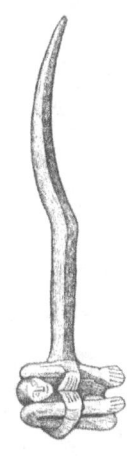

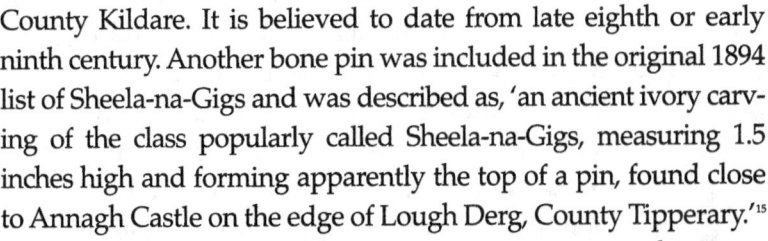

Wooden carvings are often referred to in relation to Sheela-na-Gigs and it has been suggested that the stone figures perpetuate images of wood which may have existed during an earlier period. Certainly some very interesting wooden images have come to light and indeed some of the figures have the appearance of being the direct ancestors of the Sheelas. For instance a wooden effigy

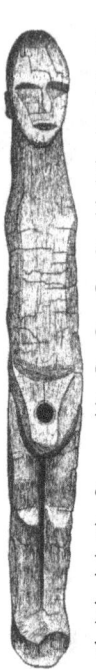

that is believed to date back to 1100–1000BC is on display in the National Museum in Dublin. This carved figure, 3 feet 9 inches high, is made of yew and was found during peat-cutting at Ralagan in County Cavan. It has a clear demarcation of a vulva and was almost certainly regarded as an idol. In Britain a wooden fetish christened by the excavators the 'God-dolly' was found. It was described as: 'Six inches in height, it has a head, flattish but clearly demarcated breasts and an emphatic phallus projecting from below the left breast.'[16]

Another fascinating wooden female figure, was found at Ballachulish in Argyll, Scotland, with the remains of the wickerwork hut in which she was presumably housed. It was preserved in the peat since the early Celtic period, possibly as early as the seventh century BC. The oak figurine, measuring about 4 feet 9 inches in length, had obvious sexual organs and frightening facial features with the eyes inlaid with quartz pebbles. The emphasis on the pudenda and the frightening facial features suggest that she is a goddess who belongs to an equivalent tradition to the Sheelas but over a thousand years before their appearance. What is most peculiar is the feature of the eyes inlaid with quartz pebbles which is also an aspect shared by the Sheela from Shanrahan whose eyes and right ear appear to be set with lighter stone, possibly quartz. The Sheela from Church Stretton also appears as if her vulva has been inlaid with a darker stone pebble, although it can not be certain whether this is the case or not. The question remains as to whether this is a remarkable coincidence or evidence of a continuity or revival in tradition?

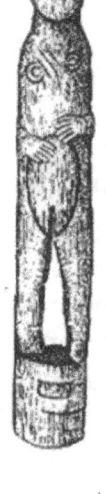

Well-preserved, wooden phallic figures dating from the late Bronze Age or early Iron Age have also been found. In some cases as on the figure from Dagenham in Essex, the phallus is separate with each figure having a hole for the insertion of this

organ. Although there are usually no breasts present, this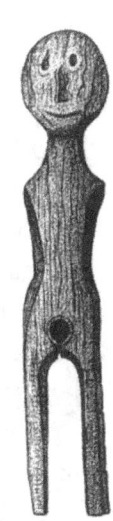
hole could be representative of a female vulva and the fig-
ures are generally interpreted as hermaphroditic in form.
Wooden figures and other devotional offerings have also
been recovered from marshes at the source of the river
Seine, in the vicinity of the Celtic-Roman sanctuary dedicated to Sequanao, the goddess of the river. It appears that
the use of such idols was widespread; similar well-preserved figures of gods and goddesses found in Danish
bogs indicate that this kind of carving probably existed in
a much larger scale in Britain and Ireland but have unfortunately been lost through decay.

In 1676 a diocesan order, issued in Ossory and Waterford,
commanding the burning of Sheela-na-Gigs provides some evidence for the existence of wooden examples.[17] At least one very
well-preserved wooden Sheela is in existence today in the medieval roof bosses of the church at South Taunton, and one can as-
sume there once were many more. Certainly, some very early
wooden statuettes have been discovered through the years, and
they may have some bearing on the matter, if only as archaic
images which have continued within traditional consciousness.

Often the only other form of decoration found in conjunction
with the Sheelas is the prolific and closely allied motif of the stone
head. Stone heads functioned as a symbol of the divine and a
source of prosperity and fertility. They were generally regarded as
an apotropaic instrument to ward off evil from the individual and
from the community as a whole. Like the Sheelas they were often
regarded in local tradition to be representations of ecclesiastics,
saints, deities or supernatural beings. Not only are the heads of
the Sheelas frequently exaggerated but physical features such as
tattooing of the face or neck are often strikingly similar as if to
suggest an overlap of traditions.

The cult of the human head was an integral part of pagan
Irish religion and ceremony during the Celtic Iron Age. This is corroborated not only by numerous examples of pre-Christian human

heads in stone but by the evidence of early literature, where the merits of heroes are judged by the number of severed enemy heads they possess. The importance of the head either singularly or in an exaggerated form as in Celtic idol sculpture did not disappear with the coming of Christianity to Ireland. On the contrary, there seemed to be an even greater proliferation of the motif on churches, abbeys and castles built during the medieval Christian period – a resurgence of its use that is contemporaneous with the rise of the Sheela-na-Gigs.

There is no doubt that heads appear in great number during the Romanesque era in Ireland, the Romanesque doorway at Clonfert Abbey being a classic example. But the origin of these heads is rarely questioned, since numerous examples of prototypes in Britain and Ireland exist and there is no need to relate them to the grotesque heads found on the continental Romanesque churches. Being fond of realism the Romanesque artists created a different style of head to the earlier Celtic prototype and after the twelfth century the Celtic head had acquired something of their flavour.

From the number of medieval examples it appears as if a kind of pagan head cult was accepted by the Church around the same time that the Sheelas were being erected, perhaps also due to the continental influence. That the motifs were often used together on the same building suggests the combination reinforced the supposed power of each. The existence of a cult of the human head within the realms of Christianity was never formally acknowledged in the same way that the existence of Sheelas within a Christian context is also denied. Through the comparison of the Sheelas with stone heads, it may be argued that such similarities go beyond mere physical likeness and that the original source of the Sheelas was the same pagan past.

Although the Sheelas are undoubtedly medieval, many of the figures have pagan features. Pre-Romanesque stone figures, such as those from Boa Island, White Island, Carndonagh and on the high cross from Clonmacnoise, are all connected to ancient monasteries and show that there were likely native prototypes for the

Sheelas. The combination of the squatting posture and the exposure of the vulva can be traced back through a number of figures carved out of stone, wood, ivory and other materials since the Celtic Iron Age which show 'the descent of the motif from pagan to Christian settings'.[18] The parallel occurrence of the stone heads also help to place the Sheelas within this long established and uninterrupted tradition from paganism through to the final blossoming in medieval Christianity.

Given such evidence it should not be surprising that a few Sheelas may actually pre-date the Romanesque era. The lack of a continuous tradition of stone figures is perhaps due to an absence of a tradition of carving figures in stone, as wood appears to have been the preferred medium. During the ninth and tenth centuries there was a sudden reawakening to the 'monumental and immortal power of stone' which during the next few centuries manifested itself in the widespread building of churches, round towers and high crosses.[19] The actual impetus for the flowering of the Sheelas is likely to have been the Romanesque movement in Europe as it was largely responsible for encouraging the trend of carving figures in stone and the use of such images to decorate churches.

It is quite likely that the prototypes for the figures were not derived from a common Romanesque original but were based in part on former archaic images once produced in wood and occasionally in stone or other materials. Perhaps the Romanesque released an image that, like the stone heads, was similar to an ancient prototype which had previously occupied many Irish stories, yet was rarely visually represented. It is quite plausible that when the influence of this art form spread to Ireland, 'it found a prepared and fertile soil – the Irish merely adapted their pagan-derived, cross-legged figure to the newly introduced Sheela motif.'[20] At the very least it is evident that pagan elements which had been incorporated into the Celtic Christian tradition strongly influenced the carving of the figures. In some cases, such as the archaic figure with holes drilled into it from Seir Kieran, they appear to have been treated in exactly the same ritualised context as pagan idols.

To appreciate such an origin or at least understand how their function was subsequently perceived by the people of that medieval era, we need to go back to the mythologies, folklore and symbolism within the context of Celtic Christianity. Then we may understand more fully what the Sheela expresses or meant to those people.

5

THE HAG OF THE CASTLE

In its original form the Sheela-na-Gig was a religious motif, primarily confined to churches dating from the eleventh to thirteenth century. However in Ireland there was a resurgence of the image during the fourteenth to sixteenth centuries and an expansion of its use to castles and other secular structures. The greater proportion of carvings in Ireland either originate from or are found on buildings which belong to this later phase. This enthusiasm for erecting Sheela-na-Gigs on castles and other non-religious structures, and the continuance of their use on churches after the fourteenth century are almost entirely unique to Ireland. What kind of culture embraced such an image and why did they choose to display it on their castles and churches are questions which lie at the very core of the mystery surrounding the Sheela-na-Gigs.

The medieval culture which is responsible for the widespread appearance of the 'Hag of the Castle' has its roots in the Norman invasion of 1169. This effectively cut the knot of the Irish dynastic or kinship system and allowed for the establishment of a feudal structure based on the continental model. While the political motive of the English monarchy and the papacy was the restructuring of the Irish political and religious system, the adventuring Norman barons were anxious to gain new lands. But in the process of achieving their aims these invaders rapidly merged into the Irish culture. In outward appearance the society that developed after this period was nominally Norman yet the speed of their assimilation into Irish culture has often been remarked upon, 'Irish and Normans intermarried freely, mingled freely and entered readily into alliances', so that within a hundred years after their arrival in Ireland, 'the principal Norman magnates were the grandsons of Irish twelfth-century kings and many of the Irish kings were the grandsons of twelfth-century Normans.'[1]

The main characteristic of this medieval culture was a deep sense of religious belief. The Normans had their own version of Christianity whereby the trade of war in which they specialised was reconciled with a pious, and sometimes superstitious, religious enthusiasm.[2] They founded and took over numerous abbeys and parish churches in the lands they colonised, and there was scarcely a church in Ireland which was not in some way altered or added to by the sixteenth century.[3] Not only did the Normans carry on the tradition of patronage of the religious foundations, as the Irish chiefs had done before them, but they also engaged in a massive campaign of castle building as they established themselves on the land. The Black Death of 1348–50, and many territorial wars, resulted in a very turbulent period characterised by the destruction of numerous castles and only minimal structural development. But a return to relative prosperity in the fifteenth century saw the advent of a new era of castle building carried on by the Anglo-Irish, the Gaelicised Normans and Gaelic chieftains alike.

The design of castles of this period is Irish and is more properly known as a Tower House. These are fortified buildings comprising a single square or rectangular tower several storeys in height, with heavily built stone walls often over two metres thick. Nearly all of the castles still standing in the countryside of Ireland today are like this as all the earlier ones were either destroyed or pulled down and rebuilt. Apart from the practical purposes of storage and defence the castles of the later medieval period are similar to the earlier medieval churches as centres of the community, and as such many were adorned with religious motifs traditionally reserved for the religious houses.

An example of this is Ballinacarriga Castle in County Cork, a well-preserved sixteenth-century tower house, which is a reminder of both the standing of the Gaelicised Norman clans of the time and the regard with which such structures were often held. The main floor, which can be reached by climbing the intact staircase to the top, was used as a chapel or church until its eventual demise in the mid-1800s, and is particularly noted for its many fine carvings, nearly all of a religious nature. Unnoticed by many visitors to this castle is an excellent example of a Sheela-na-Gig, which is located high up on the east wall.

The Sheelas from Ballynahinch, Kiltinan and Moycarkey castle were believed locally to have originated in churches. Although it is possible that a few may have been reused from earlier churches, the majority of figures found on castles appear to be contemporary with the structures on which they are found. The widespread occurrence of Sheela-na-Gigs on castles can be seen as an extension of that belief which put them on the churches in the first place, especially considering that they were still being erected on religious buildings during this later period. In certain instances the castle had a similar social standing or function as the church and the erection of the Sheelas is an example of the prominent place of Sheelas in lives of the people. Castles also employed that motif which is perhaps most closely allied to the Sheela, the human head, also considered to have had an apotropaic function.

The relatively stable period of the fourteenth to sixteenth centuries was also known for its Celtic revivalism which was probably largely due to Norman patronage of the arts and other native Irish traditions.[4] The influence of a Celtic revival is clearly visible in a number of the better-preserved castles which still retain some portion of their highly decorated lintels, window bosses, door surrounds and numerous other carvings in which there is often a liberal use of Celtic artwork. This prevailing attitude of Celtic revivalism is exemplified in the figure which is carved on a keystone over the main entrance to Ballinderry Castle in County Galway, a well-preserved, late tower house – the last of the castles built in the area. The image of the Sheela-na-Gig here is significantly set within a framework which also contains knotwork patterns, a triskele, a marigold or sun symbol and other important Celtic motifs. Another excellent and closely related example, also carved on a keystone, was recently found buried in the graveyard at Rahara church about twenty-five miles east of Ballinderry. This

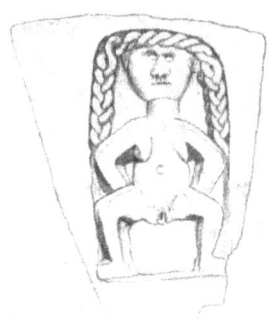

figure, now in Roscommon museum, is depicted with what looks like a long arched band of Celtic knotwork which has been described as plaited braids.[5]

The greatest density of Sheela-na-Gigs in this later period is found in areas of very rich land or places of political and religious importance such as those round the Rock of Cashel in County Tipperary and in the Shannon basin. These lands lay chiefly in the areas of Norman influence and settlement, and the spread of the Sheela motif appears to be attributable to their cultural assimilation. These were also the regions with the most affluent lands and had to be heavily defended.

While it has been established that the Normans who settled in Ireland significantly contributed to the spread of the Sheela motif, it is going a little too far to suggest that the earlier twelfth-century Sheelas were introduced into England and Ireland by the Normans. Had this been the case one would expect that the earlier wave of Normans who established themselves in England a century before they landed in Ireland would have carried on this tradition on their British castles. An exclusively Norman origin for the Sheelas also fails to account for the fact that the Sheelas can be found both prior to their coming and outside their areas of influence. Moreover, it is with the introduction of English Gothic art and architecture and not Romanesque (which had already been in existence in Ireland before the late twelfth century invasion) that the Normans are credited. Evidence to suggest that they imported the exhibitionist motif from the continent also appears quite insubstantial. Whether or not the Normans were the vehicle through which the motif travelled to Ireland it is certain that once it arrived on Irish soil it followed the same pattern as the Normans themselves, becoming thoroughly Gaelicised in a very short space of time and ending up as a unique product of an idiosyncratic Irish imagination.

Sheelas erected during this later period are larger, more eccentric than before and although the genitals are well defined they appear to depend less exclusively upon specific sexuality. Andersen suggests that these are of a more aggressive type of figure with broad, heavy shoulders becoming a consistent feature appropriate to the development of a militaristic castle-building culture. But the idol-like effect of the heavy shouldered Sheela is not new for it is evident in some of the earliest figures including those from churches at Seir Kieran, Errigal Keeroge and Lavey.[6] This powerful frontality is also evident in the figure on St Adamnán's Pillar at Tara and is even better illustrated in that most heavily built (and possibly very early) Sheela which looms out of a little spring near the old monastic settlement at Stepaside near Dublin.

There is no doubt that a more overt symbolism is used in the Sheelas erected on castles of this later period. Perhaps it resulted from superstitious belief in the power of the figures to ward off evil. A broad, open posture with feet touching the edge of the stone is a feature found on the great castle slabs with formidable hags such as Dunaman, Croomantagh, Tullavin and Ballyfinboy. Even the later more simplified Sheela on a quoin from Clenagh Castle retains the aspect of her feet turned out to touch its edge. In this aspect the feet themselves are often exaggerated, sometimes with highly stylised toes, which may symbolise their earthly nature or emphasises the point of contact with the material world. Sheelas with their feet touching the edge of the stone are also found on churches although they are by no means as powerful looking. In sharp contrast are the later examples such as the figures from the seventeenth-century castles of Bunratty and Clenagh. These later Sheelas are much more simplified in form or are depicted in a more naturalistic style, as may be seen in the figures from the holy well at Castlemagner and St Gobnait's church at Ballyvourney.[7]

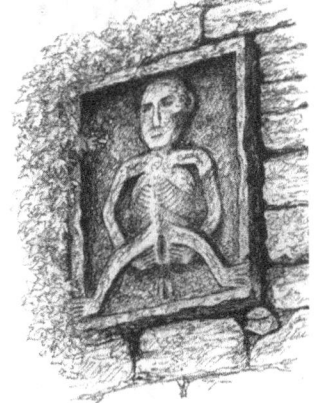

The tradition attached to the medieval castle Sheelas suggests a strong belief in their apotropaic or talismanic function. One of the earliest references to this is by Windele who, in the 1850s, reported on a figure found at Barnahealy, Co. Cork:

> This is one of those old Fetish figures often found in Ireland on the fronts of churches as well as castles, they are called 'Hags of the Castle' and when placed above the keystone of the door arch were supposed to possess a tutelary or protective power so that an enemy passing by would be disarmed of evil intent against the building on seeing it.[8]

The doorway symbolises the passage from one world to another and the placing of the Sheela above it served the function of protecting the gateway to another realm from intruders.

There are numerous early Irish examples of Sheelas located above the doorway of churches, but one of the most powerful is the Sheela from Kilnaboy situated above the main entrance to the twelfth- or early thirteenth-century church. Similarly in England,

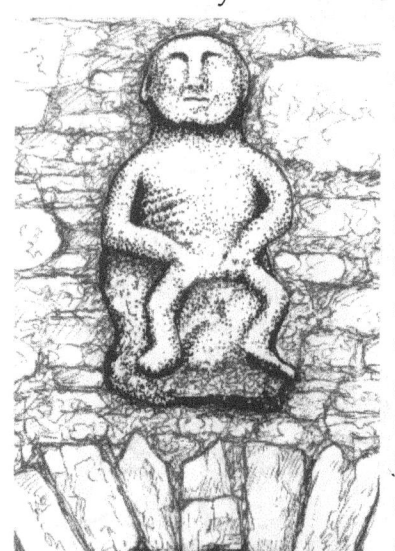

the Sheela from Buckland is found above the priest's door and that from Church Stretton is found above the north door to the church which was reserved for bringing in corpses. The tradition of placing Sheelas above the doorways was continued in the erection of the castle Sheelas. As we have already said the Sheela from Ballinderry Castle has been used as a keystone in the arch of the main doorway, and a figure from Scregg is carved on a wedge-shaped stone that probably once formed a keystone for a doorway of the now demolished castle. The later figure from Moate has also been carved in a depression on the stone over the gateway in the castle yard, which dates to 1649.

The apotropaic function attributed to medieval castle Sheelas would lead one to expect that they would be placed in more prominent situations than those in which they are actually found. The majority were located high up on the external castle wall above the main entrance, and very few are found in places that could be immediately viewed by those approaching the castle with evil intent. The larger and clearly delineated Sheela on Ballinacarriga Castle is situated at a height of about ten metres on the wall above the main entrance and so is seldom noticed unless specifically pointed out. The figure is not mentioned by one local historian in an otherwise-detailed description of the castle, and I also missed it on the first visit. Similarly at Redwood Castle in Tipperary the Sheela is even higher up and is barely visible, being tucked away under an overhanging barbican about fourteen metres above the main entrance doorway. The location of the Sheelas on the wall high above the main entrance probably signified vulnerability for this wall and the need for added protection, but perhaps it was unnecessary for the figures to be immediately seen.

Those Sheelas on quoins might give us a better clue as to their function since they are carved on a specifically designed stone which renders a fundamentally supportive role in the structure of the building. A magical role has been suggested for the quoin stones but it is easy to appreciate that these carefully worked and specifically keyed-in stones would be regarded as being an auspicious position for a protective emblem such as a Sheela-na-Gig. Figures carved on quoin stones are similarly found high up on the walls of castles and are often not easy to see. The Sheelas on the castles of Tullavin, Croomantagh, Ballaghmore and Cloghan are all very high up and though clearly visible they

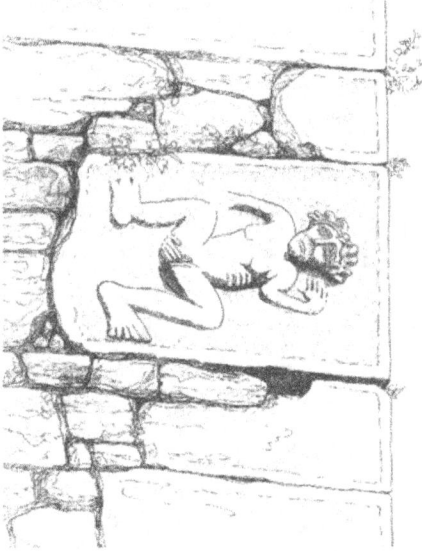

do not constitute a pronounced feature, whereas the Sheela on Doon Castle is set on a quoin only a little higher than the entrance door, and the later figure on Clenagh Castle is very close to the ground. The carving of Sheelas on quoin stones was not entirely restricted to castles as they were also used on the churches at Kiltinan, Malahide, and probably Lavey. These churches belong roughly to the same period as the tower houses and in the cases of Kiltinan and Malahide the quoin stone is situated below the roof at the springing of the gable, a vulnerable point from which the roof would once have risen. In Britain there are only two definite Sheelas used as quoin stones, on the churches of Fiddington and Pennington, both of which are places of former Celtic or Irish influence.[9]

One of the most intriguing aspects of the Sheelas is the tradition of the figures being inserted sideways or horizontally into a building, so that although the figure has been carved as if standing the stone has been set so that she appears to be reclining or lying on her side. The reclining position is also known from such twelfth-century churches as Liathmore, White Island and Buncton (the only known instance of employing a Sheela on her side in England) but is more common on both castles and churches of this later period, such as Tullavin Castle, Kiltinan Church, Cloghan Castle, Doon Castle, Croomantagh Castle and the vicar's choral at Cashel. When and why this tradition started is not known but perhaps one of the earliest example of its occurrence is the repositioning of the tenth-century White Island figure on her side in a building dated to the twelfth century. This figure is believed to be an earlier predecessor of the Sheelas and the reuse of the figure shows that she was still regarded as a relic. Andersen interprets the figure, heathen or Christian as it may have looked, as still having power but being 'employed in a state of half-disclosure' in which 'the potency of the figure, ancient or ominous, was not openly shown.'[10]

The Liathmore Sheela is another very important example, for the downward pointing pellets are carved in one piece alongside the Sheela which demonstrates that the reclining position was part of the carver's intention.[11] She is probably no older than the twelfth century and is in her original setting as the stone is integral to the structure of the church. Some of the reclining Sheelas like the later figures from Kiltinan Church, Tullavin Castle and Croomantagh Castle also have one arm raised which in their reclining position has led to their arm being below their heads. This does not seem to be a functional gesture to support lying down; rather it shows that most of these figures were originally carved as standing and then reinserted in the reclining position.

The vast majority of Sheelas are based on direct frontal view – characteristic of idol sculpture.

> In all primitive art, frontality has been relied upon for dramatic effect in an intended confrontation between a carved or painted image and the enemies, mortal or spiritual, against whom one directs that image.[12]

However, in the case of the reclining Sheela often located high up on the castle wall, the nature of her display would have been less obvious, and although this posture defies direct interpretation, a magical or apotropaic effect seems to be behind the tradition.

John Feehan has suggested that the Sheelas found on castles were protectors of a specific border.[13] He cites examples of two Sheelas – the castles in Cullahill and Ballaghmore in County Offaly – that were both built in the fifteenth century by the Gaelic chieftain Mac Giolla Phadraig (Fitzpatrick). The Fitzpatricks were the lords of Upper Ossory and they defended North Munster, strategically placed as they were on the old Irish Road. These figures are situated near the southern and northern boundaries of their territory facing out towards the border and they are the only Sheelas still to be found on any of the Fitzpatrick's castles. But territorial guardianship may be only one of their functions, for despite being situated on castles built by the same chieftain around the same time there is little similarity between the two figures.

An apotropaic function in guarding the approach or entrance to a town is clearly a feature of the three Sheelas from Fethard,

Thurles and Drogheda. The figure from Fethard is on a section of the fourteenth-century town wall overlooking the old medieval bridge over the Clashawley River at Watergate. It is strategically located facing the old entrance into the town. Curiously, just like the castle Sheelas erected high up on the walls, this fearsome and powerfully apotropaic figure is difficult to make out from a distance. It is indistinguishable from the wall until one has actually crossed over the bridge; then one is faced by perhaps one of the most terrifying looking Sheelas.

At Taghmon, a very odd four-eyed, heavy-shouldered figure thought to be a Sheela-na-Gig, is situated over a trefoil window in the north wall of the fifteenth-century, semi-fortified manorial church. The present church has a stone arched roof and an addition of a four storeys high castle-like tower, on the west end, makes the building look more like a castle than a church. The emphasis

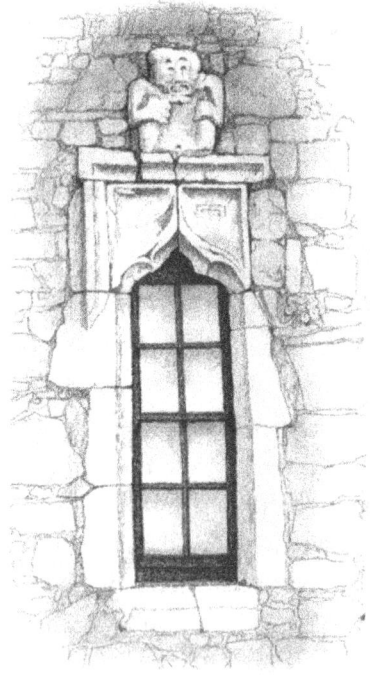

on security due to regular inter-tribal fighting suggests the Sheela is protecting the house. The two Sheelas from round towers are on or close to windows: the one at Ratoo is on the top left hand corner of the north window and the now detached figure at Toomregan is thought to have formed the lintel of a narrow, splayed, round-headed window. The figures from the churches at Kilsarkan, Bally-vourney, Cashel and Rath Blath-mac have been erected above or near the windows, often forming part of the lintel. In comparison there is very little association of Sheelas with the windows of castles, the only example being found on the inner reveal of a window at the top of the south-west tower at Bunratty Castle. Windows were not such a prominent feature of castles and as such probably did not need such additional protection.

Sheelas erected on castles of the fourteenth, fifteenth and sixteenth centuries were different to those placed on the churches before them. Larger, more hag-like figures – often placed higher up above the main entrance or on an important quoin stone – were commonly depicted. Whilst it appears that the later figures had a powerful apotropaic function and possibly also acted as clan totems, there is little association with any fertility function, let alone representing anti-lust. Indeed it seems odd that these figures were erected on castles at all if they were not taking on some sort of positive role or function.

6

THE MYTHOLOGY OF THE SHEELAS

The Sheela motif, with its added elements of superstition and magic, developed in Ireland within an environment of Celtic resurgence. It was a time when Gaelic traditions were being re-established and a period in which many of the great sagas and epics were transcribed from the oral tradition. A central and crucially important character in many of these stories, particularly those relating to sovereignty, death or warfare, was a fearsome and grotesque female of supernatural form who is known as 'the Hag', or in Irish *cailleach*.

Descriptions of the hag vary widely but many have similar features to those of the Sheelas. Typically she is described as an old woman with a bald head, cadaverous ribs, sagging abdomen and small flat breasts. In one version of the story of *Da Derga's Hostel*, the hag is described as, 'naked with a beard to her knees', while in another translation she is the woman, 'whose pudenda hangs down to her knees'.[1] It is reminiscent of a number of Sheelas, in particular the figures from Oaksey and Cavan. The suggestion has been made that the Sheelas portray 'the territorial or war-goddess in her hag-like aspect'.[2] Many Sheelas are in fact known as 'the hag' and there is little doubt that those ancient mythological Earth goddesses, the hag or the *cailleach*, influenced the origins of the medieval Sheela.

The hag is a goddess of sovereignty – the Earth goddess responsible for the fortunes, fertility and prosperity of her territory. Her association with life, fertility and death was symbolised by her ability to move between three aspects: a young beautiful maiden, a powerful sexual woman and a hag or crone. The shape-change was brought about by the annual rite of the sacred marriage, the ritual union of the goddess of the land (spirit of Ireland) with the mortal king. It was a fertility rite which symbolised and legitimised the union between the king and his land and people. The theme of an ancient hag, wandering the countryside, ugly and unkempt, recurs throughout many of the old stories. In most tales she is transformed into a beautiful young woman upon meeting and mating with a man destined to become the rightful king. In others where the man was not suitable for kingship, the hag was not transformed, and she brought about his downfall.

In the eleventh century story of the *Adventures of the Sons of Mugmedón*, Niall and his four brothers were out hunting when they were overcome by thirst. One of the brothers found a well, guarded by a hag described as 'bleary-eyed, fang-toothed, snotty-nosed with a boil-encrusted body', who demanded a kiss in exchange for water. The first brother turned her down and fled in horror, and the others reacted the same way except for Niall. He agreed not only to kiss the hag but to sleep with with her as well. As the two embraced the hag was transformed into a lovely maiden and Niall acceded to the throne.[3]

In Ireland the pattern of tribal kingship and the rite of sacral marriage to the goddess of the land did not die out until the seventeenth century, when the last of the Sheelas were being erected. The central coronation site of the high king of Ireland was Tara, and it is significant that a Sheela-na-Gig is found in proximity to a renowned and sacred site. Traditionally the inauguration of the kingship at Tara involved several ordeals that tested the candidates' fitness to be king. The *Lia Fáil*, a phallic stone situated on the hill of Tara, representing the male element, was said to cry out or shout when it came in contact with the man destined to be king. The female element was personified by a pair of pillar stones, currently standing near the present day church which are thought to be the 'Blocc' and 'Bluigne' of mythology.[4] Described as being 'but a hand's breadth between them', the

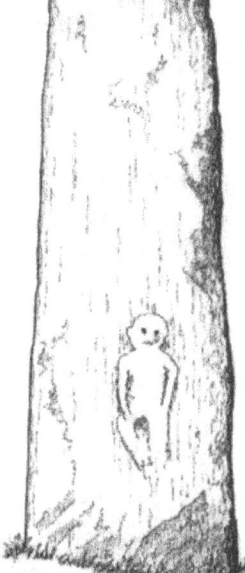

test as to whether they accepted a man as king involved their opening wide enough to give passage to his chariot. The taller one known as St Adamnán's Cross has a Sheela-na-Gig carved on it and if this mythological association could be proven it would connect the Sheela-na-Gigs with these ancient rites of sovereignty.

The hag also appears often as a goddess of war and harbinger of death. In the saga of *Da Derga's Hostel* the king initially refuses entry to the hag, as he is under a *geis* (taboo) not to allow entry to a single woman after dark. The hag curses him by, 'standing on one leg with one hand held up in the air' – a well-known magical position for casting spells. This is the same one-legged and one-armed stance that is adopted by a number of Sheelas including the figures from Tara, Kiltinan and Fiddington. Although King Conaire had already broken almost all his taboos, the hag was the final omen of his impending death. She forces him to break his last taboo by allowing her to spend the night in the hostel.

The tradition of war goddesses continues in the form of the banshee who is the current death messenger of Irish tradition. This female spirit is said to be heard to scream or cry, and on occasions be seen, at the time of a person's death. The terrifying wail of the banshee, as a harbinger of death, can be likened to that of goddesses of war. It is recorded that when Nemhain, 'raised her cry over the armies facing Cú Chulainn, a hundred warriors of them fell dead that night of terror and fright.'[5] In the south-east of Ireland she is known as Badb, one of the trio of war goddesses in early Irish literature. She, too, was seen washing the clothes of those who were about to die. A story is told of the lake of Rath (near Rath Blathmac with its Sheela-na-Gig) 'where twenty-five banshees washed the visionary clothes of the invaders doomed to die.'[6] According to the bardic tradition, the banshee was last seen washing clothes by the river at the battle of Aughrim in 1691. The fact that belief in the banshee continues strongly to this day is evidence of a strong survival of the goddess of sovereignty and her association with death.

When Sheelas were being erected, there was a great belief in the power of a female deity as a protectress of the fertility and abundance of the land. That warfare and fertility should be closely allied may seem a paradox at first sight but it reflects a recognition that giving and taking, good and evil, life and death are interdependent. If the land were to flourish and be productive then the borders of the territory needed to be defended, and war may have acted as a necessary extension of the function of guardianship. In the era of great warriors and frequent inter-tribal fighting, the representation of a goddess of war was a way of representing the goddess of death who was just as intent on ensuring that what had come from the earth should return to the earth in a form that would ensure its future fertility. The goddess of sovereignty in her form as the hag represented a protector of the territories, its rulers and inhabitants. She possessed the power of life and death and embraced both war and sexuality in a manner which ensured general fertility. It is easy to understand that the generally accepted apotropaic function of the Sheelas may also have been an extension of their original purpose of invoking prosperity and fertility.

A link between the Sheela-na-Gigs and death may be a fundamental aspect of their symbology. This association was commented on in the 1840s: 'There is, however, in the best sculptured figure a certain expression of countenance which resembles that of death.'⁷ The contrast with the open vulva, often initially taken to represent birth, has given rise to comments about the apparent contradiction between the two elements. Yet this contradiction fits the cosmology of the Celtic world where death implicitly involves a spiritual transformation or awakening. The image of death, which is integrally associated with women and portrayed in the figure of the hag, must be symbolically embraced before the cycle of life can begin again.

The nakedness of the Sheelas is one of the few features that they all have in common and there are some references to the occult power of female nakedness in Irish mythology, especially as a magical means of self-defence. In the story 'The Intoxication of the Ultonians', a female poet Richis wishes to avenge the death of her son killed in a battle with Cúchulainn and enlists the aid of another man to kill him. When Richis meets Cúchulainn she takes off her clothes and immediately Cúchulainn covers his face so that 'he might not see her nakedness'. His charioteer warns him that a man is approaching to kill him but Cúchulainn states, 'Now while the woman is in that condition shall I not rise up', and seeing him magically subdued into inaction the charioteer is forced to take matters into his own hands, throws a stone at Richis which kills her and saves Cúchulainn's life.[8]

The well-known curse of the Ulster men – whenever they needed their power most they would be overcome with pain like a woman in childbirth – is normally ascribed to Macha after the king of Ulster had forced her to run in a race when she was just about to deliver twins. An alternative version of how the Ulster men were afflicted comes from the story of the time when Cúchulainn had gone to live with the fairy, Fedelm of the Long Hair. After about a year she appeared naked before the men of Ulster and they were immediately stricken with the affliction. The above story explains not only Cúchulainn's absence and the reason he was never afflicted with the pangs but perhaps also why he did not want to look at naked females.

There are many early historical stories, recorded by Caesar and others, of Celtic women such as Boudicca and other female warriors who went into battle naked. In the mythological story 'The Death of Finn', Finn's messenger Birgad had offered terms to his opponents in the midst of a battle but their response was to threaten to kill her if they ever saw her again. 'Birgad returned upon the road and lifted up her dress above the globe of her buttocks ...'[9]

It may be assumed from the above tales that both female nakedness and more specifically the female genitals were a very powerful symbol of the goddess in her life-giving aspect and as such would be opposed to war and forms of destruction – the vulva as the source of life would naturally be opposed to death.

However, it appears that the female genitals, or less explicitly female nakedness, were the source of both life and death and as such they were an even more powerful, magical force than mere weapons. The goddess of death is no more than the goddess of life, as both life and death are mutually intertwined and are conditional and vital aspects of each other. As Nuala Ní Dhomhnaill has commented in reference to Sheela-na-Gigs:

> This image is so archaic and fundamental as to be all but forgotten in modern life. This is the as yet undifferentiated Mother-of-Life-and-Death. Her self-exhibition has nothing sexual or lascivious about it, rather it is a reminder of something which to us liberated moderns is much more obscene and frightening. 'This is where you came from, and this is where you are going to'.[10]

It should not surprise us that the hideous hag of mythology also exposed her genitals. She usually made strong sexual advances and was deeply concerned with fertility, warfare, guardianship, sexuality, prophecy and death. The many stories centred around the actions of such a goddess would have been widely and commonly told as part of the rich oral tradition of the Middle Ages. Normans and Irish alike patronised such storytellers who were responsible for transmitting the history of the land. The image of the hag would have been even more vivid at the time of the carving of the Sheelas. The concept of the sovereignty or war goddess in her various guises, especially that of a hag, was deeply rooted in the eighteenth century, although she was considered as a political or literary figure rather than a religious one. The native Irish had been conquered and poets 'pictured their land as a woman languishing in yearning for her absent spouse, or even as a shameless prostitute granting her favours to the boorish foreigner who had usurped the place of her rightful partner.'[11] Later this concept of the hag was used by Anglo-Irish writers such as W. B. Yeats in his famous play *Cathleen Ni Houlihan*.

During medieval times when the Sheelas were being erected, art was not seen as mere decoration, but formed a vital part of the transmission of the mythologies and lore of the older cultures. Although a connection with mythology, which by its very nature is obscure and vague, does not necessarily explain the origin of the Sheelas it may help to explain their great proliferation and broad acceptance in Ireland, a land steeped in mythology and tradition. At the very least, it is understandable how such stories of hag goddesses and their powerful apotropaic or fertility powers, may have become subsequently attached to the image of the Sheelas.

The image of the hag or *cailleach*, as one which corresponds to several Sheelas, goes a long way to explaining her fierce countenance, her nakedness and her otherworldly looks. This idea of local territorial goddesses might also help to explain the great diversity of images of the Sheelas as they represent localised traditions about the nature of the goddess mythology. It is possible that Sheela-na-Gigs are virtually the only surviving element of one of the most important aspects of the native Celtic tradition: its feminine orientation or belief in the ultimate deity as symbolised in the *cailleach* or hag, the goddess or the image of female spiritual power.

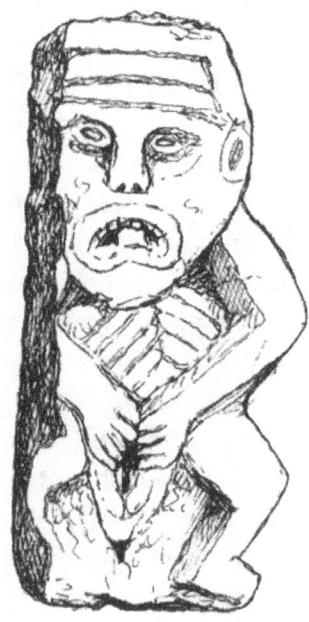

7

FROM GODDESS TO SAINT

Christianity as it evolved in Ireland until the medieval period was fundamentally an insular development, uniquely blended with the strong Celtic tradition of Irish society. It was structured on the native cultural systems: its pattern of kinship, history of learning, poetry, storytelling and druidic traditions. Similarities between the tenets of the old religion and the new meant that there was very little conflict and many of the idols, objects, beliefs and practices of pre-Christian religion were Christianised or embedded into the fabric of the Church, rather than condemned and rejected. It is not possible simply to categorise the Sheelas as either Christian demon or a pagan idol but perhaps we could look at them as representative of that merging of Christian and pagan ways.

Although the hag's association with traditional mythologies and its image suggest that the Sheelas were strongly influenced by a pagan past, the fact is that they were found on Christian churches and must have been, outwardly at least, reconciled with the Christian tradition. When we look at folklore, we see that a significant number of Sheela-na-Gigs were, and in a few cases still are, commonly regarded as saints. The Sheela at Dowth was known as St Seanachan and a second figure in the west gable of the old church of Seir Kieran was regarded as an image of its founder, St Ciarán. It has been argued that this belief in the Sheela being the image of a saint is merely a recently applied interpretation to explain away its existence. However the modern perception of what a saint represents and how the people of former times may have envisioned such saintly figures differ quite dramatically. A closer look at this idea may help us to appreciate how Sheelas were accepted on Irish churches.

People worshipping one God instead of a multitude of pagan gods and goddesses left a void in the Christian era. This was filled by saints, many of whom were former pagan deities, who still acted as intermediaries, bridging the gulf between human and the divine worlds. The Church understood the importance of the old gods and goddesses in the pre-Christian world and created a structure of saints that would allow for continuity of worship. Brigit is the best example of the transition of a pagan goddess into Christian saint as there can be no doubt that she spans the pagan and Christian tradition. Miranda Green suggested that she personifies the old pagan Earth mother goddesses, and Mary Condren described the Sheela placed above the doorway of Kilnaboy church as an image of Brigit, suggesting that she was placed there to 'allow the congregation to enter the church through her womb'.[1]

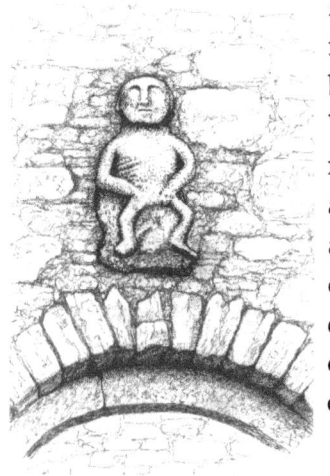

In making such a comparison Condren is aware that the Sheela-na-Gig at Kilnaboy occupies the same position as the Virgin Mary on Catholic churches of the more modern era. Although the Sheela and the later sanitised Roman model of a saint are incompatible images the perception of saintly figures by the people of the Middle Ages who built the church was notably different from that of today.

Brigit, the daughter of the Dagda, is an important deity and was a patron of poetry, smithcraft, prophecy and the healing arts. She was seen as a fertility spirit and concerned with the welfare of cattle and livestock. It has been suggested that Brigit is a title rather than a personal name as it derives from the Celtic word *bríg* or *bríog* which is suggestive of power and authority and means 'high one' or 'exalted one'. In the story of the final battle between the Fomorians and the Tuatha Dé Danann for the possession of Ireland, Brigit appears as a mediator,[2] an ancestor-deity, a mother goddess whose main concern was the future well-being of the country. While many of the old Irish goddesses were linked to particular places and intimately identified with the land, Brigit was a transportable goddess who was worshipped in many parts of Britain, Gaul and Ireland. It is no wonder Christianity quickly enlisted her into their hierarchy and turned her into a primary saint honoured above all others except for St Patrick.

Brigit, the Christian saint, is said to have lived in the fifth century AD but is easily recognisable as being the same person as the goddess Brigit. Her biographers describe her as feeding from the milk of a white, red-eared, otherworld cow, and say that flames rose from her head. The pagan fire festival of Imbolc, marking the beginning of spring and celebrated in her honour, was retained and renamed Brigit's day. On this day crosses made of rushes are still placed on buildings to guard against evil spirits. The survival of such pagan associations demonstrates that it was the policy of the Church to take over the symbols of the old religion and to convert them to Christian use.

St Brigit's traditional seat at Kildare was a renowned site of the old religion and the transformation of the pagan sanctuary to Christian nunnery or monastery was typical of the relatively peaceful way in which Christianity was introduced into Ireland. A fifteenth-century cathedral now stands on this most sacred site of St Brigit's former monastery, and recently a figure thought to be a Sheela has been found adorning a funerary monument erected inside the church. Still to be seen on the site is the foundation of a dwelling in which it was believed that St Brigit and nineteen of her nuns took turns in guarding an eternal fire surrounded by a hedge which no male might broach.

It is a remarkable fact that in her conversion to Christianity, Brigit became even more powerful – a singular goddess rising above all former goddesses alongside the development of an increasingly monotheistic Christianity. Just as the twelfth century saw the cult of the Virgin Mary spread across Europe, in Ireland the worship and devotion to Mary was translated into that of Brigit. As Mary ascended to her exalted position in the Church of Europe so too did the image of Brigit in Ireland, and she became known as the 'Mary of the Gael', being often referred to as the 'Mother of the High King of Heaven'. It is significant that the purification of the Blessed Virgin is on 2 February, the day after Brigit's feast day, and perhaps no coincidence that the expansion of the Sheela image during the twelfth century parallels the development of the cults of Brigit and Mary.

Several Sheelas are directly connected with Brigit, particularly with her healing and fertility powers. The Sheela-na-Gig over the window of the old church at Ballyvourney is venerated as an image of Saint Gobnait. Gobnait is a mysterious figure, one of those pre-Patrician saints who does not have a solid existence and whose place in Church history is uncertain. She lives on because of folk memories and the living traditions still associated with her, rather than in recorded history. Séamus Ó Catháin, who has written extensively on the subject of Brigit, not only connects Gobnait with Brigit, but regards them as being 'one and the same person' and notes that Gobnait's feast day falls on 11 February which when 'translated from the Old to New Style becomes 1 February and identical, therefore, with the Feast Day of St Brigit.'[3]

St Gobnait is also known as the 'Saint of the Bees', and Edith Guest regarded her to be amongst the most obviously pagan saints still being revered in the Irish countryside. In Gobnait, as in her *altera persona* Brigit, we are looking at a goddess of ancient origin, a personification of that primary divinity of older pre-Christian beliefs, the Earth goddess. Her association with bees, the symbol of life, death and regeneration in both pagan and Christian times, has invested her with all the attributes of the old goddesses and connected her to all those older forms of devotion.

The Sheela-na-Gig, above the doorway of Kilnaboy church, whom Mary Condren earlier likened to Brigit, is known as the image of St Ingheanne Bhuide, who is reputed to have been founder and head of the religious community of Kilnaboy. It was an important early religious foundation and there are remains of other former structures including the stump of a round tower close by the church. Just like Brigit and Gobnait, the saint was also closely associated with healing. Several curative holy wells are not far from the church, including the rock-hewn 'Seat of Inghean Bhuide' in which devotees are said to sit to cure backache.[4]

Besides these two instances of Sheelas which are believed to be an image of the alter egos of St Brigit, there is at Castlemagner a severely rubbed figure carved on a slab flanking the doorway to a well dedicated to St Brigit. This was a very popular holy well as its water was thought to be good for curing every illness, when rubbed on the painful part of the body. In the last century 'hundreds of carriages could be seen there' bringing people to the rounds, especially on Brigit's Day, when people would come from long distances to drink the water.[5] A Sheela from nearby Castle Widen-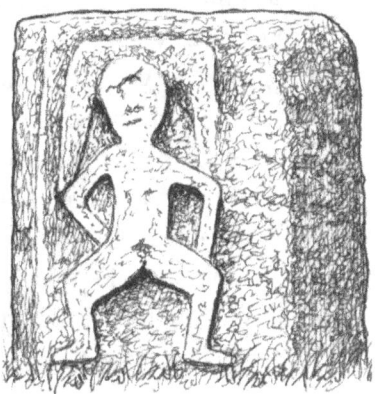ham, when first discovered, was described as lying by a holy well situated on the banks of the Awbeg River, 'and bearing an image supposed to be that of the saint'.[6] However, here the saint of the well is St Patrick, and it may have previously been dedicated to a female deity or saint, perhaps even Brigit.

Another connection to the Sheelas is hinted at in an amusing comparison made between Brigit and Priapus, the Roman 'god of gardens' who is shown 'as an old man holding up his robe to carry the fruits and vegetables for which he is responsible, and thereby exposing to view the source of all this fruitfulness ... an un-naturally large, erect phallus.' Ó Catháin suggests that it is tempting to see a direct parallel in the image '... of the fire-carrying Brigit of Irish tradition, her gown raised to accommodate the burning coals, an exercise we may be justified in assuming resulted in the exposure of more than her feet.'[7] In an account of the story in Kerry about her alter ego St Gobnait, it is said that she had a fine pair of calves and if we are to take her association with the Sheelas at face value, then she is exposing a good deal more.

For many of these early Celtic saints there are few records, but there are fascinating traditional accounts of their ancient lineage which show that holy women like Brigit and her alter egos Gobnait and Inghean Bhuide, represent an unbroken chain from pagan goddesses to Christian saints. Whilst the Christian God was superficially accepted, the Irish people continued their belief in the ultimate feminine principle, expressed through their local native goddesses turned saints.

From the very beginning the Church evolved a structure of saints and holy persons which included a primary goddess who would spearhead the gospel of God and Christ. Christianity eventually displaced the old religion but many of the pagan deities are still traceable in the characters of local saints.

Even in Britain, which compared to Ireland lacked that same continuation in tradition, there is ample evidence which suggests that paganism was not immediately suppressed by Christianity:

> In 1282, the priest at Inverkeithing in Fife had to appear before his bishop for leading a fertility dance at Easter round a phallic figure, and in the fourteenth century the Bishop of Exeter was shocked to learn that the monks of Frithelstock Priory in Devon were wont to worship a statue like 'the unchaste Diana' at an altar in the woods.[8]

Such carvings as the so-called 'green men' or 'foliated faces' that are found amongst the Romanesque art of churches in Britain, with their obvious pagan overtones, were still being erected on churches throughout the Middle Ages. Professor Geoffrey Webb found phallic symbols concealed inside the altars of almost 90% of fourteenth-century churches built up to the time of the Black Death.[9] Evidence of this nature suggests a very strong survival of pagan beliefs in Britain long after the arrival of the Christian Church and leads one to suspect that Christianity, Celtic or Roman, was not so pure and devout as we are led to believe.

The Sheela is not alone as a Christian representative of pagan elements but unlike many of the earlier images she was not easily subsumed into the Christian format. As the Church developed its veneration of virginity and advocation of higher values it became increasingly difficult to find a place for the Sheelas in the un-threatening structure of Christian deities it had created. Many of the less easily assimilated elements were made redundant, and the Sheela-na-Gigs slipped out of sight. Those figures that managed to survive into the modern era form a unique bridge with the ancient traditional structure of belief which existed until the advent of the new Christian era.

The Sheela-na-Gig on the church, which at first may seem so inconsistent with its teachings, appears a more appropriate symbol than may at first be supposed. Whether it was the original intention of the carvers to depict an image of the local founding goddess turned saint or whether a later belief became attached to an existing figure is not known. But is certainly intriguing that a number of Irish Sheelas were taken as the image of the goddess Brigit and as a general class of figures became associated with her magical, beneficent healing, fertility and talismanic female powers. The individuality of each Sheela also leads one to suspect that she was probably regarded as the local ancestor or saint whose powers were of benefit to certain clans or people who had an important territorial function.

Now that the Sheelas are once again emerging from their hiding places and people are visiting old castles and churches and appreciating our past it is an appropriate time to re-examine these much maligned figures and to acknowledge the wonder of their very existence. New tradition and beliefs are being attached to them, and they will continue to be redefined and imbued with different meanings, just as they will also continue to redefine and challenge our perception of Irish history and the role of the Church within it, making them an important part of the heritage of the old Celtic Christian world. Although debate on the figures will probably still continue, it is certain, that nothing in the whole Church ornamentation of the medieval period reaches quite as far back as they do. Our view of what is, or what is not, Christian or pagan soon blurs. Under closer examination the Sheela-na-Gigs end up somewhere in the middle – a mysterious and challenging enigma.

8

THE SYMBOLOGY OF THE SHEELA-NA-GIGS

Sheela-na-Gigs are part of an unbroken tradition of Celtic art which first flowered in Ireland around the third century BC, and continued through the early Christian period until later medieval times. In keeping with this tradition they are symbolic figures and every aspect of the carvings has a meaning: the size and shape of their heads, eyes and ears, face or body grooves, the objects they hold, the position of their arms and legs and the great variety of ways in which the central feature, the genital organs, are indicated. In Celtic art honour and reverence to a deity was visually demonstrated through use of plurality, exaggeration or schematism while energy, tension, asymmetry and opposition also played their part in enhancing the potency of the designs. All unnecessary detail was abandoned in order to capture the *numen* or the essence of an image and these images were not bound by a rigid framework of realism for, 'however bizarre and unnatural it appeared in earthly terms, they functioned as a direct acknowledgment of power.'[1]

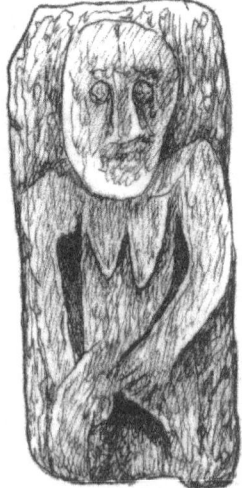

All these features of Celtic art can be seen in the depiction of the Sheelas, in particular their asymmetrical nature with the left and right hand of the body often being completely out of balance. An example of this is the Sheela in the Ulster Museum from Errigal Kierroge which has one shoulder pulled up higher than the other, one breast and one arm longer than the other and many other asymmetrical features. There are also many examples of exaggeration of parts of the body: hands, feet, head, ears and vulva. The importance of such symbolism has been overshadowed in the past by a tendency to favour literal interpretations, and the Sheelas have often been accused of being 'crudely executed', 'revolting', 'misshapen' or 'obscene'. This is to judge them on artistic competence in classical, mimetic terms which becomes irrelevant when these symbolic religious motifs are seen against a background of Celtic art.

Central to the symbolism of the Sheelas is that evocative image, the vulva or yoni. The vulva has been revered as a central and most powerful symbol for virtually all ancient cultures and its use on cult objects or depictions of various goddesses goes as far back as palaeolithic times. It is frequently exaggerated in size and its representation requires a frontal view. The symbolism of the vulva is not erotic in our modern sense of the term, and it was not intended to arouse sexual desire. It was initially thought to indicate not only human fertility but also the life force or energy emanating from the earth itself. This has led to the Sheelas being popularly regarded as 'fertility figures' but a number of factors suggest that there is more to their symbology than just fertility or fecundity.

Goddess figurines throughout history illustrate fertility by overtly emphasising the main procreative features such as the belly and the breasts, often leaving out the sexual organs entirely. In the Celtic world, mother goddesses are usually portrayed seated, often accompanied by symbols of abundance and fertility such as babies, animals, fruits and bread. In contrast many Sheelas have very small breasts, if any at all, or are so lean that their ribs show – only a few look robust enough to be symbols of fertility. When we look at what the majority of the figures are pointing to or touching we see those parts of genital anatomy not directly involved in reproduction at all. In some figures the clitoris, the labia, and even in some cases the anus, are portrayed with an anatomically realistic detail which contrasts sharply with the otherwise fantastical style of the figures. Anatomical realism of the genitalia, including the depiction of the anus can be seen on the exceptionally well preserved Sheela retrieved from an old tower at Glan-

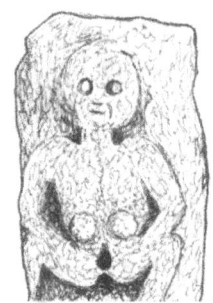 worth castle in Cork and the figure from Burgesbeg in Tipperary. It can also be seen on the similar and probably closely related figure from Clonmel which is currently on display in the National Museum, Dublin.

The purpose of this incongruous use of realism in the depiction of the genitalia may be to enhance the apotropaic function of the figures. Many references in both historic and folklore memory attest to a belief in the inherent power and ability of the female genitals to ward off evil forces. On the Isle of Man women used to stride over the ceremonial bonfires, 'exposing their vulvas to the beneficial influence of the flame, and blessing it with their own power'.[2] The power of female genitalia to avert misfortune even encompasses calming a storm at sea. In Christianity the almond-shaped *vesica piscis* symbolises the vulva and was frequently depicted surrounding holy figures. Although its origin is seldom referred to, 'it was used by early Christians to represent the mystery of God's union with his mother-bride.'[3]

The dual representation of the vulva as both an abstract symbol and as a part of the natural female anatomy can be seen as the threshold through which all life emerges. Implicit in its symbolic use is the divine power which is associated with life, death and rebirth, and the more occult notion in which the vulva or the *vesica piscis* symbolises the point at which separate forces or worlds simultaneously meet and divide. According to an expert on primitive art, Professor D. Fraser, this imagery of the displayed female is compelling, for 'it has the power to ensnare the viewer's glance and hence capture his subjectivity or selfhood.' The female genitalia is 'effective with supernatural powers ... it bends all outside forces to the will of those behind the image and thus is equally useful to attract good or to repulse evil.'[4]

While the basic seated, squatting or standing pose and widely splayed thighs of the Sheelas remains fairly constant, the ways in which the arms or hands are used to indicate and draw attention to the vulva are far more varied. The majority employ the significant gesture of both hands in front directed towards the lower abdomen or vulva, but sometimes the hands come from behind the buttocks or flexed thighs. This latter pose is an efficient means of accentuating the focus on this part of the anatomy and is often varied with one hand passing in front of one thigh

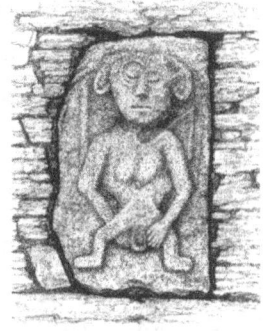

and the other hand passing from behind the other thigh in a manner of intertwining and flowing as occurs on the Sheela from Ballinacarriga Castle. A less common pose can be seen on the Sheelas from Ballylarkin and Rochestown where one hand is in front indicating the vulva and the other hand is resting on the thigh or knee.

The Sheelas from Kiltinan Castle and St Brigit's well at Castlemagner are depicted with both arms raised and are both somewhat unusual. The vulva is only slightly indicated on the Castlemagner figure and with her rotund appearance she appears to fall closer to the more stereotypic mother goddess of the ancient world than the broad range of Sheelas. It is likely that the figure would not have been classed as a true Sheela were it not for the similarity in posture with the more easily classified Sheela from Kiltinan Castle who is holding two items in her upraised hands. The motif of the upraised hands was one of great power and its use in the Celtic world is exemplified in the famous Gundestrup Cauldron where Cernunnos and other deities are shown with raised arms holding objects in a manner that is remarkably similar to the Kiltinan Castle Sheela. The raising of both hands is a uni-

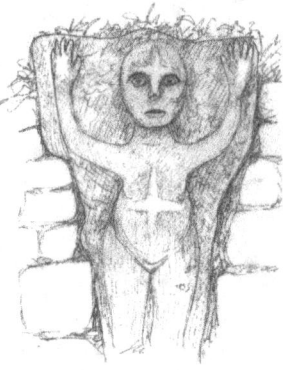

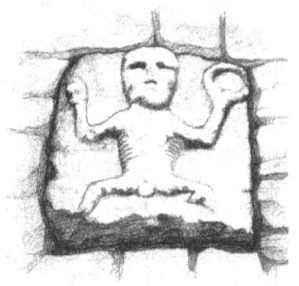

versal gesture indicating prayer, invocation or the magical conjuring of the deity, and can be traced back to very remote times, being a common feature of the goddesses of the neolithic Aegean and Cretan cultures.

A number of Sheelas have one arm raised to the side of the face, ear or eye. Although the opposite hand is, in almost all cases, indicating or touching the genitalia, the raised arm alters the emphasis of the posture since it draws attention away from the focus of the vulva. The Sheelas from Behy, Tullavin and Burgesbeg (B) have their arm raised to the ear as if to signify attention or concentrated listening. Such an emphasis on watchfulness is an appropriate attitude for a figure acting in a guardian role or having an apotropaic function. Two Scottish Sheelas from Kirkwall and Orkney have their hand or arm raised across one of their eyes, and one of a pair of Sheelas from Tugford holds her hand across her mouth and appears as if she is laughing at her partner on the opposite side of the doorway. The majority of this type have their hand located somewhere near the side of their face such as may be seen on the Sheelas from Fiddington, Tinakill, Clomantagh and Aghadoe who also holds a slender unidentified object in her upraised left hand. An English Sheela from Crofton-on-Tees rests her hand on the top of her head in what appears to be a very relaxed looking manner.

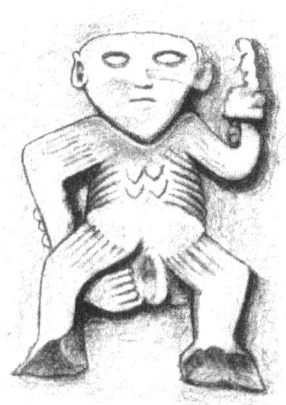

Similar to the 'one-arm-raised' type are the Sheelas who have one leg deliberately raised. This is best exemplified in the Sheelas from Swords, Ballaghmore and Kiltinan Church who look as if they are doing a jig. A number of other Sheelas such as those at Cooliagh More, Shanrahan, Ampney St Peters, Blackhall and Tara have their leg slightly raised, perhaps simply to create an asymmetrical feature. The figure from Egremont is depicted in a most unusual posture with the left leg bent and raised at the knee but

with that foot pointing downwards and
the right foot turned inwards. This inward-turned position of the feet is also re-
peated on the Sheela from Shanrahan and
the Doon Castle Sheela who is facing outwards but has both feet pointing to her
right. The only other example is the Sheela
from Ringaskiddy who has both feet turned inwards, in an almost identical manner to the male Sean-na-Gig from the gate-

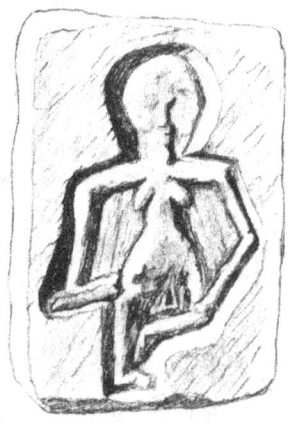

post of a former mill at Ballycloghduff. These features are unusual and can be traced to other figures, and may prove to be invalu-
able in tracing the origin of the Sheelas.

The Sheela from Kiltinan church has both one arm and one
leg raised in the renowned magical position for casting spells and
is the same stance taken by the hag in *Da Derga's Hostel* when she
cursed King Conaire because he refused to allow her to spend the
night in the hostel. There are many other instances in Irish literature of one-eyedness, one-handedness and one-footedness which
occur in magical and supernatural contexts. For instance, 'Lugh
also had recourse to his magic powers: moving around the men
of his army "on one foot and with one eye", he chanted an incan-
tation to lend them strength and courage. He thus assumed a
characteristic posture of the sorcerer ...'[5] It seems likely that the
Sheelas were carved in such a way, making symbolic use of this
magical pose.

In many Sheelas the head is one of their most striking features
and in keeping with the depiction of divine images in Celtic art it
is often abnormally large in relation to the torso. In a number of
figures the head is distinctly triangular, and on some such as those
in Fethard, Kilpeck, Ballinderry and Clonbulloge this is accentuated by a pointed chin. The figure from Lustymore Island is perhaps the best example of this style and it now stands alongside a
possibly older and classically Celtic Janus Figure with its triangular head and pointed chin. This figure is a good illustration of the

importance of the head in Celtic idol sculpture: where it is exaggerated to express regard for this part of the anatomy as the seat of understanding and the source of all human strength. The Celts had a strong belief in the occult properties of the human head, and its apotropaic use, to ward off evil did not disappear with the coming of Christianity.

The prominent or clearly demarcated, otherworldly, eyes of many Sheelas unnerved some researchers. An example of this is the Sheela from Fethard Old Wall which has large, rimmed, staring eyes with clearly marked pupils. Eyes are also frequently depicted as crooked looking or asymmetrical, as can be seen on the figures from Rosnaree, Church Stretton and Ampney St Peters. Another instance of this is the left eye of the Lustymore Sheela, which is either damaged or imperfect, or perhaps it is intentionally represented as closed or blind. This asymmetry is appropriate in the context of the many instances of one-eyedness in Irish literature which occur in magical and supernatural circumstances.

The Sheela from Ballinacarriga Castle has a benign, otherworldly, countenance which is greatly accentuated by the way the left eye appears closed but the right eye is wide open and is surrounded by a crescent. This crescent symbolises her supernatural

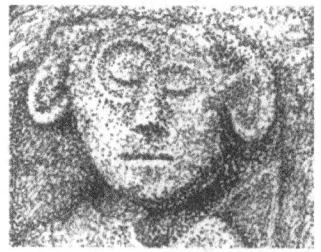

status and is also commonly accepted as a image of fertility. The eyes and right ear of the red sandstone Sheela from Shanrahan are unusual and appear to be set with lighter stone, possibly quartz, though this is difficult to establish since the figure is high up on the church tower. If it is so then it would represent a continuum of what is obviously an ancient tradition, as the eyes of the early wooden idol from Ballachulish in Argyll, Scotland, discussed earlier, were also inlaid with quartz pebbles.

Prominent ears often set at right angles to the head are another feature present on many Sheelas such as those of Ballyporty, Fethard Abbey, Ballylarkin and Ballinacarriga. However a small number of Sheelas such as Liathmore, Castlemagner and Ballyfinboy have no ears at all. The Sheelas from Pennington and Cavan have very pointed ears and some Sheelas such as those in Kilsarkan and Scregg are described as having prominent cow-like ears.[6] The cow was highly regarded by the Celts and held a prominent status in the Gaelic world. The ancestral Mother of the Gods was Boand, the white cow goddess, a divinity who is well remembered in Irish folklore and mythology.

At Fethard Abbey the right ear of the Sheela is extremely large but the left ear is smaller and again shows a deliberate use of asymmetry. The Redwood figure is more unusual as a crescent shaped ear floats by the right-hand side of her face and she has no ear on the other side. Although this Sheela is high up on the castle wall the crescent or ear is easily visible as if the carver wanted to attach some special importance to it. Freud made a connection between ears and sexuality through their identification within mythology as a sexual feature.[7] In Irish mythology the ears occur as a sexual theme in such stories as the 'Three Sons of Uisneach' in which Deirdre grabs the ears of Noíse signifying her desire for him, and it is thought that references in the mythological tales to ears being cut off may mean the loss of sexuality.[8]

The protruding tongue on the Sheelas from Cavan, Moate, Athlone, Rahara, Lustymore and Cloghan is regarded as an apotropaic symbol yet it is also possible to see this as representing fertility. Many older sacred objects of worship are depicted with a protruding tongue, its earliest occurrence in Ireland being probably on a Bronze Age cow mask discovered in a bog near the Galtee Mountains in County Tipperary. But it can also be seen on numerous stone heads in both Ireland and England, such as the Beltany stone head from County Donegal.

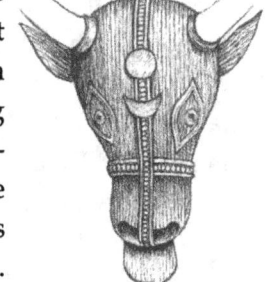

On the double-sided Janus Figure from Boa Island, the tongue is protruding out on one face of the figure but not on the other.

The showing of teeth appears to suggest a more fearsome but probably equally apotropaic message as the protruding tongue. A grim row of incised and fairly fearsome looking teeth appear on Sheelas from Bunratty, Fethard Old Wall, Moate, Lavey, Clonmel and Pennington to mention but a few. Teeth are more ambiguously represented on the Sheelas from Rahan, County Offaly, where beading around the upper lip may represent teeth, and the short vertical lines on the Sheela from Glanworth Castle are probably indicative of teeth. The Sheela from Cavan is an even more potent image as teeth are indicated and the tongue is poking out.

While the heads of many Sheelas are bald there is a rim of hair (or a type of a headdress) present on a number of them. This is sometimes simply represented as a short frame around the face, as at Ampney St Peters, Cloghan, Tugford, Romsey and Rahan. The Cavan Sheela also shows what could be a special headdress with the lines across the forehead possibly indicating some form of a band.[9] On other Sheelas such as those at Kilsarkan and Tullavin, the rim of the headdress is indicated in more elaborate detail. The Sheela from Castle Widenham has a very strange box-like headdress with pieces on both sides of the head – one goes as far as the right shoulder. The Austerfield Sheela also has what might be interpreted as a headdress which reaches down to her thighs.

Sheelas from Ballinderry and Rahara are described as having plaits down either side of their heads. On the Ballinderry Sheela what is described as hair is a pleated ornament of interlacing knotwork which increases in size as it moves towards the right. This type of knotwork decoration was typical of the Celtic revival styles of that period. At Clomantagh Castle the Sheela was mistakenly described by Andersen as having 'an absurd form of flying plaits'.[10] This is probably due to the fact that it is not easy to get a clear view of the figure for she is actually set in a recessed frame which follows closely around her body. On her left hand side is a raised slender band which seems to come from the side of her head and runs down to her arm. What this singular slender band represents is a mystery but it seems unlikely that it is any form of hair or plaits.

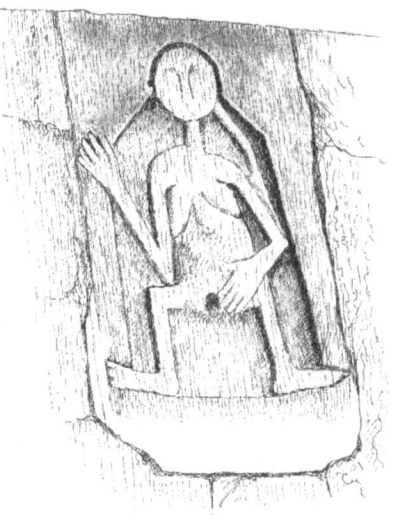

The Sheela from Tara has also been described in the past as having two braids of hair, a headdress or antlers coming from her head but she is now too badly eroded to be able to distinguish anything of the sort. It has been speculated that the two holes in the head of the Seir Kieran figure may have been intended to hold horns or antlers. This suggestion has also been made about the purpose of a drinking hollow between the two faces of the Boa Island Janus Figure and it is possible that both of these figures show a persistence of traditions associated with Cernunnos, the Horned God of the Animals, right into the Christian era. However the headdress seems to have been a form of identification, perhaps originally totemistic, whose meaning is now unfortunately quite lost to us.

One of the most intriguing features which occurs on a great number of Sheelas is the clear presence of striations or lines which are carved across their forehead, cheeks, side of the head and neck. For instance the Sheelas from Ballinderry, Moate and Cavan have strong, billowy lines across the forehead and on the Kiltinan Castle Sheela the lines are carried across her forehead to the sides of her head. At Rahan, the lines form ridges giving the impression of a heavily knitted brow. It has been suggested that these lines represent wrinkles or an intensification of an expression to suggest age, character or certain emotions. This might be the case with a few figures such as that at Rahan but such an interpretation would not be universally applicable.

On at least three Sheelas the striation marks occur across the cheek in the manner of a scar or a tattoo. The Sheela from Fethard Abbey has a streaked cheek and the fearsome looking Sheela from the old town wall has a striated chevron type pattern on her left cheek which is virtually identical to the marks on the patterned heads of the Janus Figure from Boa Island. On the Athlone Sheela there is a striated pattern of three marked lines incised and mould-ed across the left cheek and less distinct traces of tattooing on the other cheek. Clearly incised striation marks can be seen on the Sheela from Kilnaboy, beginning at the base of the neck going up towards the bottom of her chin. The neck of the Sheela from

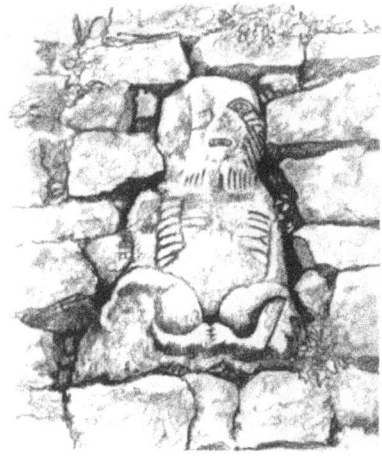

Fethard town wall is also mark-ed in a manner which adds to her terrifying presence, and the Sheela from Seir Kieran also bears slight traces of striated cheeks and more definite streaks on the neck. On the fig-ure from Clonoulty graveyard there are clear indications of stri-ations on the neck and possibly along the side of her head although unfortunately it has been badly damaged.

These face and neck striations are very similar to the deeply carved grooves which are quite a common feature on both Chris-tian and pre-Christian stone heads. A prime example is the tattoo-ing of a female head from Clannaphilip church, County Cavan, in which numerous lines extend to the back of the head. The head was said to represent a local supernatural being called *Cailleach Gearaigín*[11] and these lines surely had some significance. The cat goddess from Cashel also has streaks on her cheeks. Another stone head located on an old flour mill at Ballyboy,[12] believed to be the face of a saint, has tattooing of the cheeks and bears a striking resemblance to many of the Sheelas, especially Fethard. The early Christian cat-head from Kilcatherine's church on the Beara Peninsula, County Cork has an extraordinarily long neck carved with striation marks and on the Beltany stone head 'a shallow, pocked-out decorative feature around the neck may represent a neck ornament or collar, or possibly a tattoo.'[13]

It appears that these facial lines are a form of tattooing which perhaps indicate different classes or tribes, or a positive mark of intent of a wise woman or healer. In primitive societies it was primarily associated with a ritual of coming of age such as puberty rites. Although body and face painting were used in many ceremonies, actual tattooing which involved physically scarring the body held a much more powerful and obviously permanent symbolic importance.

These striation marks are not merely confined to the face or neck but also extend across the chest, breasts and occasionally the abdomen, in what is probably the most common secondary feature of virtually all the Sheelas. This clear presence of lines varies from slight to deep grooves depending on the extent of weathering as well as the original formation. The Sheelas from Llandrin-

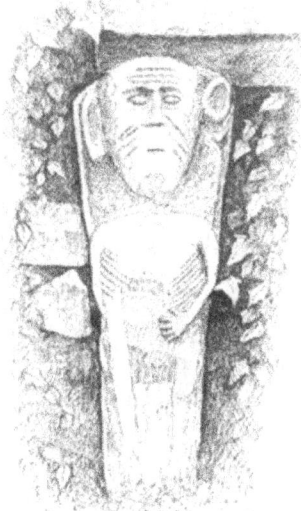

dod, Killua, Cavan, Fethard Abbey, Glanworth, Kiltinan Castle and Seir Kieran are amongst the best preserved examples of body grooves which generally start beneath the breasts, at the side of the body and extend across the chest. Great care has been taken with the detail of Sheela from Dunaman which has what looks like an incised groove with a semicircular incision to show the inner line. This feature has not gone unnoticed by other researchers and various explanations for their significance have been given. It is generally thought that the lines represent ribs, signifying emaciation, death or suffering, and seek to depict the Sheelas as 'cadaverous specimens' of womanhood. This would be similar to the description of the hag and it has been suggested, 'that we have here an illustration of a death-in-life attitude, where the upper part of the figure may mirror mortality and the lower half the source of further life ...'[14] That these lines seek to depict ribs might seem an incontestable argument, if it was not for the fact that numerous other lines are also found on the breasts and other parts of the body. This can be seen on the Sheelas from Clonmel and Lixnaw in which a distinct tattooing of the breast with downward streaks is clearly evident.

Another type of body grooving is a band-like feature across the abdomen which occurs on Sheelas from both Moate and Tracton Abbey, and interestingly on the Janus Figure from Boa Island. The Sheela from Clonlaragh was also once noted as having remarkably clear tool marks across the stomach but this feature is hardly visible now due to weathering. The Boa Island figure has striations across its arms, a feature that also occurs on the Sheela from Ampney St Peters which appears to have grooves on her lower right arm. On the well-preserved Sheela at Aghadoe there are accentuated ribs and also clearly defined linear strokes across her arms and legs. The closely related male Sean-na-Gig from the old mill at Ballycloghduff, County Westmeath has a very distinct diamond or chevron carved on the middle of the upper part of his chest.

In view of the fact that the currently accepted Irish rendering of Sheela-na-Gig is *Síle na gCíoch*, a name which is generally regarded as meaning 'Sheila of the paps' or 'breasts', one might ex-

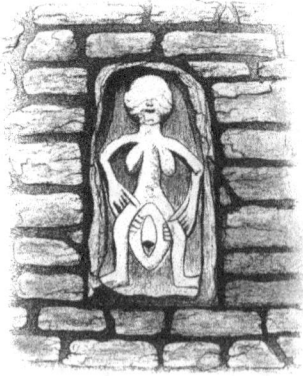

pect that these might feature prominently on the figures; yet often the opposite is the case. In most of the Sheelas the breasts are only slightly indicated but in some instances they are of normal size, but rarely large or exaggerated. On some figures they are located directly under the armpits in a manner that is characteristic of a number of carvings of pre-Christian goddesses. The Oaksey Sheela is a prime example of this type of representation with her long pendulous breasts hanging under her armpits while more modest examples are the Sheelas from Rahan and Llandrindod. On the Sheela from Birr, the breasts are shaped like round balls under the armpits and the figure from St Ives in Huntingdonshire also has breasts like flat disks in the same position.

The location of these breasts contrast sharply with the manner in which they are depicted on other Sheelas such as those of Seir Kieran, Doon and Glanworth Castles where they appear quite shrunken but are clearly indicated in the middle of the chest. On a few Sheelas the breasts are unique. The Sheela at Aghadoe Castle has what looks like four small, centrally placed breasts and the Ballylarkin Sheela has what appears to be a double set of breasts. It has been been suggested that these are meant to depict one pair of small breasts with the lower line representing a lean or sagging chest.

The Kiltinan church Sheela was unusual for having two nipples on her left breast and only one on her right, clearly the additional symbolism of triplicity accentuating her overall magical representation. At Ballinacarriga the Sheela also seems to be represented with an odd number of nipples as there appears to be only one on her left breast and none on her right breast although she is unfortunately situated so far up on the castle wall that it is difficult to be definite about such fine detail. It is quite clear that these idiosyncrasies are deliberately used to bring about an asymmetry in an image which encapsulates some form of potent, possibly divine, power.

Quite a few Sheelas are depicted holding objects which may help to illuminate their elusive nature. The Lavey church Sheela holds a circular disk that has the appearance of being under her left arm yet confusingly the outline of the circle is incised twice on top of her arm.[15] Andersen suggested that this disk could be a shield, as round, small shields occur on early Christian Irish sculpture. The English Sheela from Copgrove also appears to hold a disc or a ball in her right hand but in this case it is held away from her body and apparently by the rim, which hardly suggests a shield. A 'T' symbol which floats by the head of this figure further adds to the mystery. At first it was thought to be a stonemason's tool but Andersen could not relate it to any of the tools known to be in use, and the only other suggestion is that it might stand for Terra, a medieval Mother Earth figure.[16]

Another Sheela from Kiltinan Castle holds a circular disk in her left hand, which, it has been suggested, is either a horseshoe or a torc, and a slender object which is possibly a dagger in her right hand. Eamonn Kelly has suggested that the figure is holding a mirror and a comb similar to the objects depicted on some Irish medieval mermaid figures which belong to the fifteenth and sixteenth centuries.[17] According to Miranda Green, the mirror and comb originally formed part of Pictish iconography and 'these symbols may be pagan, magical devices stimulated by the threat of advancing Christianity',[18] though in their later medieval use they may have become symbols of vanity and possibly lust. However, the mirror and comb combination is a fairly unlikely possibility, as the circular disk is depicted without a handle and is not

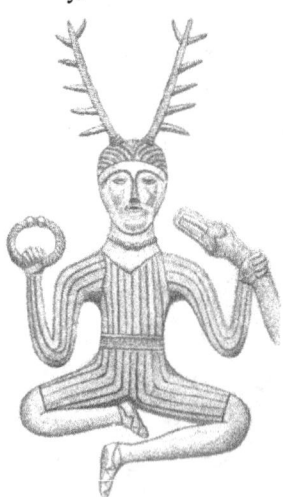

held by the Kiltinan Castle Sheela in the same way as medieval mermaid figures hold their mirrors. A better link can be made with the Celtic horned deity, Cernunnos, commonly depicted with his arms in a similar pose to the Kiltinan Castle Sheela, holding two objects in his upraised hands. One of these is the head of a serpent and this could be what the slender object held in the right hand of the Sheela represents although it is so worn it is impossible to identify as a serpent, dagger, comb or anything else. In his other hand Cernunnos holds a torc signifying his divine status and this seems to be the likely identity of the circular object held in the right hand of the Kiltinan Castle Sheela.

A few other Sheelas hold objects but due to weathering, there is some doubt as to what they represent. On the tower at Rodil, Outer Hebrides, the Sheela-na-Gig is holding what can only vaguely be described as an animal in her arms. At Romsey, a small figure set within a square frame is holding a crozier or a staff in her right hand which appears to symbolise her role as an abbess and 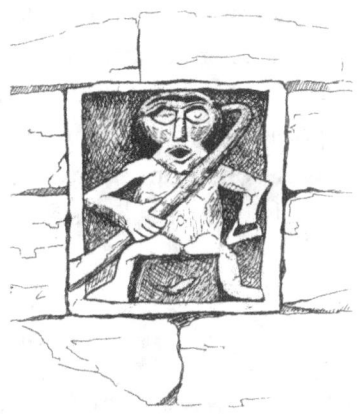 in her left hand she holds some unknown object shaped like a smoothing-iron. Similarly, the figure from Egremont, known only from a photograph, gestures towards the genitals with her left hand, but in her right she holds a cylindrical instrument. This has been described as a pair of shears which it is argued she is holding in order to remove her pubic hair and expose her pudenda more completely, so that bad luck could be warded off more effectively.[19] However the identity of the object as shears is not clear from the sole surviving photograph, and since the figure is now missing it is impossible to examine the curious object closely.

The enigmatic and unique Sheela-na-Gig from Seir Kieran also holds an cylindrical, scroll-like object in her left hand, which can only be seen clearly from the side. This Sheela is most notable for its series of strange holes, nine of which are drilled through her stomach, her lower abdomen, and a further two holes have also been drilled down deep into the stone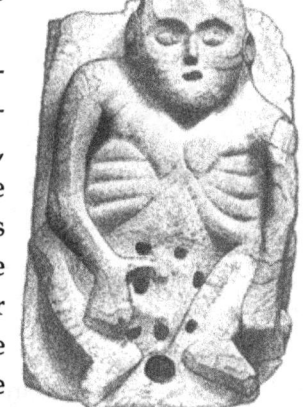

from the back of the head. These two holes have no practical purpose for attachment as the figure was originally probably abutting from the wall, and their function might possibly be for the purpose of applying headgear in the form of horns or antlers.[20] The holes may result from a long forgotten tradition as they look like the remains of rites rather than representations of female features. Yet the largest hole is just below the normal place of pudenda and goes up into the body in a direction which suggests the drilling was done from below. Despite speculation to the contrary, it is likely that these holes are an original feature of the sculpture.

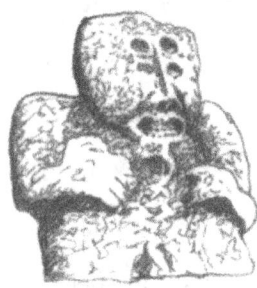

Another very strange, free-standing figure from Knockarley also has a small neat hole drilled through the top of her head and another below her vulva, and the Sheela from Swords has what looks like a tiny hole just above her vulva. A small deep hole most likely representing the anus has also been noted on Sheelas from Cloghan, Abbeylara, Aghadoe Castle, Burgesbeg, Glanworth Castle and Clonmel. The Abbeylara Sheela also has three holes or weathered cavities around the area of her breasts. Two further peculiar figures are the Taghmon Sheela with her four eyes or four drilled holes across her forehead, and the figure from Holgate also has two round holes in place of a mouth.

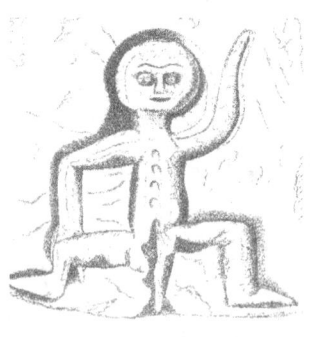

A round circle, which is possibly a navel but seems too high to be so, appears midway between the chest and stomach on a few Sheelas. This symbol can be very clearly seen on the Sheelas from Ballinderry, Rahara, Ballyporty Castle, Llandrindod, Caherelly East and Crofton-on-Tees. Even more peculiar is the Burgesbeg Sheela which has two large round circles above her vulva on her lower stomach, and the Sheela from Fiddington church has worn traces of three or possible four round circles extending from her lower stomach up to her chest. The circle is also associated with other early Christian and medieval figures and those which relate more closely to the Sheelas are the so-called 'cat goddess' from Cashel and the mermaid from Clonfert cathedral.

The overwhelmingly strong presence of the circular form, whether it be in the guise of a circular object, round hole or simple engraving on some part of the figure's body, is perhaps the most surprising and prevalent aspect of the Sheela's symbolism. The most unique features of the Sheela from Aghadoe Castle are the strange, round nodules clearly carved into the wrists, three on her downward pointing right arm and at least two but possibly originally three on her upraised left arm. She also holds a slender unidentifiable object in her upraised left hand. The Ballinderry Castle Sheela also exhibits the circular motif as she is surrounded by three geometric circles as part of the design which encircles her on the keystone block. What these holes, circular motifs and round disks symbolise probably varies enormously between each figure and should be subject to individual interpretation wherever possible. However, as a recurring theme they could be generally interpreted as solar symbols and the positioning of these symbols on the breasts, near the genitals and belly emphasises the link between the sun and fertility. The circle is the basic sun-symbol, its derivations formed an essential aspect of Celtic Art where it may have been used to represent specifically godlike qualities in both male and female deities.

Another peculiar feature that has been hitherto unnoticed amongst the Sheelas is an unexplained object descending from their vulvas or lying underneath the legs of at least seven Sheelas which originate from Ballinderry, Kilnaboy, Fiddington, Romsey, Bunratty, Cloghan and Dunaman. At Cloghan Castle, County Roscommon, the Sheela is depicted with a well-defined vulva and a secondary vulva-like shape carved into the background just below the genitals. On the Sheelas from Kilnaboy and Ballinderry it is more like a tail descending from the vulva, perhaps meant to represent her sacred essence or sexual potency, in the form of menstrual blood descending to the earth. It could also be implying that they are urinating as the bladder serves as an analogy for the vulva, and the bladder size, as seen in the amount of urine, is equivalent in Irish mythology to a person's sexual capacity.[21]

The Sheela from Behy Castle in County Sligo is unusual as she is painted red and has been this colour as far back as the current occupants can remember. Similarly when the Sheela from Llandrindod was discovered in the last century, the colouring of the stone was thought by a medical man to have been caused by blood. Whoever made the fake Sheela now in the Devizes Museum may have known something of this tradition since red paint once covered its upper surface. In Irish mythology, red was the colour most frequently associated with the otherworld or the supernatural, and to be stained red meant to be chosen by the Goddess as a king, for in Irish, *ruadh* meant both 'red' and 'royal'.[22] The hag in some of the old stories was also associated with this colour. In the *Táin Bó Regamna* 'the Mórrígan appears before Cú Chulainn as a red woman in a chariot drawn by a red, one legged horse', and in the tale of Da Choca's Hostel, Cormac Conloinges, sees the hag as a red woman.[23]

Although originally found in a Christian religious context, there is no doubt that with the Sheelas many of the figures, 'carry on shapes and postures derived from paganism, or at any rate employ gestures with pagan associations',[24] and while it is important to note these various features, it is impossible to fully understand this world of rich symbolic beliefs personified in the images. Many attributes will probably remain a mystery to us. Often it is the more subtle nuances that have the greater importance, such as the shape of the ears, face lines, body grooves or the presence of a small drilled hole. What may have seemed an unusual feature on one isolated figure can now be seen in the wider context. Despite the vast difference in the depiction of the various figures there are certain prevailing characteristics. All gestures and symbolic nuances are subservient to the display of the vulva which is fundamental to the figure. What comes through most clearly is their deliberate asymmetry and the various poses or postures which appear to establish a supernatural context for the display of the vulva. The postures and the symbolism of the figures can be seen as the background against which representation of divine power, the exhibiting of the genitalia, takes place. Other important features such as face and body tattooing and the holding of circular objects, imply a divine status for the images.

Such features may well have been inspired by the vivid descriptions of the hag in mythology as she was responsible for the fortunes, fertility and prosperity of her territory. She was seen as a divine figure who probably encompassed some general fertility associations, yet her primary purpose was one of warding off evil and misfortune. Viewed in the light of the symbolic tradition of Celtic art the Sheelas come to represent a ritual, a divine rite, frozen in symbolic enactment – around the central all powerful images of life and death.

9

THE SHEELA-NA-GIG ARCHETYPE

When the Sheela-na-Gigs were first discovered it was assumed that such an archaic looking image must be a pagan relic. This view held sway until Guest's work of the 1930s established them as part of Christian iconography. Before this it seemed natural to compare them with similar goddess imagery from the pre-Christian world and various analogies were drawn which now, in the light of more recent research, are regarded as untenable to the modern scholarly mind.

Although they appear out of context, apparently popping up out of nowhere in the medieval period, Sheelas are the latest manifestation of an archaic and constantly recurring theme. They are the last of an ancient lineage of female goddesses depicted in a state of displaying their genitalia that can be traced back to ancient times. It is not possible to discern a direct lineage between the Sheelas and the earlier goddess imagery but then neither do they fit comfortably into any of the modern theories which try to explain them. We should bear in mind the possibility that cultural traditions which inspired certain imagery in an earlier period might well have a bearing on the mystery of the Sheelas. As Guest stated 'the surprisingly late date for the Sheelas in no way reflects the antiquity of the ideas that they embody'.[1] To dismiss the connection between the Sheela-na-Gigs and the ancient archetypes is to the deny the very existence of these as yet unresolved mysteries.

Whilst most of the earlier researchers speculated on the pagan appearance of the Sheela-na-Gigs it was the Egyptologist and anthropologist Margaret Murray who first identified the divine goddess aspect of the figures and began investigating parallels with earlier sacred art forms. To her the Sheela-na-Gigs represented clear evidence of the survival of goddess-orientated beliefs into the later Christian age.

Murray divided female figures into three classifications:

The Universal Mother – The 'true' Mother Goddess, usually depicted with full breasts and/or a child in her arms. The protector and nourisher of all human kind, past, present and future she is worshipped equally by men, women and children.

The Divine Woman – Represented by a beautiful young woman who is both desired and worshipped, principally by men.

The Personified Yoni – 'In which beauty or form or features is disregarded, the secondary sexual characters, such as the breasts, are minimised as the whole emphasis is laid on the pudenda.'[2]

According to Murray the Sheela-na-Gigs fitted into the last class and she likened them to the curious Greek figures known as Baubo. These small figurines are often found near or within women's rooms in Egyptian houses of the Greek period, the second and third century AD, where they appear to be connected with childbirth and fertility. Baubo's are usually depicted wearing an elaborate headdress and are generally portrayed as seated on the ground with the legs spread to display a clearly marked or exaggerated pudenda. The position of the legs is horizontal, with the knees bent and the feet turned inwards, although sometimes the figure is squatting with the knees raised and turned outwards.[3] Although the Baubo figurines 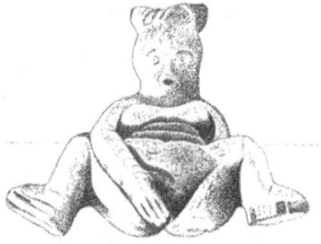 differ in that they often have a swollen belly, they have the characteristic gesture of the Sheelas with the hand indicating the pudenda, sometimes even with one hand passed beneath the thigh and the other on top.

According to a Greek legend when Isis was mourning for Osiris, Baubo exposed her genitals and the shock of the display made Isis laugh and cease from lamenting. The fact that there is only this one popular reference to Baubo in existing writings from ancient times gives the impression that her cult was destroyed, though there is mention of later erotic rites carried out in her honour. Murray believed that the Sheela-na-Gigs were worshipped in the same way as Baubo, that is exclusively by women. She then went on to express the belief that they played a role in teaching women of the pleasures of sex. Such views did little to endear her to the scholarly world and it is not surprising that her suggestion of a link between the Sheelas and Baubo have largely been ignored in recent years.

Even leading proposers of the clerically-inspired anti-lust Sheela, Weir and Jerman, discussed the possibility of a link between Baubo and the Sheelas. In *Images of Lust* they propose a connection through the early Christian cleric Clement of Alexandria (b. 150 AD) who is said to have been initiated into certain Hellenistic cults at the time when many of the Baubo figures were being created. It is known that Clement's work was still highly influential during the eleventh and twelfth centuries and Constantine Psellos is said to have inspired the creation of three female figures on churches in northern Italy which are shown 'lifting their robes to reveal their private parts in the way described by Clement'.[4] Constantine Psellos was an influential Byzantine monk and politician who drew heavily on Clement's writings to 'pour scorn on pagan beliefs and practices'.[5]

The rites associated with the Elusinian cults, to which Baubo is related, involved the drinking of a special intoxicating beverage, which echoes the traditions associated with the goddess Meave of the Celtic lands where she is know as the 'intoxicating one'. Weir and Jerman also note that the later Greek name for Baubo was Iambé, a name which is still used to describe an old hag in parts of Greece much as Sheela-na-Gig is recorded as having been used as a synonym for 'Hag' in Ireland into the twentieth century.[6]

The pre-historic divine goddess with displayed genitalia was considered as an exceptionally powerful image and examples occur sporadically throughout the archaeological record. In the earliest period, the Palaeolithic, the vulva is often depicted in disembodied form, and as such it is found in rock shelters and caves throughout Europe. According to André Leroi-Gourhan the earliest art from this period consists of 'sexual symbols realistically represented and some 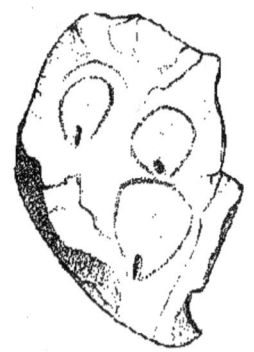 animals extremely crudely rendered'.[7] Most of the sexual symbols are vulvas, male sexual symbols being quite rare, and the earliest of these, from sites in the Dordogne, France, are thought to date to around 30,000 years ago. Often the disembodied vulva is carved in relief but it is also painted in black or red ochre.

The so-called Venus figurines, such as the Goddess of Willendorf and the female figure carved into a rock at the entrance to the Laussell cave in France are the better known examples of a wide range of imagery dating to this period. Most of these are of the mother goddess type although there is a great variation in the styles of the figures suggesting that the concept of the female divinity was complex and included a wide range of conceptual imagery.

The goddess of Life/Fertility/Death as perceived throughout the pre-Christian period seems to have its origins in the late Mesolithic/early Neolithic era, around 10,000–8,000 years ago. Many mythological elements connected to the worship of the goddess developed into traditions that endured until the Christain era.

According to Maria Gimbutas the gesture of one arm raised up and the other arm pointing down suggests a divinity whose function was the regeneration of life and the hands pointing to or holding the vagina emphasises the goddess as 'protecting, promoting and aiding the act of birth.'[8] Such representations of figures appear in many areas of Europe on pottery and plaques from the Neolithic era. Gimbutas illustrated many images which relate closely to the Sheela-na-Gigs but it is only possible here to represent a small selection of those which have the most striking similarities.

The Neolithic culture of Malta (fourth millennium BC) left many goddess images, most of which are depicted as plump universal mother types. But one unusual figurine has been discov-

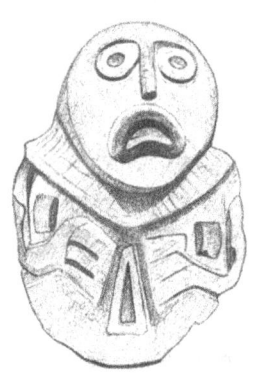

ered which is depicted in a pose reminiscent of the Sheelas, with one hand touching her pronounced vulva and the other touching the side of her head. Pregnant belly, large breasts and widely splayed legs exposing a large vulva suggest that she is in a birth-giving posture.[9] On her back nine lines are also incised perhaps indicating the months of gestation.

Some of the most compellingly Sheela-like images are found amongst the so called Fish Mother figures from the ancient sanctuary of Lepinski Vir situated on the banks of the Danube in former Yugoslavia. Approximately fifty-four red sandstone sculptures, dating to the early Neolithic times, were discovered inside the shrines of the sanctuary laid out on red, triangular floors at the head of vulva/uterus-shaped altars. They are unique in that they incorporate elements of an egg, a fish and a woman and several of these figures are depicted in a classic Sheela-like pose of both hands pulling apart a triangular shaped vulva. Several of these vulva-pulling figures are also engraved below the face with interconnected diamond bands and columns of chevrons or zig-zags. Gimbutas considered the Fish Mother to represent 'a generative womb', a 'primeval creatrix' or a 'mythical ancestress' in whose power was the renewal of life.[10]

Nancy Sanders gives many examples of god and goddess figurines from sites in the Baltic region that are depicted with triangular heads, the female figurines having a triangular incision depicting the vulva. In the prehistoric art of this area it is possible to discern most of the symbolic nuances that are evident in later Celtic art and which form elements of the symbolism of the Sheelas: striations on the head and body, stylised posturing and sometimes a large number of holes drilled into parts of the figures that defy explanation.[11]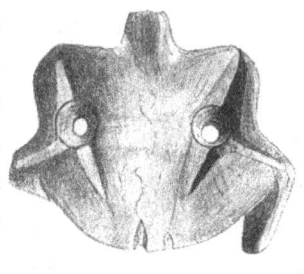

Although the display of the vulva is prominent on various ancient figurines, there is one particular aspect of the goddess with which the Sheelas appear to be related. This is the effigy of the Frog Goddess, a woman/frog hybrid. This is characteristically portrayed in an early Sesklo figure of the seventh millennium BC which has outstretched limbs and a human vulva or a large pubic triangle. The image of the frog/toad is often equated with the uterus and according to Gimbutas '... does not represent, as often hypothesised, a birth giving posture, rather the shape is that of an anthromorphisised frog which is connected by its symbolism to regeneration.'[12] The function of the frog/toad was to both bring death and restore life.

The totem of the Hecate, one of the oldest Greek versions of the trinitarian goddess, is the toad or frog and is sometimes called 'baubo'. This is significant since Hecate is derived from the Egyptian midwife goddess, Heqit, and she was specifically diabolised by the medieval Christians who gave her the name of 'Queen of the Witches', and condemned as those most dangerous to the faith, 'those whom Hecate patronised: the midwives'.[13]

Toads were also believed to have healing powers, in Bavaria on the Virgin Mary's holy days, a toad would be killed and nailed to the doors, houses and stalls for the protection of animals and humans from illness and death. The frequency of other such frog/toad/vulva designs running through the Old European belief system testifies to the considerable role of the frog goddess. That it may play a role in the tradition of the Sheela-na-Gigs is suggested in the unique figure at Studland in Dorset.

The snake goddess was another very important image in the

ancient world and perhaps we can also see aspects of her survival in the Sheelas. According to Gimbutas the snake is a transfunctional symbol and 'its vital influence was felt not only in life creation, but also in fertility and increase and particularly in the regeneration of dying life energy ... a vertically winding snake symbolised ascending life force ... a column of life rising from caves and tombs.'[14] Viewed in this light the strange object which descends from many Sheelas may possibly represent a snake/umbilical cord, linking the subterranean womb with the living world. Many Sheelas and their Celtic predecessors appear to show direct evidence of the snake goddess such as the Sheela from Rath and the Cat Goddess at Cashel with her inter-twined snake-like legs. The early La Tene figure from Reinheim, Saarbrucken, could also readily fit into the half human/half snake goddess archetype, and the carved Pictish figure from Scotland is another possible example of the continuance of the snake goddess prototype with her legs represented as twisted snakes and her snake-like hair.

Also related to the Sheela archetype are the figurines made of stone or clay which are thought to portray the owl goddess, a manifestation of the fearsome goddess of death, revered as a divinity and respected for her grim but necessary part in the cycle of existence.[15] Characteristic of the owl goddess is the face with the beaked nose and connecting arched brows, and regeneration is emphasised by large vulvas or serpentine umbilical cords. An Anatolian vase of the Early Bronze Age displays these features having a sec-

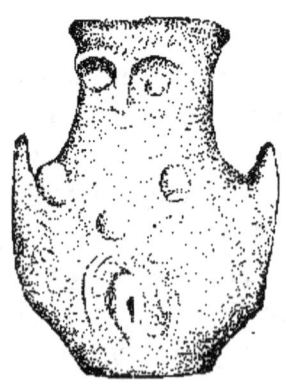

ond face on the reverse as well as a small spiral on the opposite side the the large vulva. The eyes were regarded as having sacred power and as such the owl is credited with profound wisdom, oracular powers, and the ability to avert evil. Although the owl was a harbinger of death the large vulva also emphasises regeneration.

A seated figurine found at Nudra, central Turkey, early third millennium BC (Anatolian Early Bronze Age) reaches down to pull apart her vulva in a very Sheela-like manner. She wears a crossband and 12 necklaces or circles around her neck and also has three depressions on the abdomen and six on the back. Another interesting large stone sculpture dating to c. 4,000 BC from Capdenac-le-bout, Lot, Southern France, is depicted with enormous three fingered hands which are centred around the vulva area. She also has a deep V or triangular sign above her breast and a round hole for a mouth which appears to symbolise that she is the divine source.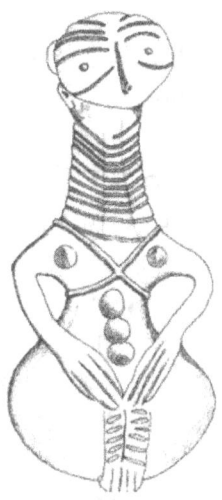

The fearsome face of the Sheelas may also be related to the hideous grinning mask with glaring eyes and pendant tongue of the ancient Greek Gorgon Medusa. The stare of the Medusa could 'turn men to stone' and it was said to be also capable of taking the breath away. The Gorgon certainly shares many characteristics with the Sheelas and was also erected on town walls, buildings, shields and portable ovens. It is certain that the Gorgon acted as a prophylactic mask and her gruesome features – lolling tongue, projecting teeth, and writhing snakes for hair – were believed to be a protection against the Evil Eye.

The concept of the 'Great Goddess' figure is universal, often underlying the belief structure of those societies which appear to be exclusively god worshipping, and figures with Sheela-like characteristics can be found in almost all traditional cultures throughout the world. Many Oceanic tribes still commonly use the displayed female as an apotropaic, rather than a fertility, motif and the Sheela-like Bargini, an important goddess of the Australian Aborigines, is quite distinct from those images connected to fertility.[16]

The similarities of some Hindu figures was also noted by some researchers, one commentator referred to a Sheela-like figure seen in the highly decorated tower of the old Royal palace in Katmandu, Nepal,[17] and Andersen published a picture of a Tantric figure from the same region.[18] In the Hindu and the older Buddhist traditions the yoni is believed to be the centre of divine power and an image of the displayed female in India is deeply associated with the serpentine energy of Tantric beliefs. Throughout India, yonic statues of the great goddess Kali still appear at the doorways of Hindu temples where visitors lick a finger and touch the yoni, the most revered of sacred icons, for good fortune.

Whilst the meaning and purpose of the Sheelas is very much dependent upon the cultural context from which they evolved and developed, comparisons with other figures are useful for in many ways they speak a universal language. Throughout varying cultures, ages and traditions, the powerful image of displayed females encompassed aspects of fertility, averting evil, and primarily the inter-relation of life, death and regeneration. Though they may appear widely dissimilar to our modern way of thinking these functions do not necessarily exclude one another.

Memories of the role played by the feminine principle are carried in the stories and mythologies handed down from generation to generation and revolved around such ancient goddess figures as the Morrigan, Badb, Macha and Brigit. The 'Hag' of the Irish legends appears to be the goddess of death and regeneration, she who decided who should live and who should die, as is vividly described in many mythological stories.

CATALOGUE

A list and description of the known figures with details of current location.

This catalogue lists all the figures that can reasonably considered to be, or in the case of those now missing, to have been, Sheela-na-Gigs. Sizes of figures where given are approximations corresponding to the greatest length or width of figures or the size of the stone on which the figure is carved.

IRELAND

1. *Abbeylara, County Longford:* Abbeylara is a small village about 3 km east of Granard and the ruins of the thirteenth-century Cistercian Abbey can be found on the east side of the village. A deeply sculpted but rather weathered figure protrudes from the inside wall of a fifteenth-century tower. There are three deep indentations around the area of the breasts, the vulva is oval shaped with a raised vertical section and the anus is clearly indicated. (36 cm x 21 cm)

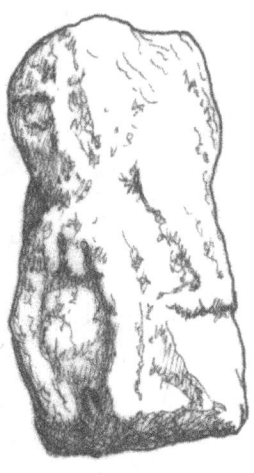

2. *Aghadoe Castle, Killeagh, County Cork:* The remains of this castle are incorporated into farm houses about two kilometres north of Killeagh. This unusual Sheela-na-Gig has recently been re-erected on the old dovecote, which is all that remains of the castle. It has been carved in high relief and is well preserved with clearly defined linear strokes across arms and legs, accentuated ribbing, four small

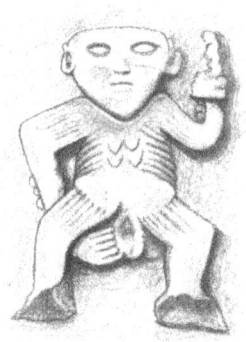

centrally placed breasts and clearly defined genital features. The raised hand holds the rather indistinct form of a pointed object and there are strange nodules very clearly carved into the wrists, three on her downward pointing right arm which reaches towards the vulva and at least two but possibly originally three on her upraised left arm.

3. *Aghalurcher, County Fermanagh:* Aghalurcher church is about three kilometres south of Lisnaskea and west of the main Newtownbutler road. A Romanesque type figure was discovered here in 1970, with a large head and legs raised in the acrobatic fashion, heels touching ears, which because of a depression in

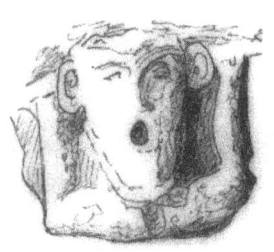

the genital area is thought to be female. A report on the figure surmised that the stone was cut in such a way that it formed the under-section of a cornice or a gable-coping rather than a corbel. Remains of a medieval church established by St Ronan in the seventh century are on the site. On the gateway leading into the churchyard is a good example of a Romanesque head. The figure is now kept in storage at the Archaeological Survey, Department of the Environment, Belfast.

4. *Ardcath, County Meath:* Discovered during the 'removal of a masonry gate pillar at the entrance to a farm' a mile southwest of the parish of Ardcath.[1] It was obviously at some point

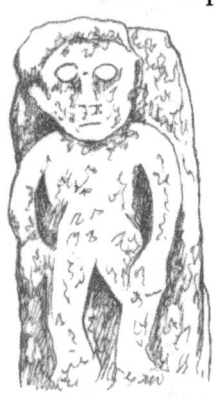

intentionally concealed from view as it was built into the filling of the gate pillar and is now badly weathered but recognisable as a Sheela-na-Gig by the well-defined vulva. Although the left foot is missing it appears as if the heel may have been pointing upwards. The arms hang symmetrically across the body and and the hands which have a faint suggestion of fingers rest on the thighs close by the pudendum. In 1984, the figure was in the private possession of the land owner, John Corry. (54 cm x 28 cm)

5. *Athlone, County Westmeath:* The figure was previously set up over a gateway to the laundry of the convent of St Peter's Port, established in the eighteenth century. It is thought to have originated from the nearby twelfth-century Cluniac monastery of which not a trace remains. It is now on display in the castle museum in Athlone. The figure is carved in deep relief and is depicted with her arms around her legs. The pudendum is shown by a bulge and she has a distinct striated pattern incised and moulded across the left cheek.

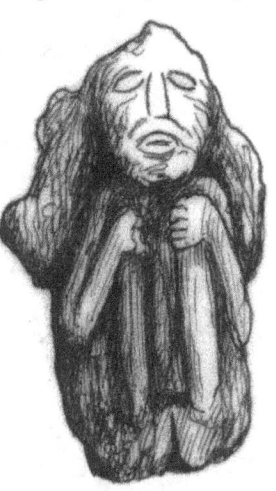

6. *Ballaghamore Castle, County Laois:* Ballaghamore Castle, built by the Fitzgeralds, is situated about seven kilometres east of Roscrea. The Sheela-na-Gig can be seen on a quoin stone about ten metres from the ground, on the south-west tower wall of this late fifteenth-century castle. The left arm rests on the left thigh and the right arm appears to rest on the right hip. The feet are pointed and turned outwards and the left foot seems also to be slightly raised. According to John Feehan and George Cunningham, who recorded the figure in 1978, it is 'considerably weathered and sand grains at the surface are easily rubbed off'.[2] The figure has been carved in bold relief in soft, white sandstone of local origin and although her facial features are no longer discernible she is described by Feehan as having 'a devilish expression'.

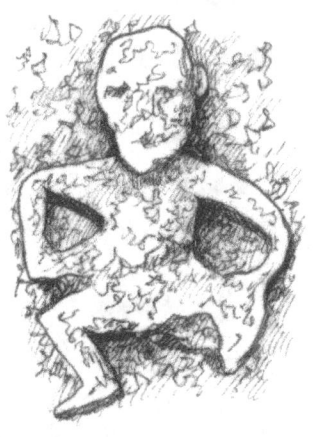

7. *Ballinacarriga Castle, County Cork:* The castle, a listed national monument, is situated about seven kilometres south of Dun-

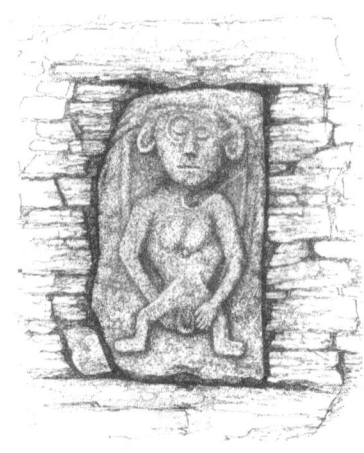

manway. The upper floor was used as a chapel until the last century and is renowned for its decorated stones depicting religious motifs. This well-preserved Sheela-na-Gig is located quite high up on the east facing wall of the castle, above the main entrance door. The right hand passes beneath the thigh while her left hand passes on top of the other thigh and what looks like a lunar crescent encircles her right eye. (45 cm high)

8. *Ballinderry Castle, County Galway:* The castle is about five kilometres south of Tuam on the west side of the Tuam–Athenry road. The Sheela is located on the keystone on the archway of the main doorway of this sixteenth-century castle. The breasts are located like folds under the armpits and the hands are

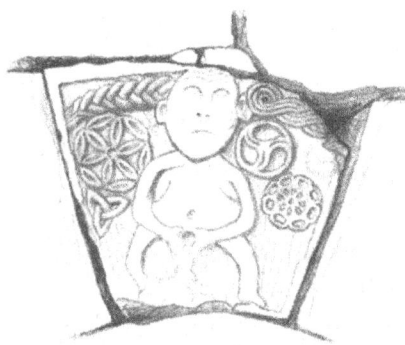

joined around the vulva. It is a unique and important example since the figure is depicted on a background of Celtic-style patterns which include Celtic knotwork based on three strands passing behind the head of the figure and a triskele or triquetra, a hexafoil rose and a marigold motif with eight divisions. What appears to be a rush of liquid, perhaps indicating urine or menstruation, or some other unidentified object is depicted between the figure's legs. (25 cm x 35.5 cm)

9. *Ballyfinboy Castle, County Tipperary:* The castle stands close to the Ballyfinboy River about two kilometres west of Borrisokane. It is actually a fifteenth- or sixteenth-century tower house, and the Sheela is considered contemporary with its construction as it is carved on a quoin stone which appears to harmonise

with the other stones. The figure, which has been kept clear of the encroaching growth of ivy, can be found some four metres above the ground 'at the height where the batter of the lower wall ends'.[3] The hands pass below the thighs and meet

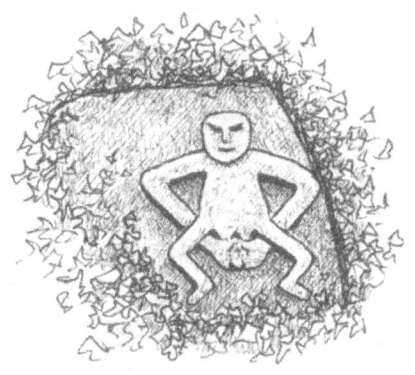

around the 'sagging middle of the abdomen'.

10. *Ballylarkin church, County Kilkenny:* This excellent example was removed to the National Museum in Dublin from its original location on the thirteenth-century parish church of Ballylarkin about one and a half kilometres south-west of Freshford. It is undoubtedly the most refined image of a Sheela-na-Gig currently known to exist and is interesting due to several unique features. The figure is depicted in an almost seated yogic-like pose with one finger of the left hand delicately touching the pudendum and the right hand resting on the knee. Even more remarkable is the fact that the

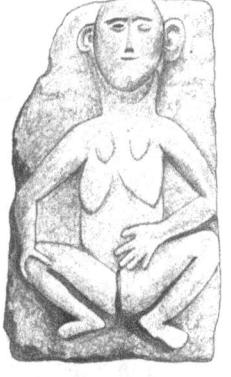

Sheela appears to have two pairs of breasts, although it has been suggested that they are meant to depict a sagging chest or small breasts with the lower line representing a lean chest. The benign facial expression, large ears and bulging eyes with slits in them are also notable features. (58 cm x 32 cm)

11. *Ballinaclogh Castle, County Tipperary:* This small round Norman castle is situated about four kilometres north-west of Golden, which is about seven kilometres west of Cashel. This figure was listed by the National Museum but there is no trace of a Sheela on the remains of the original castle though she could be underneath the rampant ivy that currently covers virtually the whole south-west side of the castle.

12. *Ballynahinch Castle, County Tipperary:* Ballynahinch Castle is

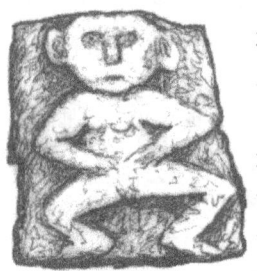

about four kilometres west of Cashel, on its northern side, but near the west bank of the river Suir. The Sheela-na-Gig is over the door about six metres from the ground on the main tower and was said to have come from the ruins of a nearby church to the north of the castle. The hands are joined above the pudenda and the legs are widely splayed. The head is large and round, the eyes have pupils clearly marked and there are wavy lines across the forehead. (60cm high)

13. *Ballynamona Castle, County Cork:* Ballynamona Castle, built by the Nagles, stands on the banks of the little Awbeg river about eight kilometres south-east of Mallow and two kilometres from Shanballymore. The Sheela-na-Gig was apparently displaced from the castle and built into a gate pier, until around 1820 when a mason carrying out repairs 'somewhat injured' the figure, 'on account of its characteristics'. A later search for the figure was made around the turn of the century and she was discovered some distance away from the castle 'but so smashed up that she was beyond repair'.[4] She was regarded as a talisman and 'it is certain that once she left her place in the castle, the Nagles did not long survive her.'[5]

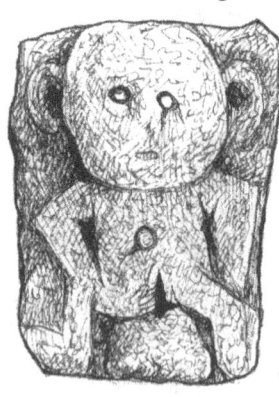

14. *Ballyportry Castle, County Clare:* This Sheela-na-Gig, carved in limestone, was found a short way from the late fifteenth- or early sixteenth-century castle and taken to the National Museum in 1942. It is an excellent and curious figure with an over-large head, deep-set, round eyes with pupils, broad shoulders, a large round navel, signs of teeth and possibly an anus. The hands reach behind the thighs and her fingers hold open her vulva. (53 cm x 38 cm)

15. *Ballyvourney, County Cork:* St Gobnait's church or abbey is sign-posted at the southern end of the village of Ballyvourney, which is about fifteen kilometres west of Macroom on the

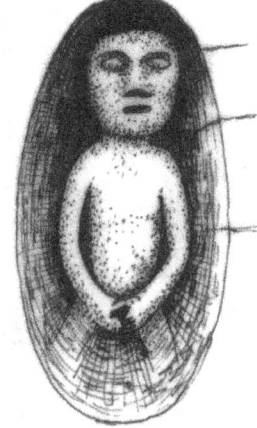

main Killarney road. This very small and benign Sheela-na-Gig can be found carved into an oval recess at an odd angle on a reused lintel over a window on the south wall of the church. The hands point towards her lower abdomen or genital area and although the legs are missing, the figure appears to be standing. She is prob-ably a later but important example of a Sheela-na-Gig as the old church is an important pilgrimage centre and the prac-tice of touching the Sheela-na-Gig, which is regarded as an actual image of St Gobnait, is still part of the ritual rounds at this shrine. (18 cm high)

16. *Barnahealy Castle, County Cork:* This figure is said to have been found at Barnahealy Castle or Castle Warren a short distance to the south-west of Ringaskiddy but has since gone missing. The antiquarian Windele, who was familiar with the repre-sentation of the Sheela-na-Gig, recorded that 'a brown gritty stone with a rude representation of a female figure' was found in the ruins of the castle.[6]

17. *Behy Castle, County Sligo:* Behy Castle is on the north side of the

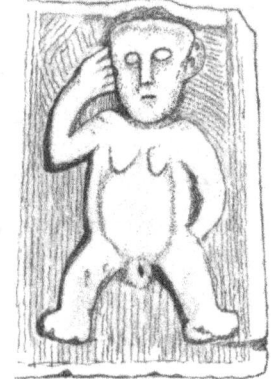

Sligo to Dublin road about eight kilo-metres south of Collooney and about six kilometres north of Castlebaldwin. Only one wall of the castle remains standing but the Sheela is in a nearly perfect state, having been re-erected on the gable wall of an outhouse. It is a very well-preserved example and all the finer details both of the carving and of the highly decorative nature of the dressing-marks on the stone are clearly preserved. The oddest feature about the figure is that she has been painted red and according to the owners of the farm it has been this way for as long as they can remember.

18. *Birr, County Offaly:* This limestone figure was acquired by the

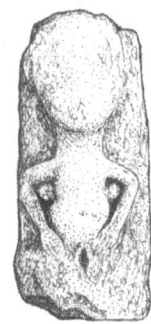

National Museum in 1956 and although its exact former location is not recorded, it is likely that it originated from St Brendan's church.[7] It is a curious but badly worn Sheela-na-Gig with small hands reaching down towards the abdomen. Small, round breasts are located under her arms and an odd feature is that her neck and head are rolled backwards. (53 cm x 30 cm)

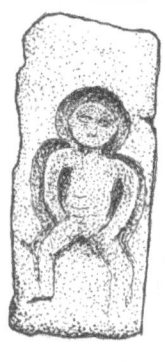

19. *Blackhall Castle, County Kildare:* Blackhall Castle is about ten kilometres south of Kilcullen and about two kilometres north of Narraghmore. The Sheela-na-Gig has been set in stonework of recent origin by the doorway of the peel tower of the thirteenth-century castle which faces south-west. It has a groove around the head similar to the Clenagh castle figure and her right leg is slightly raised. It appears as if both hands pass under the thighs and are joined below the abdomen.

20. *Boyle Abbey, County Roscommon:* This carving is on a capital at the western end of the nave of this late twelfth-century Cistercian abbey. The figure mainly consists of a very large triangular head with its arms descending towards the pelvic area. There is little sign of the body or legs and it is uncertain if this figure can be regarded as a true Irish Sheela-na-Gig.

21. *Bunratty Castle, County Clare:* This famous castle is situated between Shannon airport and Limerick. The Sheela-na-Gig was originally at the top of the seventeenth-century south-west tower, on the inner reveal of a window. During restoration it was set into the wall of the Hall of the Great Keep. She appears to be a late example depicted with eyes set into hollow

sockets, bared teeth and widely splayed legs. The arms pass below the legs and make up almost a full circle with the hands placed on the rim of the pudenda. This most famous of Irish castles was built about 1460 and was the seat of the

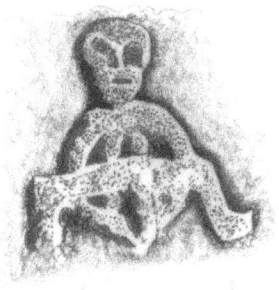

O'Briens, Earls of Thomond until the early eighteenth century.

22. *Burgesbeg (A), County Tipperary:* Two Sheela-na-Gigs, carved of sandstone, originating from the old church of Burgesbeg, are located about ten kilometres west of Nenagh. The figure, on loan to the National Museum, was found in 1932 by a Mr Wallace inside the church at the base of the wall of the only remaining gable. Mr Wallace thought it formed part of an arch of either a door or a window. Carved in

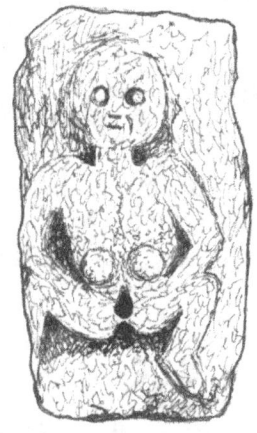

relief, the hand gestures towards the deeply hollowed out vulva, and appears to depict a clitoris. (71 cm x 38 cm)

23. *Burgesbeg (B), County Tipperary:* This is presumed to be the second figure from Burgesbeg for in her brief article entitled 'A Sheela-na-Gig at Clonmacnoise' Edith Guest stated, 'Mr Wallace has informed me of the finding of two Sheela-na-gigs found lying outside the south wall of Burgesbeg churchyard.'[8] This figure is currently kept in a store room adjoining the cathedral at Clonmacnoise and has bent legs, bulbous eyes and clearly defined ribs. According to Weir there is 'a small protuberance, like an uvula [which is described as a 'hesitant penis'] immediately below what is a small deep hole which

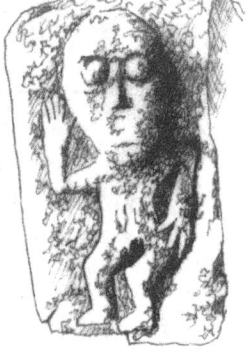

most likely represents the anus'.[9]

24. *Caherelly Castle, County Limerick:* The site of the castle is about twenty kilometres south of Limerick city near the Lough Gur prehistoric centre. This headless Sheela was discovered by workmen repairing a culvert on a small stream about a hun-

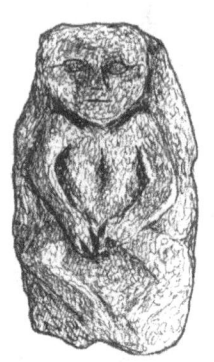

dred metres from Caherelly or 'Black' Castle which was the former seat of the O'Hughes. The figure had been built into the wall guarding the road and is presumed to have originated from the castle which had been dismantled in the nineteenth century. An unusually rotund figure with large breasts and an exceptionally large opening for the vulva, it was recognised by the renowned collector of antiquities John Hunt and is now included in his collection on view in the Hunt Museum in Limerick. (48 cm x 33 cm)

25. *Carne Castle, County Westmeath:* The Sheela was found in the ruins of Carne Castle, at Coolatore, one and a half kilometres west of Moate and was acquired by the National Museum in 1956. Carne Castle was a sixteenth-century tower house, seat of the O'Melaghlin family, whose ancestors were kings of Meath. The Sheela is a bulky figure with heavy shoulders and bulbous breasts, but an unusual feature is the widely splayed thighs with feet meeting at the heels. The hands are joined in the usual gesture towards the vulva. (63 cm x 36 cm)

26. *Carrick Castle, County Kildare:* Around the turn of the century a figure called the 'Evil Eye Stone of the Castle' is known to have existed in the area. It was transferred with the Murray Collection around the turn of the century to Cambridge University Museum of Archaeology and Ethnology in England and has since disappeared.

27. *Cashel, County Tipperary:* A reclining Sheela-na-Gig is carved

on a quoin stone on the south-east corner of the Hall of the Vicar's Choral on the Rock of Cashel. This fifteenth-century building is said to have housed the clergy and now functions as the visitors' reception centre and museum. The Rock of Cashel was a place of religious and political importance, the royal residence of the Kings of Munster until

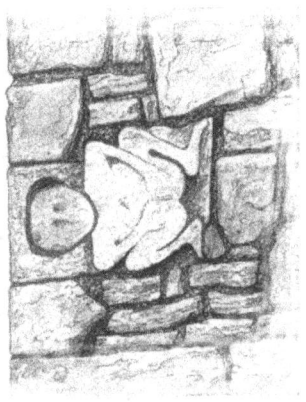

AD 1101 when King Muirchertach O'Brien handed it over to the Church. The figure can be described as squatting and the hands of the figure reach down from broad shoulders towards the slit of the vulva. In 1840, O'Donovan referred to a Sheela here as 'The Idol' but he may well have been referring to a figure with a cat-like head, rotund belly and intertwining legs known also as the 'Cat Goddess' that was previously regarded as a Sheela and can now be seen inside the museum. Local tradition also refers to a Sheela-na-Gig here that was said to have had the power to avert the Evil Eye.

28. *Castlemagner, County Tipperary:* Castlemagner is about eight kilometres south-east of Kanturk near Ceciltown. On the north side of the road about a kilometre west of Castlemagner is a path by the river Catra leading to a popular holy well dedicated to St Brigit. Flanking the opening is what is thought to be a later Sheela, while on the opposite side is a smaller figure which has been likened to a Roman soldier. The Sheela is standing or kneeling with her arms raised and her face has large staring almond shaped eyes and a incised mouth. Unlike most Sheelas she is not overtly emphasising her sexual organs which has led some researchers to dismiss

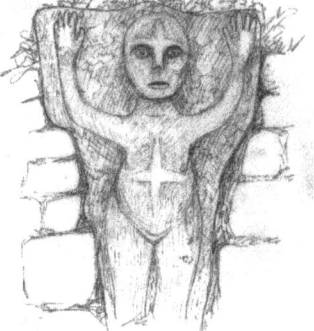

her as a true Sheela, yet the pubis is clearly marked. Andersen suggested 'an adaptation of the Sheela idea by a polite age' and refers to Du Noyer's estimate of a seventeenth-century origin.[10] The tradition of rubbing the figure with a pebble or stone has left well worn cross marks on the forehead, hands, belly and thighs. Although her whole stance and demeanour are unusual amongst the Sheela-na-Gigs the figure falls within the category of the current list because of her similarities to the Ballyvourney figure and and where she has been placed. (50 cm x 30 cm)

29. *Castle Widenham, County Cork:* Castle Widenham is near Castletownroche on the Fermoy–Mallow road. In the mid-1800s this Sheela was recorded as lying by a holy well situated on the banks of the Awbeg River but in 1906 it was found in a backwater and was re-erected by the well. In 1934 it again disap-

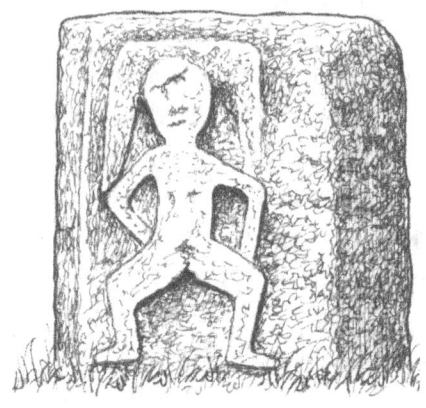

peared but was rescued and re-erected by the tower of the nearby castle. More recently it was removed to the safer environment of the castle and can only be seen by permission. The Sheela is carved on a large slab of rock and has an unusual headdress. She a lean torso, no sign of breasts, and hands pointing to the prominent pudenda. According to the *Ordnance Survey Field Book* of the late nineteenth century the figure was 'bearing an image supposed to be that of the saints',[11] and the well beside which she was found is dedicated to St Patrick. The Sheela looks as if she had been carved on a quoin stone, so her original setting would not have been the holy well.

30. *Cavan:* This is one of the better known Sheela-na-Gigs, carved in sandstone, and one of the earliest figures to be acquired by the National Museum. There is no record of the church from

which it is said to have originated. The legs are widely splayed and hands are joined around the extremely large genitalia. The right side is badly damaged but she retains many interesting features particularly the beading or bands around the forehead and around the lips, as well as a protruding tongue, a feature that may have been lost by weathering on other examples. (43 cm x 23 cm)

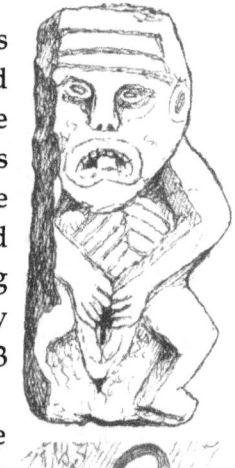

31. *Clenagh Castle, County Clare:* The castle, a late sixteenth-century tower house built by the McMahons of Clonderlaw, forms part of a large farm behind Shannon airport. A curious spindly figure is situated very low down on a quoin stone on the south-east side and appears to be contemporary with the castle. It is almost totally symbolic in form and the squat-legged, bridge position of her legs has

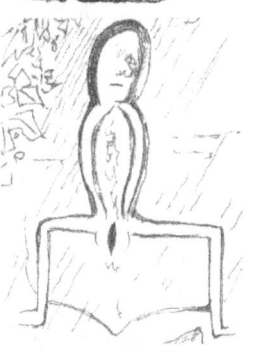

been seen as relating to the Sheela in nearby Bunratty Castle. The pudendum is well defined by an oblong, diamond-shaped, depression which shows signs of rubbing while the head and neck are outlined by a deep groove. (50 cm x 37 cm)

32. *Cloghan Castle, County Offaly:* A figure was reported as originating from the castle at Lusmagh, on the river Brosna a short way south of Banagher. This was according to information given by a Mr Cooke who in 1906 stated that he had in his possession an image called by the peasantry, 'The Witch' that was carved out of limestone. It was supposed that the figure represented 'an Hermaphrodite, one of the breasts being like the sun and the other a crescent like the moon.'[12] It was said to be preserved in a museum in the south of Ireland but there is no record of its existence.

33. *Cloghan Castle, County Roscommon:* The castle is close to Athleague which is on the main Roscommon–Galway road. Much

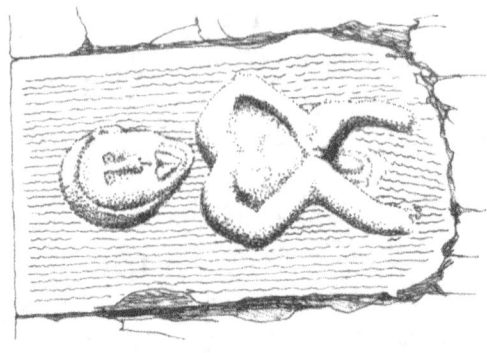

of the old castle has been dismantled but the tower with its well-preserved Sheela-na-Gig is intact. It is carved on a quoin stone 'some distance from the ground' on the south-east corner of the tower and is in a reclining position.[13] Both hands gesture towards the defined vulva. The main features are a protruding tongue, a second uvula-like shape carved into the background below the genitals and a fringe of hair or hairpiece that frames her head. (60 cm x 30 cm)

34. *Croomantagh or Clomantagh Castle, County Kilkenny:* This castle on the Urlingford–Kilkenny road is five kilometres from Freshford. The Sheela-na-Gig is approximately ten metres high, on a south-west quoin or corner-stone of the castle in a reclining position. She is a large figure with her feet touching the edge of the quoin. Her right hand is raised up towards her face and

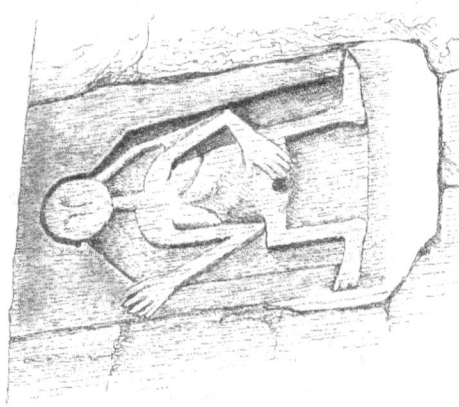

her left hand is clearly depicted touching her pudenda. She shares a similarity to the Sheela from Kiltinan church, with the same pendulous breasts and pipe-stem neck. The Clomantagh Sheela is mistakenly described by Andersen as having 'an absurd form of flying plaits'.[14] She is set within a recessed frame that follows the contours of her body and a raised slender band on her left-hand side stems from the side of her head to the side of her body. The quoin on which she is carved appears to be of a slightly darker grey than the rest of the quoin stones.

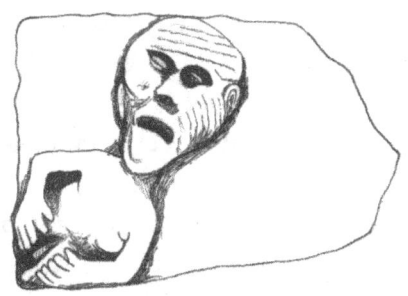

35. *Clonbulloge, County Offaly:* This unique figure was discovered in the 1970s in the Figile River below Kilcumber Bridge, near Clonbulloge. The figure is carved into the corner of a limestone quoin in high relief and is depicted without legs. Large hands pull open the vulva and the clitoris is clearly delineated. Other pieces of decorated stone found in the river suggest the destruction of a medieval building in the locality but the lack of any nearby castle or other structure leaves doubt over the origin of these remnants. The figure is now in the private possession of James Lawlor of Ballynalart, Clonbulloge who made the discovery.

36. *Clonlara, County Clare:* The figure is situated on an old canal bridge at Clonlara about midway between Limerick and Killaloe. It is a badly worn and damaged figure and is said by Westropp to have come from nearby Newtown Castle which was built in the 1380s. It is also possible that it comes from another nearby castle of the Earls of Ormond since a later earl was instrumental in building the canal and erected this bridge about the same time that the castle was pulled down. The date of 1769 which is inscribed above the left shoulder is thought to have been added later and relates to the construction of the bridge after the building of the canal which began in 1755. The figure was known locally as 'The Witches Stone' and also by the strange name of Peadar Taigdhe Buidhe. It is damaged below the waist and the legs and pelvic area are not visible but earlier researchers found traces of splayed legs and the right hand probably resting on the right thigh 'with the left

hand on or close to the pubic area' and was noted as having remarkably clear tool marks across the abdomen.[15] According to Guest it was said 'to have been defaced by the landowner about three generations ago'.[16] (62 cm x 47 cm)

37. *Clonmacnoise, County Offaly:* One of the few Romanesque Sheelas in Ireland is to be found on the 'Nun's Chapel', a classic piece of Romanesque architecture, standing within the former enclosure of the 'Abbess' which is outside of and to the north of the main complex at Clonmacnoise. On the inside of the larg-

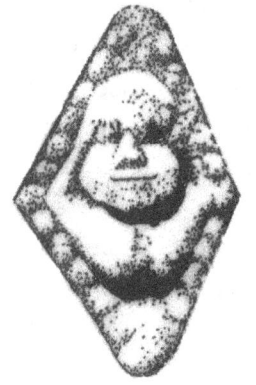

er decorated chancel arch, the seventh voussoir from the left, is a very small figure embracing its head in the manner of the continental acrobatic figures set into a lozenge-shaped stone, and with its feet raised. Other faces and animal heads are also set within a similar ornament on the arch. The 'Nun's Chapel' was erected by Derbforgaill Ní Mhaelsechnaill, wife of Tigernán Ó Ruairc, king of Bréfne and according to an entry in the *Annals of the Four Masters* it is said to have been completed in 1167. Clonmacnoise was important because of its position on the banks of the Shannon, formerly an essential trade route in Ireland, and its position on the Eiscir Riada, an ancient roadway across Ireland which follows a ridge of eskers that can be traced across the country from county Dublin.

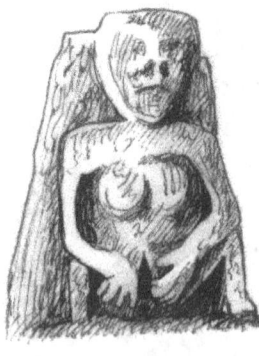

38. *Clonmel, County Tipperary:* Acquired by the National Museum in 1944, having been discovered in the wall of a bank opposite the site of a former Dominican priory. The figure became known as the 'Idol of Blue Anchor Lane' referring to where she was discovered. She is seated, with thighs splayed, and the hands touching the genitals. The lean ribs are carved in relief and a heavy streaking pattern of parallel lines is clearly delineated.

There is tattooing on the breasts. There are two curious holes, one to the left of vulva and one in the position of anus, and the top half of her face is partly destroyed or badly weathered. She is currently one of the two Sheelas on public display at the National Museum. (62 cm x 36 cm)

39. *Clonoulty, County Tipperary:* This magnificent Sheela was found in January 1989 during a clean-ing-up scheme in Clonoulty church; she was buried up to her neck at the foot of a yew tree. The age of the tree indicates that the stone was buried at least some time prior to 1800 and it is thought to have been placed in this position as a marker, possibly of a grave. Unfortunately the face and right arm of this otherwise very fine Sheela has been so damaged that no features sur-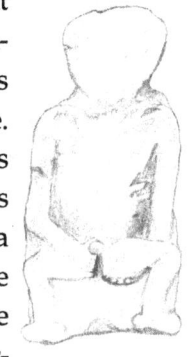
vive. The left hand passes under her thigh and the right hand on top is sculptured in deep relief. There are rib marks and despite the facial damage there are still clear indications of neck striations and possibly striations along the side of her head. Clonoulty is the site of a former Preceptory (temple) of the Knight's Templars and at the end of the Crusades when the Templars were disbanded, Clonoulty was the wealthiest of their Irish foundations. The figure is located in the GPA Bolton Library in Cashel. (70 cm x 35 cm)

40. *Cooliagh More, County Kilkenny:* This Sheela-na-Gig was un-earthed during clearance work on Cooliagh church near Kells priory and is now in private possession at Rothe House in Kilkenny. Local tradition relates that the Sheela was previously found in a well at Kyle and brought to the churchyard of Cooliagh early in this century. There is speculation that it could have derived from a pre-Norman church which is now no longer visible. There are a number of other nearby sites in the area from which the Sheela could originate such as the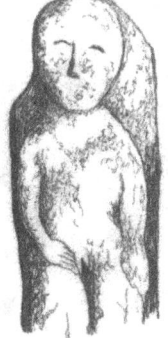

ancient monastic site of Kilree with its old church and round tower. The left hand of the figure appears to rest on the thigh and the right hand is clearly gesturing towards the genitals. The position of her feet is unusual with the left leg outstretched with the foot inclined towards the left, the right leg

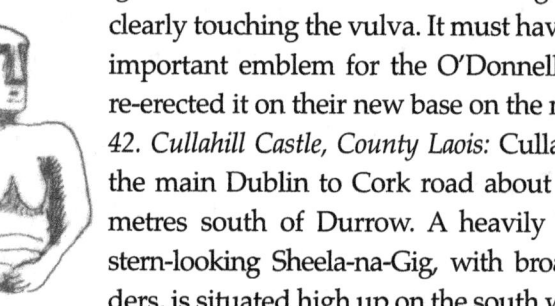

bent tightly at the knee and the heel seems to be tilted to indicate the genitalia.

41. Corveen Castle, County Donegal: Corveen or Lough Eske Castle, the island stronghold of the O'Donnells, is a few miles east of Donegal town, but the Sheela-na-Gig is now missing despite several thorough searches made in recent years. Thomas Fagan's *Ordnance Survey Letters of 1846–7* records a 'female exhibitionist figure' which was said to have been originally on the older castle in the lake and then re-erected on the coach house of the new castle on the mainland. Fortunately, he made a fairly good sketch of the figure – the legs are raised to the head and the right hand is

clearly touching the vulva. It must have been an important emblem for the O'Donnells as they re-erected it on their new base on the mainland.

42. Cullahill Castle, County Laois: Cullahill is on the main Dublin to Cork road about five kilometres south of Durrow. A heavily built and stern-looking Sheela-na-Gig, with broad shoulders, is situated high up on the south wall of the peel tower. Her hands reach down to her abdomen but the lower section may be missing. The breasts are fairly large and

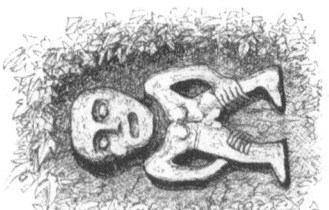

a few lines are carved across the lower half of the chest. Cullahill was one of the more important strongholds of the Fitzgeralds and the date given for its construction is 1425.

43. Doon Castle, County Offaly: Doon

Castle is on the east side of the Athlone to Birr road about a mile south of Ballynahown. This is a well-preserved Sheela, carved as standing but found in a reclining position on a quoin stone on the south-east corner of the tower a short way to the left of the main entrance. The right hand passes underneath the thigh and the left hand passes over the thigh. The legs are carved as standing but both feet point towards the right.

44. *Dowth, County Meath:* The Sheela-na-Gig is on the south wall of the old church, which is situated eight kilometres south-east of Slane. The figure has been badly damaged; when Dr Guest visited the church in the 1930s she was disappointed to find that the prominent abdomen characteristic of this figure had been hacked off to accommodate a modern tombstone. An earlier photograph confirms that the figure at one time had legs with thighs splayed with the hands directed towards her genitals.[17] The Sheela was formerly known by the name of St Seanachan (or St Shanahan), who was probably the same saint as St Senach – the brother of St Senan, a sixth-century patron saint of the Shannon estuary. It has also been noted that the Sheela is carved from a type of stone that is different to that used in the walls of the church.

45. *Drogheda, County Louth:* This rather worn and flat example of a Sheela-na-Gig was recognised by Dr Peter Harbison on the wall of a house at 18 John Street in Drogheda and removed to the Millmount Museum, Drogheda when that part of town was demolished for road improvements. It is thought to have come from the old town wall which once ran through this area. The hand are joined together just above a round hole or a depression which marks the genital area.

46. *Dunaman, County Limerick:* Dunaman Castle, now in ruins, is

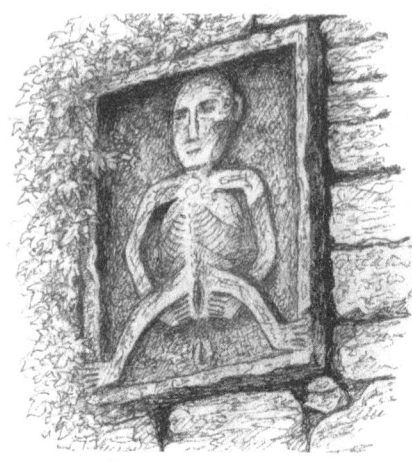

incorporated into the present farm, and and lies about three kilometres south of Adare and west of Croom. This is one of the largest and most overt Sheelas in Ireland and is situated about halfway up on the main south-facing wall of the castle where she could be clearly seen by everyone who visited the place. This wide-shouldered figure is set within a square frame and the broad toes of her big feet extend to the outside edge of the frame. Her large hands go under her legs to the the pudenda. The ribs are heavily incised and there is a strange uvula-like shape below the actual vulva.

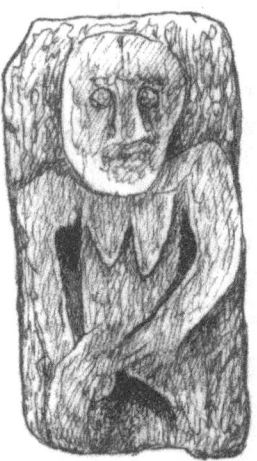

47. Errigal Keeroge, County Tyrone: This figure came from the early church of St Dachiarog about five and a half kilometres west of Ballygawley, Co. Tyrone but is now located in the Ulster Museum, Belfast. The church is situated on a hilltop and is thought to have been built on the ancient site of a Celtic shrine or sanctuary.[18] When the Sheela was first handed into the museum it was described as having come from somewhere else but it was later revealed that it had come from the old church. Andersen commented on the impressive ugliness of this carving and it is certainly not intended as a portrait of beauty with a large, bald head, crooked nose and wide mouth. The hands are pointing towards the pudenda with the right hand passing beneath one thigh and the other hand passing in front. Deliberate asymmetry is also at play here with one shoulder raised higher than the other and one breast longer than the other.[19] (46 cm x 25 cm)

48. *Errigal Keeroge, County Tyrone:* A second figure from this site came to light during the final days of research for this book and was brought to our attention by Cary Meehan. The Sheela-na-Gig has been built into the low masonry that constitutes the remains of the old church and is about 70cm high and carved from a dark grey sandstone. The figure has been carved in quite high relief and is depicted squatting with arms reaching straight down to the abdomen and there are deeply carved indentations beneath legs and arms. The head is represented by a recessed circular depression above the body and there is a deep groove on the stone to the left of her head which gives the impression of having been carved for a particular function. A crack running from this carved notch to the left cheek gives the impression of a pipe-smoking sheela. Unfortunately she is rather worn or weathered in the lower areas and the hands and details of the area around the pudenda are unclear. It is particularly significant that this figure should be found at a site that has deep connections with St Ciaran from whose main centre at Seir Kieran in Tipperary two figures have also been recorded.

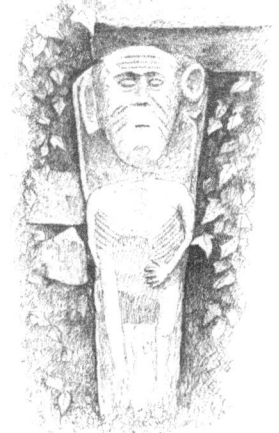

49. *Fethard Abbey, County Tipperary:* This Sheela is on the north face of the wall, at the east end of the ancient Augustinian friary, next to the priest's modern house. It was possibly erected originally on the earliest church at the abbey founded c. 1300, now in ruins. The figure is finely carved with signs of ribs and streaked cheeks, and prominent asymmetrical ears. The legs are thin and widely spaced but it does not appear that her lower regions have been hacked at, as is sometimes suggested, although the right hand appears to be missing. The left hand gestures towards

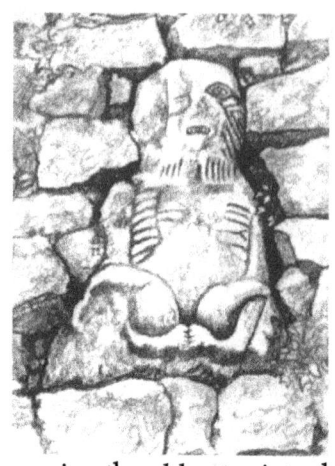

the abdomen and the figure is kept clear of the ivy which encroaches on the rest of the wall.

50. Fethard Wall, County Tipperary: This most startling Sheela-na-Gig can be found on a section of the old fourteenth-century town wall overlooking the medieval bridge on the Clashawley River at the entrance to the medieval town of Fethard. Although the figure is strategically located facing the old entry into the town it blends in with the rest of the wall and is only really visible from close up. The hands meet below the thighs and the fingers are joined in the opening of the vulva. This Sheela is one of the few examples that could be described as ugly as she has an emaciated look, incised ribs, an incised, striated chevron pattern on the left cheek, striations on her neck and a large growth on her right ear. Grimly set teeth and large, rimmed staring eyes with pupils add to her hideous appearance. James O'Connor commented that 'it

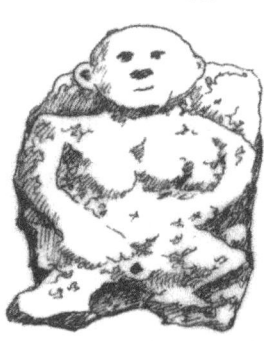

must be one of the most powerfully apotropaic of all the Sheela figures'[20] and Jorgen Andersen called this figure the 'Witch on the Wall', from which his most erudite book is named.

51. Garry Castle, County Offaly: Garry Castle is situated about midway along the Birr to Clonmacnoise road, between Cloghan and Banagher. This figure is only about two meters from the ground on the east wall of the old castle and is described as being a rotund figure with round head and one hand pointing down towards a clearly defined vulva. It was discovered by Anthony Weir and described as being, 'curiously sited between the fine large corbels which supported a collapsed bartizan parapet or machicolation'.[21]

52. *Glanworth Castle, County Cork:* The figure was found during an archaeological dig beneath a layer of rubble in a vaulted ground floor chamber of the gate tower and is thought to have been deliberately hidden here sometime in or before the 1600s.[2] The figure is sculpted in deep relief and since it has been preserved from weathering such 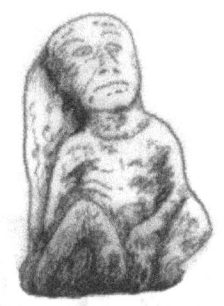 small details as the anus are still clearly defined. Both hands meet at the vulva with the left arm passing over the left thigh and the right arm passing under the right thigh. This castle was originally built of limestone in the thirteenth century by the De Caunteton or Condon family and the Sheela, sculptured from red sandstone, would have stood out clearly from her position on the castle walls. At present, this figure is stored for safekeeping at the National Monuments Depot, Mallow, County Cork. (52 cm x 35 cm)

53. *Holycross Abbey, County Tipperary:* Situated on the river Suir between Cashel and Thurles, Holycross Abbey was originally founded by the Benedictines in the twelfth century and not long afterwards passed on to the Cistercian order. The Sheela was discovered during restoration work on the abbey in 1970 and is located on the south wall of the west range about two and a half metres from the ground, on the same side as the entrance to the cloister. However the figure has been badly damaged and almost entirely hacked away, making her fairly difficult to discern.

54. *Kells, County Meath:* A grotesque female figure was recorded by Wilde in the catalogue of the RIA collection, as being in the church at Kells but there is no trace of any female figures now.

55. *Kildare Cathedral:* A small, nude figure of a woman spreading her legs adorns the crypt in Great Connel Abbey where Bishop Arthur Wellesley is buried. One must bend down to see her as she is above a crucifixion panel under the left hand corner of the top slab. This Sheela was identified by John Hunt

and is conceived of in a much lighter vein, being carved in a much more naturalistic manner, with the decorative treatment of her pubic hair and lack of explicit reference to the genitals.[23] The funerary monument is thought to have been 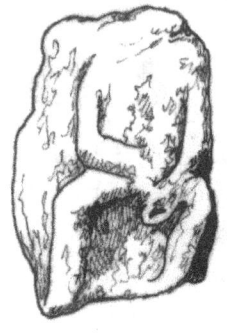 carved in 1539 and is now in St Brigit's cathedral which was built on the site of the famous monastery founded by St Brigit in the fifth or sixth century.

56. Killaloe, County Clare: A headless Sheela is situated over St Flannan's holy well opposite the Romanesque church which is dedicated to the same saint. The Sheela-na-Gig may have originally been erected on the church but it is now situated in a small garden at the rear of a bank. Access to this headless Sheela-na-Gig is restricted but one would hope she is at least in safe keeping from further dam-

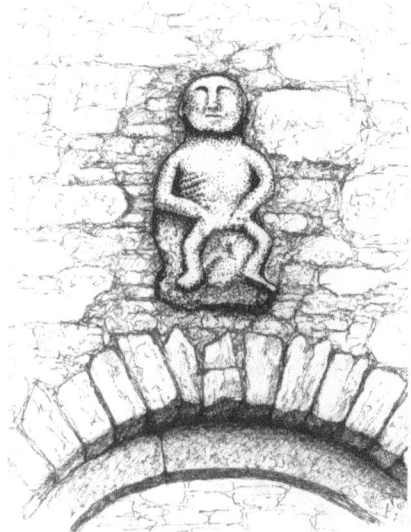

age. She has long dangling breasts with her hands touching above her thighs and her her legs are widely splayed.

57. Kilnaboy Church, County Clare: The twelfth or thirteenth century church of Kilnaboy overlooks the road just north of Corofin. The church was built on the site of an early monastery founded by St Inghean Bhaoithe but all that remains of this former foundation is the stump of the round tower. The Sheela, carved in deep relief, is prominently displayed above the entrance door to the church but unfortunately is worn. Incised ribs and folds of the neck are still visible and there is something like a tail descending from the vulva. Her hands meet above the vulva. She is regarded as an image of the first abbess St Inghean Bhaoithe (daughter of Baoth), pro- nounced locally as 'Innan Wee'. An odd fig- ure with a small cross marking her vulva and possible horns on her head is inserted side- ways just inside the doorway.

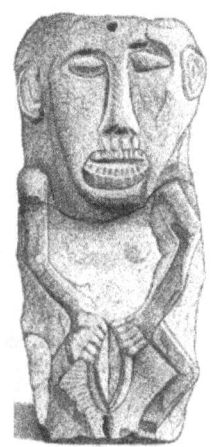

58. *Killua, County Westmeath:* This figure, now in the Witt Collection of the British Museum, was found in a field in 1859 on an estate called Old Town and was known to have been in the possession of Sir Benjamin Chap- man of Killua Castle, Westmeath. In 1866 Thomas Wright in his book *The Worship of the Generative Powers during the Middle Ages of Western Europe* re- corded it as Chloran. It is thought to be made of granite and appears like the Cavan Sheela with similar depiction of ribs, visible teeth, squatting position of legs and hands joined in a gesture around the extremely large genitalia. (47 cm x 20 cm)

59. *Kilmacomma, County Waterford:* In 1937 it was reported that a figure which appears to have been a Sheela-na-Gig existed at Kilmacomma about a mile south east of Clonmel: 'The antiq- uity was found about fifty years ago by the late John Gibbons, farmer, when raising sand in his sand-pit, and as he was building a barn at the time, he inserted the affair in one of the gables. Some time after a high bank of sand in the sand-pit fell on Gibbons and killed him, with the result that his death was attributed to the malign influence of the Sheela.'[24] The death of Mr Gibbons however may not have been the only reason for the removal of the Sheela-na-Gig for it is also recorded that 'subsequently, on account, of trespass by persons coming to see the Sheela-na-gig, Michael Gibbons, son of John Gibbons, removed the affair from the barn gable, and hid it, and is un- able to find it ...' The Sheela was inadequately described as being 'about two and a half feet high and had eyes, a mouth and a nose'.[25]

60. *Kilmainaham, County Meath:* Edith Guest recorded that she was

told of a figure, which she took to be a Sheela-na-Gig, buried in a churchyard near the railway station shortly before 1900.[26]

61. *Kilsarkan, County Kerry:* Kilsarkan church is about six and a half kilometres east of Farranafore. This Sheela-na-Gig is car-

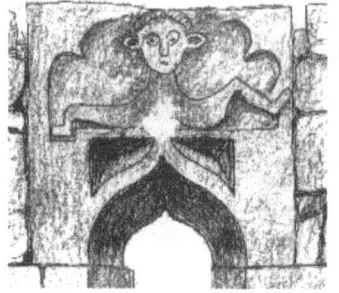

ved into the lintel of the south window of the medieval parish church and both the genital area of the figure and several places around the window frame are extensively rubbed in a cross pattern with a stone or pebble, obviously as part of the rounds. According to local information, it was 'the mullion of the window' that was formerly rubbed, which presumably means the edges of this narrow slit of a window.[27] It appears to be a relatively late carving, perhaps a contemporary of Ballyvourney or Clenagh, but no earlier than the fifteenth or sixteenth century. Notwithstanding her late origination the figure has the curious features of prominent cow ears, a strange rope-like headdress and one leg raised.

62. *Kiltinan Castle, County Tipperary:* Kiltinan Castle, which dates

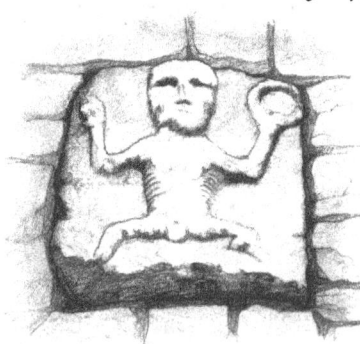

back to 1215, is a short way to the east of Kiltinan church (see below). Called the Guardian of the Well, she is now on one side of a round, fortified well-house overlooking the stream. This is not its original position; the figure was first identified in 1840 and described in *PRIA* 1840–1844 as being discovered at Kiltinan Castle, but she may have originally come from Kiltinan church, as mentioned by the owner of the castle, Colonel R. Cooke in 1909. This grim looking figure holds two objects in her upraised hands. These objects are subject to various interpretations such as a dagger, a torc or horseshoe but they may also portray goddess symbolism, such as the circle and the serpent.

63. *Kiltinan Church, County Tipperary:* Kiltinan church is located about five and a half kilometres south-east of Fethard. This Sheela-na-Gig (the first to be described by O'Donovan in the last century and the figure from which the name entered into common usage) was stolen on the 9 January 1990. She was a curious figure that appeared as if she was dancing or doing a jig, with her left arm and left leg uplifted and her right hand holding her vulva open. 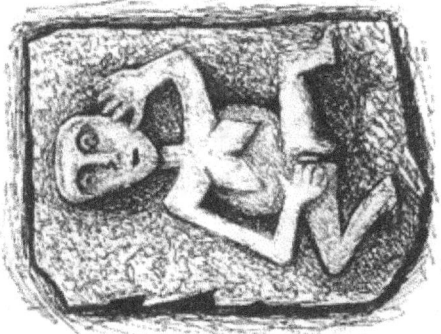 Other unusual features are her thin neck and two nipples on her left breast. She was originally in a horizontal position and used as a quoin in the south-west corner of the church. She was, however, not part of the original fourteenth-century building as the limestone quoin did not fit in with the normal alternating-size pattern of the other quoins.[28] An replica carved by James O'Connor, local author of a book on the subject of the Fethard Sheela-na-Gigs, has not yet been erected in place of the original. (81 cm x 51 cm)

64. *Knockarley, County Offaly:* Knockarley is only about two and a half kilometres south-south-east of the old monastic centre of Seir Kieran (see below). This dramatic sculpted figure is of the same genre as the Sheela-na-Gigs but is clearly an unique example. It is carved from a local sandstone and appears as if this particular piece was chosen for its shape which the carver evidently modified using the existing contours. It is obviously a free-standing figure as it would have been nearly impossible to erect on a building and as such its age, which one suspects may be quite early, is difficult to judge.

The face is inclined towards the right on top of an elongated neck and although she is fairly weathered it is clear that her right hand lies across the belly and the left hand is laid on the thigh. The figure does not appear to have legs but there is a small yet clearly defined vulva marked by a small incision surrounded by a very thick raised oval. Like the Seir Kieran figure, which originates from a church nearby, the Knockarley figure also has two small neat holes drilled into the top of her head and another below the vulva. (55 cm high)

65. *Lavey, County Cavan:* This figure, carved on a limestone slab, 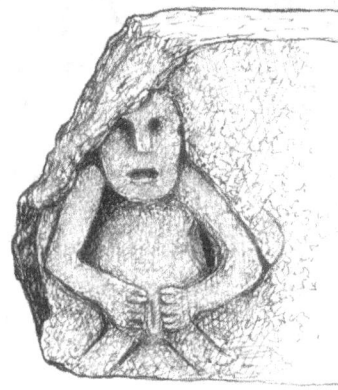 was found in 1842 by a Dr Charles Halpin on top of a new gate pier built at the entrance to the old graveyard at Lavey. It was supposed by the finder to have been a quoin stone originating from the old church, 'of which scarcely a trace was left then'.[29] Lavey church is thought to date no earlier than the late twelfth century and is dedicated to St Dymphna, an early Irish saint who is patroness of the insane. One of the most interesting aspects of this figure is the unidentified discoid object which appears to be located under her left arm, yet the outline of the circle is also incised twice on top of her arm. The fingers of the large hands rest on the raised rim of a box-like slit of her prominent vulva. She has deeply set eyes, indications of teeth and extremely long toes on turned-out feet. The figure is now located in the National Museum, Dublin. (47 cm x 58 cm)

66. *Lemanaghan Castle, County Offaly:* The castle is three miles from Firbane on the road to Ballycumber. Thomas Cooke of Birr, wrote a history of the area, had a [1870] drawing of the Sheela.[30] Unfortunately neither the drawing nor the stone can be found.

67. *Liathmor (Leighmore), County Tipperary:* The site of this seventh-century monastery lies on the south side of the main Cork to

Dublin road, approximately nine kilometres from Urlingford. Remains on the site 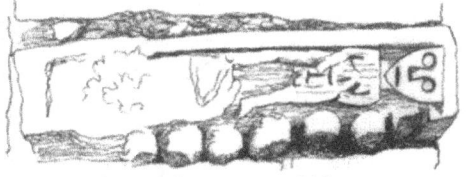 include the remnants of an eleventh- or twelfth-century church (the larger of the two churches on the site) on which can be found the Sheela-na-Gig. The figure, carved in sandstone, is on the Romanesque north doorway above a row of pellets. She is on her side but can be described as standing with straight legs, with hands joined around the genital organs and with a large triangular head and eyes. There is a decorative motif at her feet, a foliate design of six lobes, which Dr Guest suggests is a degenerate form of the palmette.[31] She is probably not later than twelfth century and is in her original setting, as the stone is integral to the church's structure.

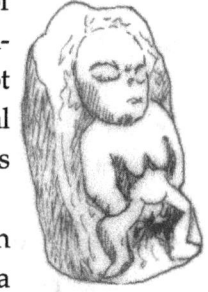

68. *Lixnaw, County Kerry:* Lixnaw is about eleven kilometres south-west of Listowel. This Sheela was acquired by the National Museum in 1964 having been found in a river bed near The Court, a castle built in 1320 by Baron Lixnaw, from which the figure may originate. She is carved in relief, has small, flat, breasts and her hands pass under her thighs to grasp and pull apart her vulva.

69. *Lusk, County Dublin:* A figure fitting the description of a Sheela-na-Gig, was recorded by an antiquarian Austin Cooper as having existed in the church at Lusk in 1783 but in 1844 the Rev. Mr Tyrell presumably buried the figure then known as 'The Idol'. Cooper's description gives us an idea of the physical characteristics of the figure: 'the human features [were represented as] fancifully hideous; the face being seven inches broad, and the head without neck or body, being attached to a pair of kneeling thighs and legs.'[32] Perhaps that kneeling implies the kind of reduced body which is typical of the Sheelas.

70. *Lustymore, County Fermanagh:* On Boa Island is the ancient

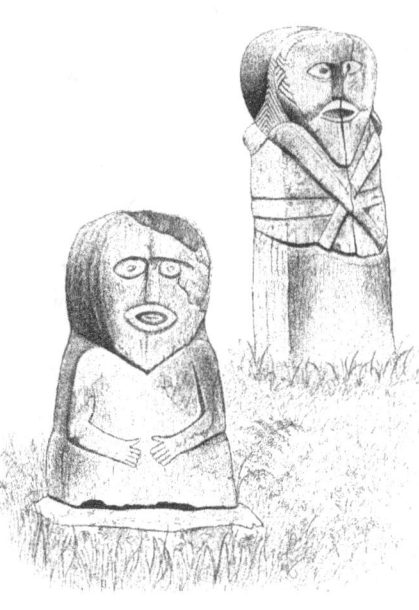

church site of Caldragh, at the northern end of Lower Lough Erne. It best known for the double-headed Janus Figure, found in the old overgrown graveyard. Close by is the less well known Sheela which comes from nearby Lustymore Island, on which there was once a monastery. Originally preserved in a house on Lustymore, in the early years of the twentieth century she was removed to Lustybeg Island, before finding her present resting position on Boa Island. The figure is similar in style to the Janus Figure and many features such as the pointed chin and the broad open mouth gives the appearance that the figure is carved in the same tradition. The left eye of the Sheela is either damaged or

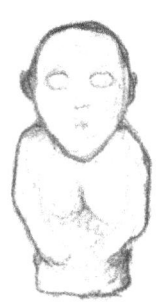

imperfect, perhaps deliberately represented as closed or blind, and the legs of this figure are also too worn to make out. The vulva is no longer clearly marked but the hands point towards the lower abdomen.

71. *Maghera, County Derry:* About six metres from the ground on the northern side of the tower of the old church at Maghera is a Sheela-na-Gig. Unfortunately, the lower part of the sculpture appears to have broken away although the pointing of the hands towards the lower abdomen can be clearly made out.

72. *Malahide (A) and (B), County Dublin:* In 1954, P. J. Hartnett reported that workers clearing up the church, also known as the abbey, for Lord Talbot de Malahide had revealed a Sheela-na-Gig on a quoin or corner-stone at the north-east angle of the old church. This is a fifteenth- or sixteenth-century church

dedicated to St Sylvester and, like the Kiltinan church Sheela, the stone is situated
just below the roof, at the springing of the
gable. The Sheela-na-Gig carved from red
sandstone at Malahide is unusual and is
one of the better examples of the figures set
within a frame. But the figure, which had
been formerly preserved by its covering of
ivy, is now only a vague outline. Several
features visible on an early photograph are
no longer clear:[33] the fingers of the left hand
rest on the thigh but the other hand is not

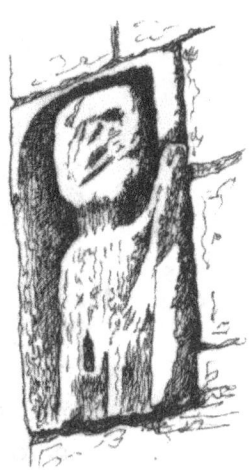

recognisable, although there is a clear trace of the slit of the
vulva. A second stone of similar origination and of the same
material is probably another Sheela and is also endangered.
This figure can be found at the springing of the gable on the

opposite side of the church.
Only the head with a tongue
slightly protruding is left and
the stone appears to have been
broken off at the junction of
neck and body. (48 cm x 25 cm)

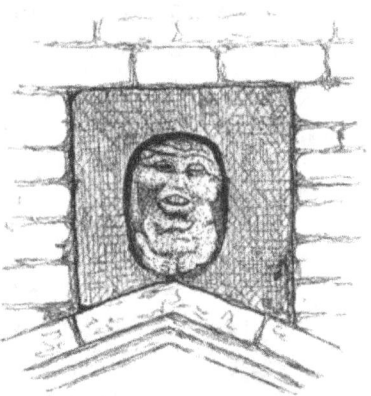

73. *Moate Castle, County Westmeath:*
Moate Castle is on the north
side of the road from the village towards Kilbeggan. This
figure, in a cement sunken
oval, is only 3.35 cm high, and is over the gateway in the wall
of the castle yard which was built in 1649. It has a wide mouth
with thick lips showing teeth and a protruding tongue, a striated hair style and a waist belt or band across the abdomen.
Both hands, with fingers clearly indicated, are shown holding
the vulva to leave no doubt about her classification as a
Sheela, although it is suggested that it is a later grotesque
treatment of the subject.[34]

141

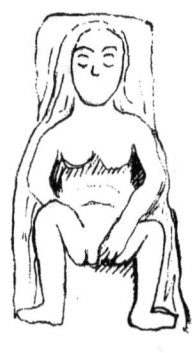

74. Moycarkey Castle, County Tipperary: Just off the Cashel road about five kilometres from Thurles are the remains of Moycarkey Castle which was described as having a Sheela-na-Gig set in the south wall. A nineteenth-century sketch of the figure in the RIA library, Dublin has the caption 'the country people have a legend and call it Cathleen Owen', which refers to the figure in mythic terms, Cathleen meaning the Hag and Owen meaning a river.[35] Local lore relates that the Sheela was procured from the ruins of the nearby church to bring luck to the house. The figure appeared seated and the left hand passed in front of the left thigh while the right hand passed from beneath the other thigh.

75. *Moygara, County Sligo:* The castle is known as O'Gara's Fortress and is about half a mile from the north-western end of Lough Gara. It is an impressive fortress built during times of protracted troubles in Connacht. It was attacked several times and was finally burned down in 1581. The Sheela-na-Gig is said to have been on the barbican over the entrance and to have been part of a pair of 'inverted pyramid shape' corbel stones. Guest records that, 'the limestone block, on the corbelled end of which the figure is rudely carved, now lies on the ground near the castle entrance' and published a picture of the stone lying in the grass.[36] Unfortunately Guest's photograph is rather unclear and there is now a heap of rubble piled up beneath the entrance making it difficult to locate the

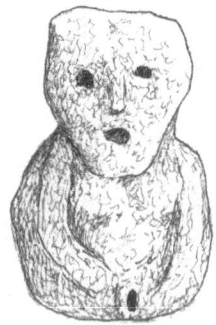

stone at all. However Weir describes an acrobatic or dancing figure on one stone and on the corresponding corbel stone, a 'couple apparently coupling'.[37]

76. *Newtown Lennan, County Tipperary:* Remains of the old church of Newtown Lennan, which is possibly of twelfth-century origin, can be found about five and a half kilo-

metres north of Carrick-on-Suir at the foot of the Slievenamon Hills. This rather worn Sheela was found in an exposed position in the church yard. The face is quite badly worn but fortunately it can be clearly identified as a classic Sheela with arms hanging loosely from the body and the hands pointing towards the clearly marked vulva. (37 cm x 27 cm)

77. *Portnahinch, County Laois:* The castle from which this figure originates has been destroyed and the Sheela-na-Gig has been missing since the 1930s. The figure is described from a photograph as 'standing, with legs awkwardly apart and arms slightly akimbo suggesting usual gesture towards the abdomen' and a large, low-set head.[38] It was discovered at the same time as the Tinnakill Sheela, which is also missing.

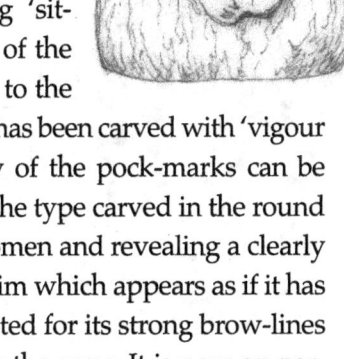

78. *Rahan, County Offaly:* According to D. Newman in his report to the Royal Society in 1972 this Sheela-na-Gig was discovered during grave-digging 'sitting upright on the ruined walls of the chapel or church in the cemetery to the south of St Carthach's Church'. It has been carved with 'vigour and attention to detail', as many of the pock-marks can be seen.[39] It is also a rare example of the type carved in the round with legs flexed up over the abdomen and revealing a clearly defined vulva with an indented rim which appears as if it has been rubbed. The figure is also noted for its strong brow-lines and its pronounced breasts under the arms. It is now on permanent display in the Castle Museum, Athlone. (28 cm x 21 cm)

79. *Rahara, County Roscommon:* Rahara is about thirteen kilometres south of Roscommon on the Athlone to Athleague road but the Sheela can be viewed at Roscommon County Museum, which is located in the old Presbyterian Church, Roscommon. The Sheela-na-Gig from the old church at Rahara came to light during cleaning-up work in the graveyard when a vous-

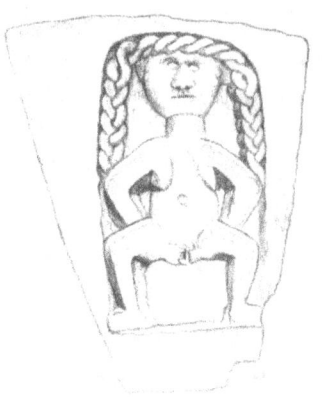

soir-shaped stone with one face deeply sunken into the ground was found. On turning it over it was discovered that it had a female figure carved on it and because the stone was face downwards in the soil the fine details were in excellent condition. It is carved in low relief, has quite large breasts and very pronounced nostril channels. Both arms are shown reaching down beneath the widely splayed thighs. This figure has many similarities to the Ballinderry Sheela, as it is also surrounded by a Celtic knotwork which falls down to her arms like hair. It was carved into a wedge-shaped stone which denotes that it would have been a keystone, and like the Ballinderry figure would have probably been erected over

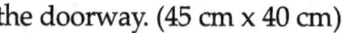

the doorway. (45 cm x 40 cm)

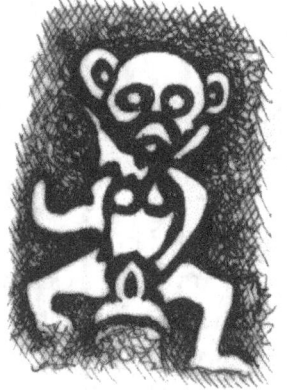

80. Rath (Rath Blathmac), County Clare: Rath church, named after St Blathmac, is about three kilometres south-east of Corofin and about one and a half kilometres north of Dysert O'Dea. The remains of the old nave and chancel date from various periods and the Sheela-na-Gig is found carved to the left of an ornamented panel of a lower window lintel inserted upside down. The animal carvings on this stone have been related to a figure found on a window at Annaghdown, County Galway, *c.1180,* and a Scandinavian origin has also been suggested. A figure reported to have come from Carrowfield church is illustrated by M. A. Murray and proves to be identical to the Sheela from Rath.[40]

81. Ratoo, County Kerry: Ratoo round tower is about eight kilometres south of Ballybunion, near the village of Ballyduff. This is the only example of a Sheela-na-Gig placed on a round tower and the figure is stated to be carved on the top left-hand corner of the north window, facing the interior of the round tower.¹¹ The figure is carved in relief on two stones with the head and shoulders on the end of the lintel stone and the rest of the figure on the jambs below. It was discovered in 1880–81 during restoration work and a cast was made of it for the Old Kilkenny Historical Society. This cast is in the National Museum,

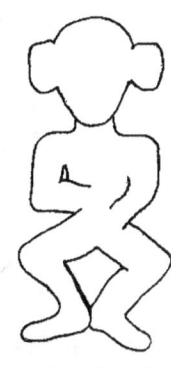

Dublin. Ratoo is one of the finest round towers in Ireland and the Sheela is clearly part of the tower and not a later insertion.

Its finely carved doorway and various other unusual features suggest that this round tower was built at a quite late date possibly the eleventh or twelfth century. (30 cm x 14 cm)

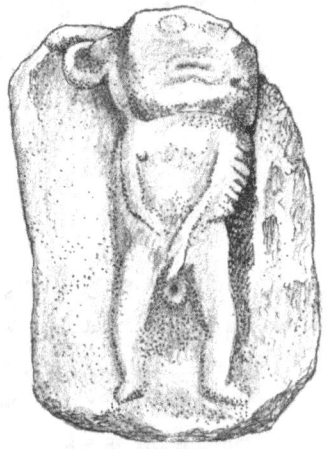

82. *Redwood Castle, County Tipperary:* Redwood castle is about ten kilometres north-east of Portumna. The Sheela is located very high up on the east-facing wall about fourteen metres above the main doorway, slightly to the right and just underneath the overhanging barbican. She is sculptured in deep relief and has a large head, large eyes, nose and mouth, and a prominent 'C'-shaped right ear. The body is long and slender with tiny round breasts and is grooved at the sides of the head and body. Her legs are only slightly splayed and she is touching or pulling the vulva from above.

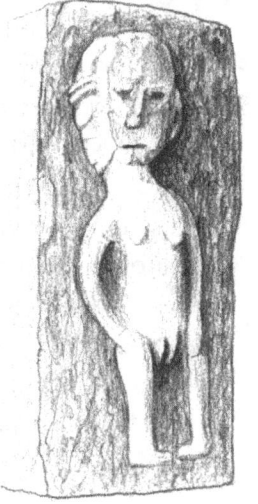

83. *Ringaskiddy, County Cork:* In the mid-1980s a figure was retrieved from a

garden of a deserted house near the village and was acquired by the Fitzgerald Park Museum in Cork where it is now kept in storage. The Sheela has a disproportionately large head with arms hanging down, a long, slender body and almost straight legs, and both hands are directed towards a slit indicating the vulva. She is one of the unusual type that has inward-turned feet. It is possible that this is one of the two Sheelas in a private garden at Ringaskiddy in the early years of the century but Guest was unable to verify this in 1935.[42]

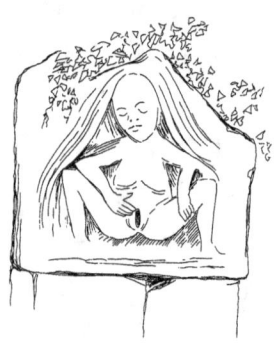

84. Rochestown, County Tipperary: The old church, in which a Sheela-na-Gig was once set in the east gable, can be found about four kilometres south-west of Cahir. This figure was reported by R. P. Coles at the same time that O'Donovan noted the Sheela on Kiltinan church and is the first Sheela-na-Gig to have been discussed in print. It is now missing having disappeared some time between the late 1800s and Guest's visit to the site in the 1930s. All that remains is a sketch made by T. J. Westropp shortly after its initial discovery which depicts a benign-looking, seated figure with large breasts and the knees widely splayed. The left hand is resting on the left knee and the fingers of the right hand is clearly touching her pudenda.[43]

85. Rosenallis, County Laois: Rosenallis is about six kilometres northwest of Mountmellick. The figure was discovered in 1992 in the Church of Ireland graveyard and removed to the National Museum. The stump of a round tower and other remnants including the ruined church from which it is presumed the Sheela-na-Gig originated, attest to Rosenallis' former importance as an ancient holy centre. The figure is carved from sandstone and is rather weathered with the facial features and other finer details virtually obliterated, although there are still traces of ribbing below the small oval breasts. (51 cm x 31 cm)

86. Rosnaree, County Meath: About four kilometres south-east of Slane, a curious and barely discernible Sheela-na-Gig can be found adorning the wall by the door of an old watermill, where the grain used to be carried in. Many coats of lime-wash obscure her and give the figure a ghostly appearance but she remains distinguishable as a true Sheela-na-Gig. The figure was remembered by the former owner of the mill as an original goddess, and

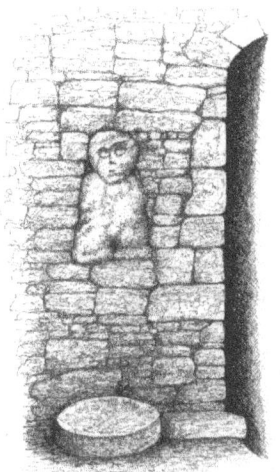

an old photograph published by Murray shows her to be a rather worn squat figure with a big head that was curiously erected above a large stone basin." This is the only Sheela found in connection with a water mill and is probably a secondary relocation.

87. & 88. Scregg Castle (A) & (B), County Roscommon: Scregg is about ten kilometres south-east of Roscommon and about two kilometres south of Knockcroghery. The two figures at Scregg probably both originated from the old castle, a tower house of the Uí Maine clan, most of which has now been dismantled. The present structure on the site of the castle is a period house and the Sheelas have been re-erected on either side of the entrance to a carriage house which is built of stone from the old castle. One of the figures is small, only about ten centimetres high, and is depicted with legs widely splayed in an almost acrobatic fashion. The larger figure is just under thirty-five centimetres high and would have formed a keystone, possibly over a window or door. This figure is

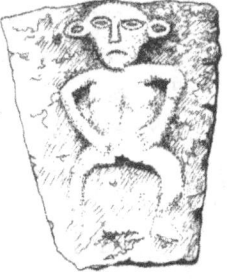

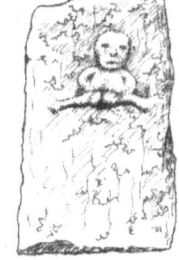

depicted in a posture similar to the Ballinderry Sheela but has ears that are strikingly similar to the cow ears of the figure at Kilsarkan in Co. Kerry. It is perhaps also worth noting that Scregg is less than four kilometres from the north-east of Rahara church and the finest figure in the region.

89. *Seir Kieran, County Offaly:* Seir Kieran is about six kilometres south of Birr and is a ancient monastic site and pilgrimage centre. It presently consists of a relatively modern church standing within a large hilltop enclosure extending over twenty-five acres in which can be found the remains of a round tower, ancient tombstones and traces of earthworks. The site is recorded as the burial place of the ancient kings of Ossory and is dedicated to St Ciarán 'the Elder', a contemporary of St Patrick. Around 1200 it was reorganised and a religious foundation was established by the Augustinians. The old church from which the Sheela originates was destroyed but the figure was depicted in the *Dublin Penny Journal* of 1834 as protruding from the eastern gable near 'an old freestone window frame', and was found later 'abutting on the vallum

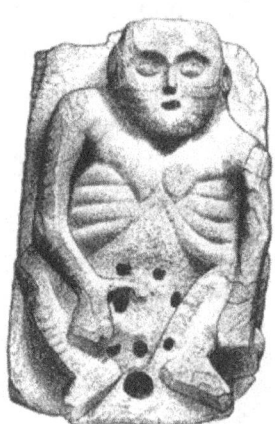

of the ancient enclosure'. This 1834 article also made reference to another figure in the west gable of the old church known as St Kieran, which has subsequently disappeared.[45] The Seir Kieran Sheela is now on display in the National Museum and is probably one of the most remarkable and important examples in Ireland and the British Isles. The right arm reaches down towards the abdomen and the left arm hangs loosely by the side of the body holding an unknown cylindrical object. A strange series of eleven holes are drilled through the figure's stomach, lower abdomen and deep into the stone from the back of the head. These holes serve no practical function and suggest that this idol-like figure served some sort of ritualistic purpose. (42 cm x 25 cm)

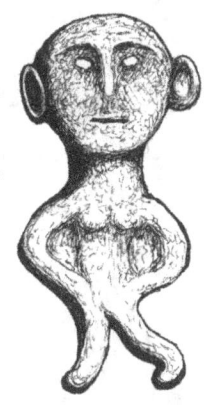

90. *Shanrahan, County Tipperary:* The bell tower of Shanrahan church can be seen on the south side of the road about six kilometres east of Ballyporeen. A distinctive Sheela-na-Gig is deeply carved in red sandstone and set into the west-facing wall of the old church tower, at about mid-height and directly over the main entrance. It is difficult to gain a clear view of the finer details but her eyes appear to be set with lighter stone, possibly quartz as is her right ear, and her left leg is turned outwards with the foot in-turned.

91. *Stepaside, County Dublin:* Situated on the public golf course which is on the east side of the road going south just outside of Stepaside, in the middle of an old laneway lined with trees about 100 metres to the east of the ruins of Jamestown House.

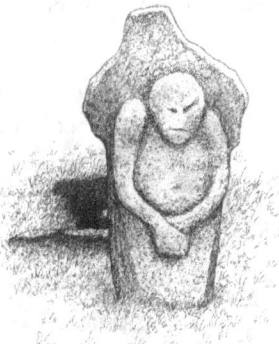
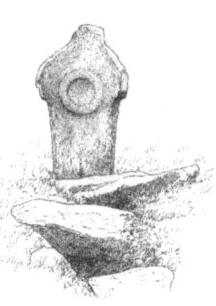

This Sheela-na-Gig looms out of an old well and is on an cross slab on the site of an early monastic settlement. The cross is a little over a metre tall and may be as early as the eighth century. The figure has been carved in relief on the cross, her head hanging down between powerful shoulders and her vulva represented, or covered by, a worn box-like object, though this is possibly her hands. On the reverse side is a circle and other symbolism too worn to decipher. The figure has been largely ignored by researchers, despite its closeness to Dublin, and is rarely commented upon. This is probably one of the earliest Sheelas and the only one that is in its original setting by a holy well.

92. *Summerhill, County Meath:* A figure that appears from the description to be a Sheela-na-Gig was recorded as being 'in a rock garden' at Summerhill House, the seat of the Earl of Longford. This house is now a ruin and 'no figure is to be found'.[46]

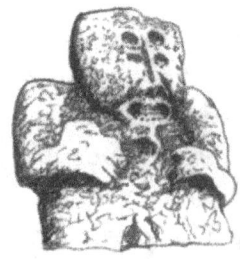

93. *Swords, County Dublin:* This Sheela-na-Gig is carved on a tall limestone pillar stone of uncertain age which was used as a gate post at Drynam House near Swords, County Dublin. The stone was moved to the National Museum for preservation and is thought to have possibly flanked the doorway of one of a number of ruined medieval buildings in the general vicinity. It is carved in high relief and one leg is raised as if the figure is doing a jig. The hands gesture towards the vulva, with the left hand resting on the thigh. (*Pillar:* 148 cm x 34 cm; *Figure:* 67 cm x 28 cm)

94. *Taghmon, County Westmeath:* Taghmon church is on the Mullingar–Castlepollard road about one and a half kilometres east of Crookedwood, and about ten and a half kilometres south of Castlepollard. This four-eyed Sheela-na-Gig is situated above a trefoil window in the north wall of the fifteenth-century fortified manorial church of St Munna. An arched stone roof and a four storey castellated tower have been added to the western end which, together with the battlements on the older section, make the building look more like a castle than a church. There is little indication of the vulva on this crouched figure but the posture of both hands directed towards the abdomen would place her in the same class as the Sheelas. There is something like a beard beneath her mouth, and apart from the holes in her head which look like an extra pair of eyes there is also a hole at the position of the navel. The concern for security would suggest that the figure acted as a protective icon and along with the stone head above the entrance door perhaps

emphasises a need for guardian spirits.

95. *Tara, County Meath:* Possibly one of the most significant Sheela-na-Gigs in Ireland is found on the east face of a standing stone in the churchyard at the ancient sacred site of Tara. The stone is one of pair of standing stones, the other one is a squat, rounded pillar, possibly the 'Blocc' and 'Bluigne' of mythology. Tara is the most important sacred ceremonial centre of Ireland, the place where the ancient kings ceremonially entered into sacral marriage with the goddess of the land. The existence of a Sheela-na-Gig here has far-reaching implications. The Sheela-na-Gig is rather worn, carved in relief with the left leg straight down and the other bent inwards. It is hard to make out the position of the 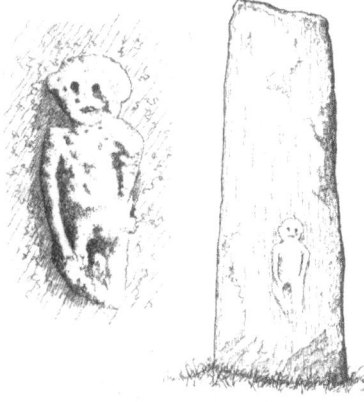 arms but a 'vaguely discernible gesture towards the abdomen' has been noted by previous researchers.[47] There has been a good deal of speculation about the Tara Sheela; some people have likened it to the figure of the god Cernunnos because she was believed to be wearing headgear or antlers, whereas others have disputed whether the figure is a Sheela-na-Gig or not. The age of the figure and the nature of the stone are perhaps the most contentious issues with dates varying from early Christian times to the later medieval period. The stone on which the figure is carved is known as St Adamnán's Pillar, a name which commemorates the saint who was St Columba's biographer and who championed the rights of the women of Ireland.

96. *Thurles, County Tipperary:* Surviving sections of the old town walls are now intermixed with later buildings and the Sheela can be found on a surviving section in a yard on the south side of Liberty Square near Black Castle. The figure is badly

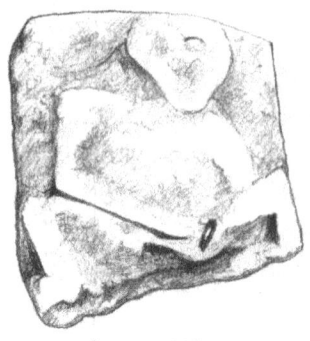

worn and her feet have broken away but her legs can be seen to be widely splayed and her right arm reaches down to a well-defined vulva. It is similar in appearance to the Sheela found at Cashel. The walled town was largely created by the Butlers, Earls of Ormond and though dates as early as the twelfth century have been suggested for the construction of the walls it is more probable that the section of wall which holds the Sheela is not older than the fourteenth century.

97. *Timahoe, County Laois:* Timahoe Castle is about thirteen kilometres south-east of Portlaoise and eight and a half kilometres south-west of Stradbally. It is possible that there were formerly two figures on Timahoe Castle, one of which was said to be 'a strange figure ... at the doorway'[48] and another on part of the north wall. The is no description of the figure, or figures, nor are there any illustrations. The castle has disinte-

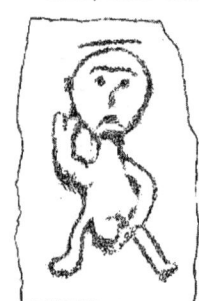

grated a good deal and the north wall has since collapsed but it is possible that the figure or figures may still exist within the fallen rubble.

98. *Tinakill, County Laois:* This Sheela-na-Gig, from a ruined castle, was discovered by the early pioneer of Sheela-na-Gig hunting, Helen M. Roe, in a lane in Mountmellick. It is not certain what happened to the carving, but a photograph taken by Ms Roe[49] shows details of a standing figure with a long neck, straight thin legs, the left hand indicating the genitals and the right hand raised to the head.

99. *Toomregan, County Cavan:* Sitting inside the doorway of Toomregan church, Ballyconnell, is a most peculiar figure with a large scowling face and sagging genitalia – horrific and hag-looking. It is often described as having serpents or animal

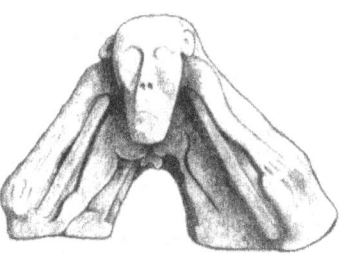

heads biting the fingers or having heads dangling from the hands but her right hand is shown as normal with fingers marked and her left hand appears to be holding some object. The figure was found in a ditch in 1961 half a mile outside the site of the monastery of Toomregan (Túaim Drecáin) founded by St Bricin in the seventh century, where traces of both a church and a round tower survive. It suggests that it may have been part of the outer face of a narrow, splayed, round-headed window, from a round tower rather than a church. Túam Drecáin was an old-established druidical school turned into an early Christian monastery and was famous for 'the trepanning of the skull'. (60 cm x 70 cm)

100. *Tracton Abbey, County Cork (Fitzgerald Park Museum, Cork):* In the Fitzgerald Museum in Cork City is a Sheela-na-Gig that, along with other carved stones, was found in a garden on the site of the ruined abbey. Tracton was a Cistercian establishment founded in 1224 and the Sheela and a few other stones are all that remain of

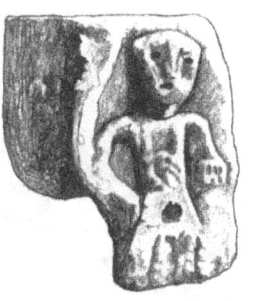

this ancient site. Guest thought that the stone on which the Sheela is carved originally formed part of the jamb of a window or door and is contemporary with its construction. The figure was included in Guest's list of 1935 and again by Andersen. The arms hang parallel to the torso but do not touch it. A band-like feature set partly across the flank of the figure is an unusual feature but there can be no doubt as to her

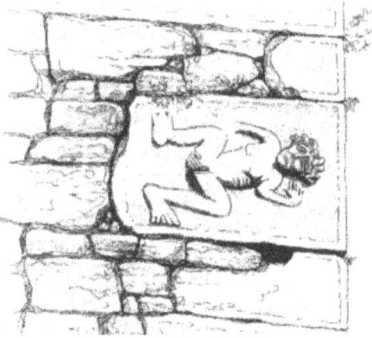

authenticity as a true Sheela.

101. *Tullavin, County Limerick:* Tullavin Castle is about five kilometres south of Croom. The Sheela-na-Gig is placed high up on the south face of the late fifteenth century peel tower. It is a well-preserved figure, carved in relief and depicted in a reclining position on a quoin stone. Her left hand points to her head upon which is a very unusual head-dress and her right hand reaches down below the thigh to touch the rim of her pudenda.

ENGLAND

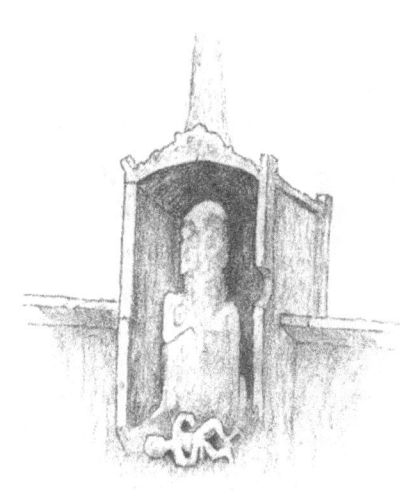

1. *Abson, Avon:* The village of Abson is about seven kilometres east of Bristol. High on the east wall of the tower of the church of St James the Great a Sheela-na-Gig can be seen. It is uniquely situated at the base of an unidentifiable effigy, set within a box. The Sheela, though weathered, can be clearly seen to have splayed spindly legs which are bent at the knees. This is the only Sheela in Britain so far recorded that is set on its side and the only one so far found in this context of being laid at the foot of another figure. Although the Sheela appears to be carved in a classic pose what is possibly a long protuberance is visible below the right arm extending from the lower abdomen which could perhaps delineate a different gender for the figure. This figure was brought to our attention by Keith and Gillian Jones.

There are many other carvings on this church, nearly all of

side the church and is erected on the south 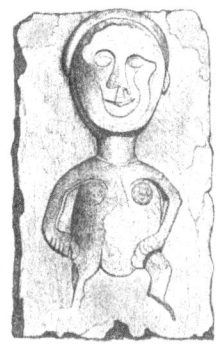 wall of the nave, about two metres from the ground. The lower half of this sandstone figure is damaged but her other features are well preserved. She has well marked breasts set high near the armpits, indication of ribs and an outline of the vulva can be see. Earlier visitors to the church saw the genitalia well-defined.[1] (40 cm high)

3. *Austerfield, Yorkshire:* Inside the twelfth-century nave of the Norman church of St Helen (c.1180) a Sheela-na-Gig can be found placed at one corner of a capital replacing the foliate design of the other capitals. She is seated and wearing a head-dress which reaches to the stiff leaf of the foliage decoration. Her right arm extends towards the genitalia and the other passes under her widely splayed, chubby thighs. (28 cm x 32 cm)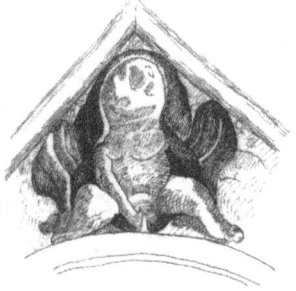

4. & 5. *Bilton (A) & (B), Yorkshire:* In Bilton in Ainsty, north Yorkshire, is a twelfth-century church, dedicated to St Helen (c.1160), with two Sheela-na-Gigs set beside one another, close to the east wall. They have been carved at the east end of a series of carvings that include mermaids, bearded masks and animal heads. Originally they were on outside corbels but after renovations were relocated inside the church. One of the Sheelas has been damaged, hacked at, presumably because her remaining right arm and leg indicate a striking spectacle. The second figure is very worn but wide shoulders and a sharply defined mouth can be seen. Andersen considered the figure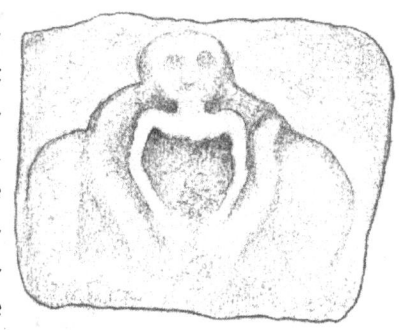

to have been deliberately damaged.[2] (Measurement of corbel: 20 cm x 25 cm)

6. *Binstead, Isle of Wight, Hampshire:* This Sheela-na-Gig can be found 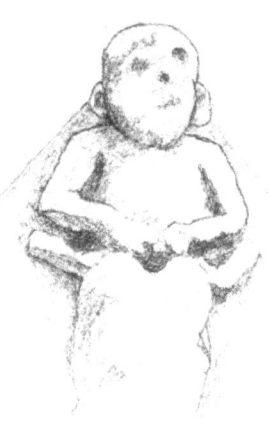 on the twelfth-century Holy Cross parish church on the Ryde–Fishbourne road close to Quarr Abbey. The figure is badly weathered but a squatting Sheela, with her hands pointing towards a deep hole-like vulva can still be detected. It is thought to have been originally on the old church at the site but it is now over a gate leading to the churchyard. In 1781 Richard Worsley wrote in *The History of the Isle of Wight* that when the church was being repaired around 1770 the figure was removed, 'but the inhabitants were displeased at it, and procured its restoration.'[3] (56 cm high)

7. *Bray, Berkshire:* The figure can be found inside St Michael's church on a ledge at the top of a pillar close to the west wall. Andersen says that it is '... a small figure, dressed but raising the lower hem of the garment so as to exhibit the genitalia'.[4] The vulva is shown to be sagging but above is something that is said to appear like a small penis or a clitoris, which leads Andersen to suggest that the figure is 'ithyphallic but reported as a Sheela'.[5]

8. *Bridlington, Yorkshire:* This figure is situated in the late twelfth- 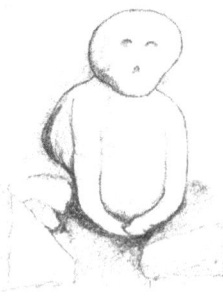 century cloister of the reconstructed priory church at Bridlington. The cloister (c.1175) is lined with decorated colonnettes and the Sheela-na-Gig can be found at the western end. She is depicted with thin arms joined towards the abdomen, a clearly defined pudendum and with one shoulder powerfully moulded and pushed forward.[6]

9. *Bristol, Avon:* Due to the height of the church of St Mary Redcliffe it is often impossible to gain a good view of the fasci-

nating oddities created by the master masons. However, it is possible to discern high up on a section of decorated stone eaves a Sheela-na-Gig wearing a curious head-dress. She has a large nose, sunken eyes and both hands gesture towards her vulva.

10. *Buckland, Buckinghamshire:* The Sheela-na-Gig is above the Priest's Door of the old parish church of All Saints just off the Aylesbury–Tring road. She has large shoulders coming over her head and her arms hang down. Lightly cut long fingers surround a sunken indentation, indicating the genitalia show evidence of constant rubbing.[7]

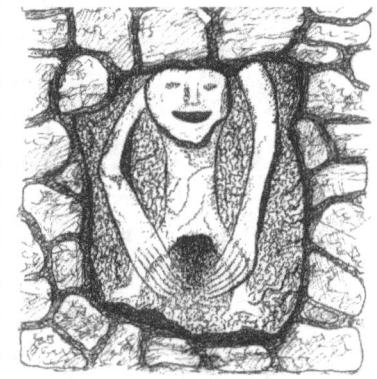

11. *Buncton/Wiston, Sussex:* This figure can be found inside the twelfth-century All Saints Chapel (1150–1180) at Buncton-with-Wiston, which is about midway between Steyning and Storrington on the north side of the A283.[8] A slim female with small breasts, pulling her vulva, is on the left side of the Romanesque chancel arch of the old church. The figure is unusual as she is the only British example discovered lying on her side. Weir conjectures that she has been deliberately rubbed before entering the building but the figure is so high that it could not have been casually rubbed, although there are definite scratches around the genital area.[9] A sign inside the church states that the figure depicts 'the mason'.[10]

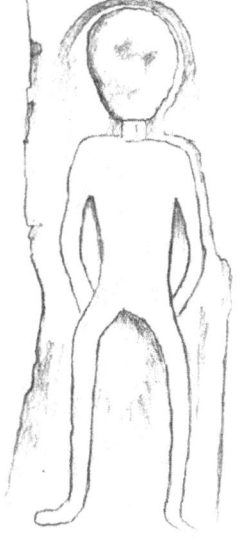

12. *Church Stretton, Shropshire:* Directly above the north door to the church dedicated to St Lawrence in Church Stretton is a Sheela carved in a niche-like depression. It is recorded that

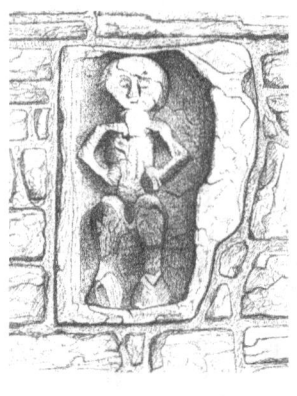

this doorway was reserved for bringing in the dead. She is quite similar in appearance to the figure from Oaksey in Wiltshire but is in a sitting position and has huge protruding knees and large feet. She also has very clearly outlined genitalia and it appears as if a lighter coloured stone has been inserted in this area. (60 cm high)

13. *Copgrove, Yorkshire:* In Copgrove church (dedicated to St Michael and All the Angels), West Riding, Yorkshire, is one of the more remarkable Sheela-na-Gigs remaining in England. The figure is now on the north-east corner of the late Victorian

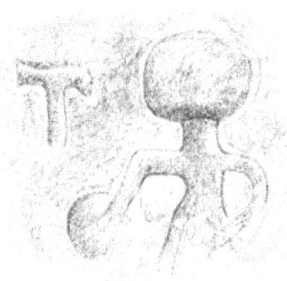

extension, having been removed from the north chancel of the old church in 1897. She was carved on a quoin stone and has a thin neck, a large and round head and no breasts. Her left arm reaches down to a large slit vulva and the one leg that is not worn is straight. In her right hand she holds a large round disk slightly away from her body and there is a capital 'T' above her right shoulder. Popular belief interprets her as a Celtic or pre-Christian figure. (Height of figure: 31 cm x 26 cm; Slab: 40 cm x 47 cm)

14. *Crofton-on-Tees, Durham:* This well-preserved Sheela-na-Gig

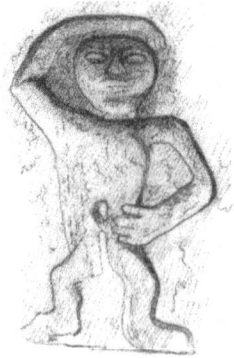

carved in relief on a slab is set into the wall immediately inside the south entrance to the church. She is depicted as standing and has broad, powerfully raised shoulders.[11] The right arm is raised above and across the head, while the left hand is clearly shown reaching towards the top of her vulva.

15. *Cross Canonby, Cumberland:* The carving from Cross Canonby is reported to have been found in the same region as the Pennington figure but seems to have disappeared without any record of its design.[12]

16. *Darley Dale, Derbyshire:* This figure can be found on a keystone on the Gothic style archway above the former entrance to the parish church in the village of Darley Dale. It is badly weathered but carved in a similar style to the 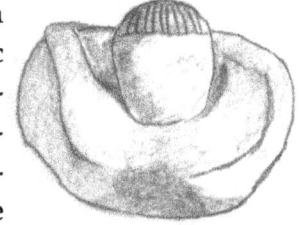 nearby Haddon Hall figure with its legs raised above its head and its heavy set arms reaching around its buttocks. What looks like a small cap can be seen on its head. (Information kindly supplied by J. Harding)

17. *& 18. Diddlebury, Hertfordshire.* Diddlebury is about ten kilometres south-east of Church Stretton. There are two figures on adjacent corbels on the outside of this church. *Figure (A)* is badly worn in 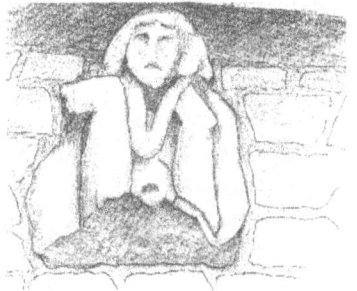 the lower section and her right leg is broken off below the knee. This leg appears to bend outward whilst it seems that she is holding her left leg over her shoulder and her left arm extends towards the vulva. *Figure (B)* is also badly worn in the lower portion and it is difficult to gain a clear idea of how her 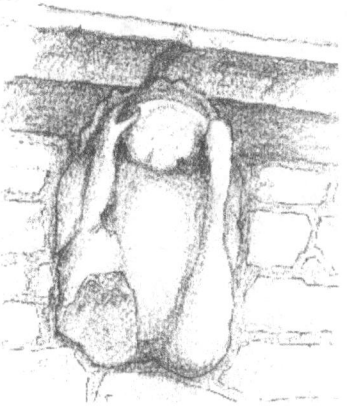 right leg is supposed to be positioned but it seems that her right hand touches the side of the face. These figures were brought to our attention by Keith and Gillian Jones.[13]

19. Easthorpe, Essex: This Sheela-na-Gig has been removed to the Col-

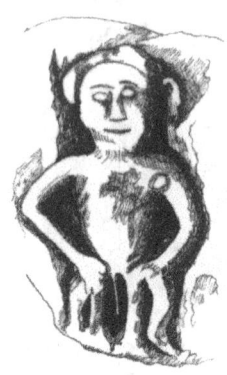

chester and Essex Museum from its original location above the south door of Easthorpe church.
It was known locally as the Clunch Stone and
is a remarkable figure with a very large, de-
tailed and deeply carved vulva. Carved letters
ELUI on her left may post-date the Sheela by
some centuries and according to Andersen
shows signs of erasure although he speculates
that the inscription might refer to the unlikely
St Eloi, patron saint of goldsmiths.

20. Egremont, Cumbria: This figure was discovered during the de-
molition of Egremont church in 1880 and was subsequently
noted in 1902 by Dr C. W. Parker, who recorded that it 'was said
to have been used in the earliest part of the church'. Apparently, 'the original structure of the building embodied two
medieval phases, the one Norman and the other early English',[14] which would fit in with well with the general dating of
the figures in England. Although the stone itself has since disappeared, a photograph of the Egremont Sheela-na-Gig sur-
vives depicting a figure with broad shoulders, small breasts
under the armpits and a well-marked navel carved in shallow
relief on a square stone, possibly a quoin stone.[15] The posture

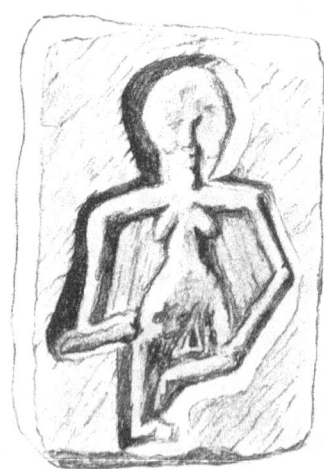

is most unusual as the left leg is bent at
the knee with the foot raised and the
standing right foot is turned inwards.
The left hand leans towards the genitals but in her right hand she holds a
cylindrical instrument which has been
considered to be a pair of shears. It is
suggested that the shears were used to
remove her pubic hair, in order to expose her pudenda, so that bad luck
could be warded off more effectively.[16]
(30.5cm x 17.5 cm x 50 cm)

21. *Fiddington, Somerset:* The Sheela-na-Gig can be found on a quoin stone of the south-east wall of the eleventh- or twelfth-century church of St Martin. It is portrayed in a near-seated position with widely splayed knees. 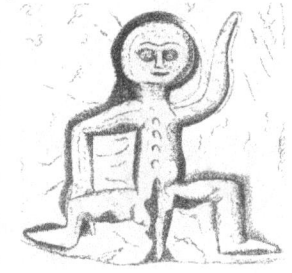 The left arm is raised parallel to the side of the head and the right arm is resting on the knee. Worn traces of three or possibly four round circles extend from her lower stomach up to her chest. While the head, arms and feet are finely executed and clearly demarcated, the body, hands, legs and genitalia are very poorly represented. A closer examination of this figure has shown that the lower half of the figure may have been damaged sometime after the carving was placed *in situ* probably in an attempt to disguise its erotic nature. Although the figure was known locally, early drawings of the church fail to depict the Sheela-na-Gig which is contemporary with the rest of the south wall of the nave.

22. *Haddon Hall, Derbyshire:* This figure was placed above the doorway to the stables on an Elizabethan estate, built around 1600, but it has been moved to the inside of the stable to prevent further weathering. It is said to have been found in a field nearby and is a 'somewhat comic figure' with her legs raised above the head and the hands reaching from below to pull open the well-marked vulva which is shown as a square-shaped hollow.[17]

23. *Hellifield, Yorkshire:* Hellifield is near Grassington in north Yorkshire. This curious figure made of coarse gritstone was found in 1967 as an ornament in a garden and is still in private ownership.[18] It is a small, standing figure, flatly carved in a niche-like depression with a disproportionately large head and arms joined pointing to-

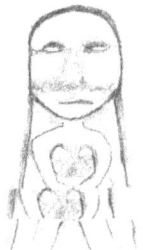

wards the lower abdomen. (51 cm high)

24. *Holgate, Shropshire:* This Sheela-na-Gig is carved almost in the 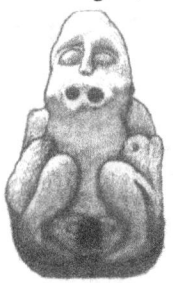 round and protrudes from the south wall of the thirteenth-century church of the Holy Trinity. The hands pass underneath the bent knees and the fingers of both hands hold open the outer labia to reveal the genitalia in a clearly visible manner. An unusual feature are two round deep holes in the place of the mouth. (30 cm high)

25. *Kilpeck, Herefordshire:* The Sheela-na-Gig on the Church of St Mary and St David at Kilpeck is the best known example in Britain. The church is noted for its carvings which are a masterpiece of the local school of Norman carvers and the south doorway is one of the most elaborately carved in Britain.[19] The 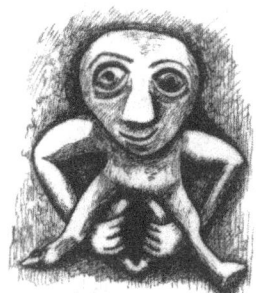 Sheela-na-Gig is in its original setting on the corbel table which decorates the outside walls of the church and can be dated to c.1140. The hands pass behind the legs and pull open the large vulva. The facial features are stylised with the eyes set within a deeply inscribed rim and a small hole clearly marks the pupils. This well-executed figurine was disrespectfully known as the whore of Kilpeck while in 1842 it was described as a fool.[20] There are many other carvings but sadly some of the originals were removed in the last century by a vicar who considered them too obscene for his congregation.

26. *Oaksey, Wiltshire:* Oaksey is about eleven kilometres southwest of Cirencester and the Sheela-na-Gig can be found on the outside of the thirteenth-century church. It is set about three metres from the ground into the north wall, close by a large window. It would be hard to miss her as she is a most stunning figure with dangling breasts, a well marked clitoris and with very large genitalia. Her large hands pass underneath her thighs, the clearly marked fingers grab the rim of her

pudenda. She is carved in the same stone as the church itself and is probably contemporary with the church. (36 cm high)

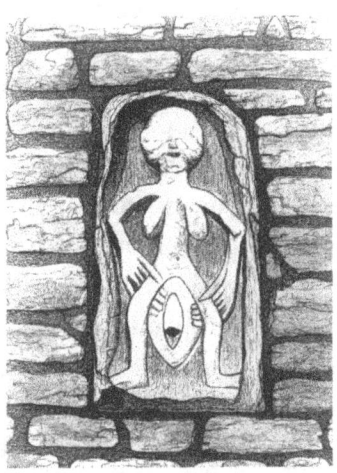

27. *Oxford:* The Sheela-na-Gig was originally set high up on the west wall by a belfry window of the eleventh century tower of St Michael's church but was removed in 1928 to the vestry to save it from weathering. She can now be found on the first floor of the church which forms part of a small museum. The figure is set in a square, niche-like frame with both legs stretching straight out to the edge of it. One hand reaches from behind the thighs and the other from in front, gesturing towards the genitals. It was the custom for brides to look upon the Sheela-na-Gig as they entered the church. (30 cm x 30 cm)

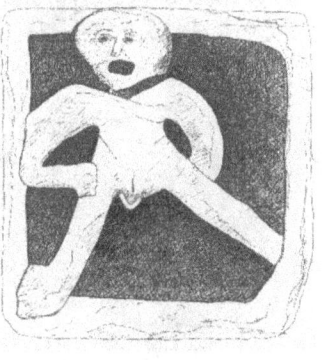

28. *Pennington, Cumbria:* Pennington church is about ten kilometres north-east of Barrow-in-Furness but the Sheela-na-Gig is now to be found in the museum at Kendall. The figure is depicted with strikingly pointed ears, small but clearly marked breasts, bared teeth and with both hands pointing towards the vulva. It is thought that it was originally facing outwards on a quoin stone high up on the south-east corner when the church was built in 1160 and turned inwards during rebuilding of the church in 1826. A 1929 report by John Satchell relates that the workmen who

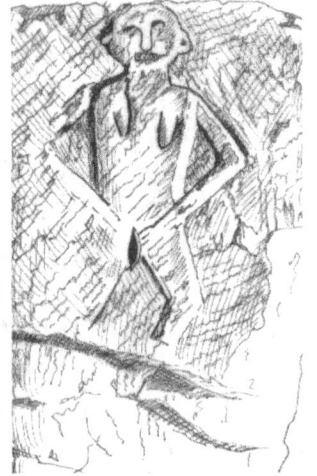

discovered the stone while repairing a corner of the old church were going to destroy it as they feared that 'the parson should not see this'.[21] Fortunately their foreman saved the figure, placed it in a box and hid it in the boiler room where it lay forgotten until a later vicar discovered it and put it on display on the porch. The Sheela was not the only unusual discovery from this church for inscribed in runes on the original tympanum was 'Gamel built this church, 1160', which demonstrates that a script of Viking origin was still in use locally in the twelfth century. Due to this Nordic influence in the area the Sheela is identified by the local people as the fertility goddess Freya, the Viking earth mother.

29. Romsey, Hampshire: This Sheela-na-Gig can be found on the old abbey at Romsey on the west wall of the north transept above

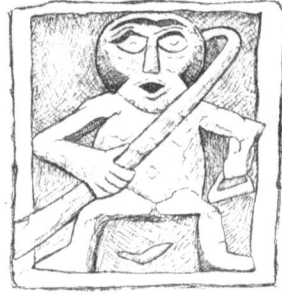

a Romanesque window. The left arm of the figure is holding a small unidentifiable object and the right arm is grasping a crook or staff indicating a form of a crozier, perhaps the staff of an abbess. The abbey, which is of Norman date, was originally a Benedictine nunnery and 'was one of the most important religious houses of the Middle Ages in the South of England.'[22] However, due to its insufficient size the Nun's Church was extended when it was later taken over for use by the parishioners and the wall with the Sheela formed part of these extensions. Interestingly, according to a local historian Professor Zarnecke, the Sheela is 'in a place where it had no chance of being seen'.[23]

30. Royston, Hertfordshire: A female figure forms part of a large composition of carvings in an extraordinary rock-cut chamber. She is set between a horse and a big sword and part of a large area of pockmarked carvings which cover one wall of the mysterious Royston Cave, a chamber six metres in diameter, sunk into the chalk beneath the village. The cave is very old, possibly a neolithic flint mine and the carvings have perplexed historians since they were discovered in 1742. They look most ancient but are presumed to be of a late medieval date, approximately fifteenth century. The genitals of the Sheela figure are clearly marked but her arms are hanging loose beside her body reminiscent of cave drawings from palaeolithic Europe.[24]

31. *St Ives, Huntingdonshire:* In 1956 some discoveries were made in the river meadows near the site of St Ives Priory including this Sheela-na-Gig. The priory, built between the tenth and eleventh centuries, was subsequently burned down in 1207 and traces of burning have also been found on the figure. It is much worn and is carved in high relief on a block of Barnack stone but cannot be mistaken for anything other than a Sheela-na-Gig. According to a description by Andersen: 'The eyes are two small holes, the nose is slightly V-shaped, and the mouth is strongly worked at the corners.'[25] The genitals are described as having been carefully worked and the breasts are indicated by flat disks.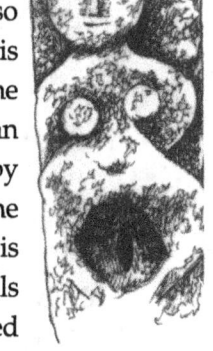

32. *South Taunton, Devon:* The only known example of a Sheela-na-Gig carved in wood can be found among the carvings of the medieval roof bosses on the fifteenth-century church at Okehampton. With her head bent backwards, she is shown emerging from a background of floral designs which may indicate fertility. The thighs are widely splayed and both hands are resting on her vulva. The impressive roof of wood dates from the 1400s and the Sheela-na-Gig appears to be in its original but not very prominent location.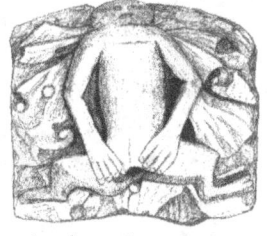

33. *Studland, Dorset:* A unique female figure can be found on a corbel of the old church at Studland, a village on the coast about 3km north of Swanage. The vulva is very rounded and over-enlarged and she is holding it with an over-sized left hand. In

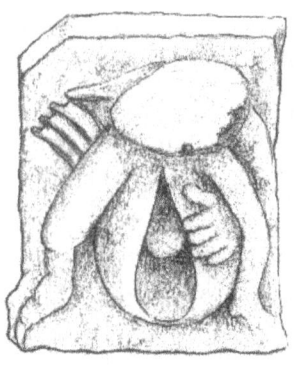

this figure only the left arm is depicted whilst on the right there is a well defined but quite incomprehensible fan-like shape towards which her head is inclined. Within the enormous opening of her vulva a rounded clitoris is well defined and her right leg is rounded with a pointed end where the toe should be, in contrast to the other more conventional leg. This figure appears to embody aspects of the toad or frog as well as the egg.

34. *Torksey, Lincolnshire:* A very worn Sheela-na-Gig can be found inside the church of St Peter 'fitted into a pointed arch-like frame' on the south wall. The thin-legged Sheela-na-Gig is probably gesturing towards her pudenda but because of the weathering it is impossible to say whether the figure originally had breasts or not. It has been noted that it is not in its original location and Margaret Murray suggested that it may be a late type of Sheela that was removed from another church.[26]

35. & 36. *Tugford (A) & (B), Shropshire:* There are two Sheela-na-Gigs carved in high relief immediately inside the doorway of St Catherine's church. They must be amongst the smallest examples of Sheela-na-gigs in England, being a mere sixteen centimetres in height. It is reminiscent of the famous Kilpeck Sheela with the haunched shoulders and the hands passed below the slightly pulled-up legs. The other, on the opposite side of the door has her hand to her mouth in a comical pose almost as if she is pondering her friend across the other side of the entrance. The support of the rear arch of the south door on which they are situated is thought to be of the late twelfth century.

37. *Wells, Somerset:* St Andrew's cathedral at Wells is famous for its highly decorative west front, completed in 1230.[27] One of the figures is shown grasping her legs and exposing the vulva whilst the second figure has her arms and legs bent back and seems to be exposing her whole body.

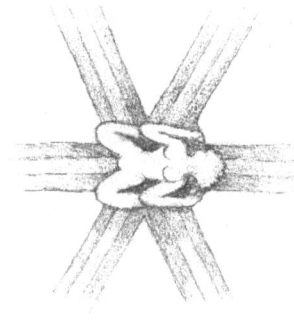

38. *Whittlesford, Cambridgeshire:* On the twelfth-century church of St Mary and St Michael is to be found a unique British carving. It is 'on an irregular block forming the arch of a Norman window' on the south side of the tower and consists of a well-defined Sheela-na-Gig shown in classic squatting pose with an ithyphallic man/beast straddling the window towards her.[28] The Sheela figure is depicted with her right-hand fingers clearly clutching the open vulva and the male creature has been likened to the Saxon god Baal. Although this is the only instance of a Sheela in male company there is a similarity with a crouching phallic male found at Abson Church in Gloucestershire.

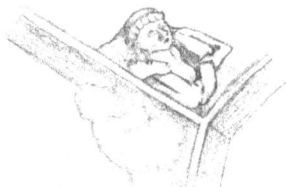

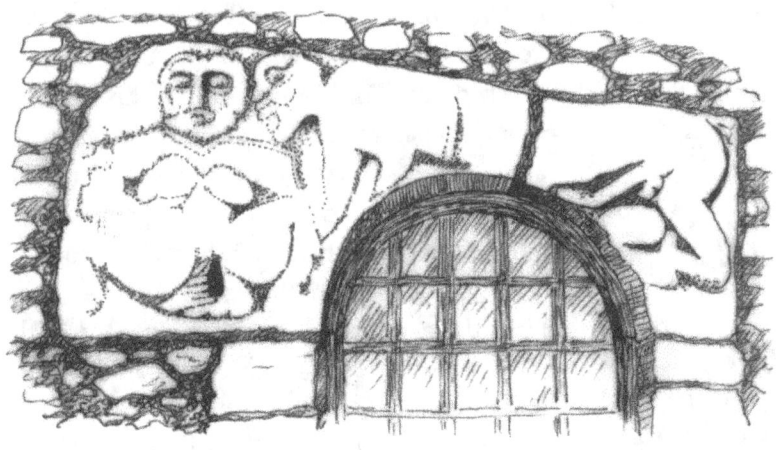

39. Llandrindod Wells, Powys (Radnorshire): This is one of the best examples of a Sheela-na-Gig in Britain and is said to have been found 'on October 24, 1894, concealed and built into the north wall of the church, face downwards, in pulling it down for rebuilding'.[29] The figure has incised ribs, large ears and breasts set almost under the armpits. The tool markings are very clear on the figure and show that it may have been

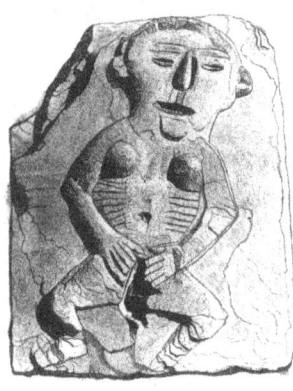

buried at some early date. Incised marks worked over the top of the forehead may indicate a hair or perhaps tattooing. A cross crosslet has been carved on one side of the thick stone slab, obviously at the time of burial. The church where it was found is dated 1746 but there are traces of an earlier church nearby called Llanfaelog, named after the sixth-century St Maelog. (75 cm x 45 cm)

40. Penmon, Anglesey: Now preserved within the twelfth-century church of St Seiriol at Penmon Priory is a Sheela-na-Gig, which was originally located on the west wall of the south transept of the old church. The figure is weather-worn but is sculpted

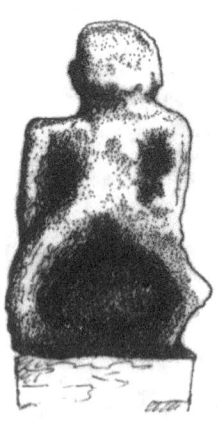

in high relief and stands out from the stone in a pose very similar to the figure at Iona. The right hand passes over the right leg and the left hand passes under her left thigh. It is not possible to distinguish the facial features apart from the ears. A second figure situated in the dark interior of the church may also be a Sheela-na-Gig but very little is known of it. Anglesey is *Mona mam Cymru*, the 'Mother of Wales', and the island has an ancient affinity with Ireland stretching back to the earliest neolithic period. (45 cm x 30 cm)

SCOTLAND

41. *Iona, Mull, Strathclyde:* This very significant figure is thought to be in her original position being seated on a lintel above a window of the Nun's Refectory on the ancient island sanctu-

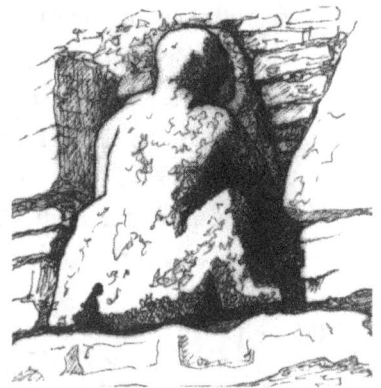

ary of Iona. Described by Andersen as 'a badly weathered, nearly blurred carving of a female shown in a displayed state, with small legs and sagging pudenda.'[30] It appears that her arms reach down towards her abdomen or genitals and a fifteenth-century date has been suggested. Iona is very strongly connected with Ireland, ever since St Columba established what is known as the first Irish monastery there in 563.

42. *Kilvickeon, Mull:* A badly weathered figure thought to be a Sheela-na-Gig is situated by the door of the medieval parish church of Kilvickeon. It can be found close to the road going to Assapol and Scoor. This is the only medieval parish church on Mull with any ancient remains and it was closely connected to the nearby island of Iona.

43. *Kirkwall, Orkney:* A good example of a Sheela-na-Gig can be

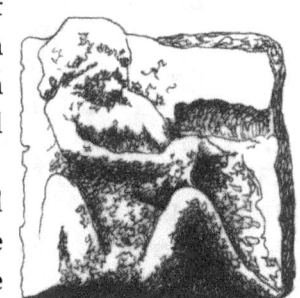

found on a capital in the nave of Kirkwall cathedral. She is unique in that one hand holds her vulva open from above and the other is held across her left eye.

44. *Rodil, Isle of Harris:* A badly weathered Sheela-na-Gig can be found on the tower of St Clement's church on the

most southern island of the Outer Hebrides. The figure is depicted with widely splayed legs but is also holding something that has been best described as an animal in her arms. According to Andersen, in the upper right hand corner of the panel a curious rectangular object with a spout can be discerned.[31]

45. *Taynuilt, Strathclyde (Argyllshire):* On the south wall of Muckairn parish church built in 1829, about sixteen kilometres east of Oban, is a badly weathered Sheela-na-Gig. From what can be discerned she is a plump and undemonstrative goddess figure. At the eastern end of the same wall is the head of an ecclesiastic, also carved in sandstone. The Sheela is thought to have originated from the nearby thirteenth-century church of Killespickerill, dedicated to the (Norman) Bishop Harold. (35 cm x 18 cm)

IRELAND

1. ABBEYLARA, Co. Longford – Church/*In situ*
2. AGHADOE CASTLE, Killeagh, Co. Cork – Castle/Re-erected on dovecote
3. AGHALURCHER, Co. Fermanagh – Church/Storage – Archeological Survey
4. ARDCATH, Co. Meath – Origin Unknown/(Private)
5. ATHLONE, Co. Westmeath – Church/Castle Museum, Athlone
6. BALLAGHAMORE CASTLE, Co. Laois – Castle/*In situ*
7. BALLINACARRIGA CASTLE, Co. Cork – Castle/*In situ*
8. BALLINDERRY CASTLE, Co. Galway – Castle/*In situ*
9. BALLYFINBOY CASTLE, Co. Tipperary – Castle/*In situ*
10. BALLYLARKIN CHURCH, Co. Kilkenny – Church/ National Museum Dublin
11. BALLINACLOGH CASTLE, Co. Tipperary – Castle/*In situ*
12. BALLYNAHINCH CASTLE, Co. Tipperary – Castle/*In situ*
13. BALLYNAMONA CASTLE, Co. Cork – Castle/Missing
14. BALLYPORTRY CASTLE, Co. Clare – Castle/National Museum Dublin
15. BALLYVOURNEY, Co. Cork – Church/*In situ*

16. BARNAHEALY CASTLE, Co. Cork – Castle/Missing
17. BEHY CASTLE, Co. Sligo – Castle/Re-erected on outhouse
18. BIRR, Co. Offaly – Original Location Unknown/National Museum Dublin
19. BLACKHALL CASTLE, Co. Kildare – Castle/*In situ*
20. BOYLE ABBEY, Co. Roscommon – Church/*In situ*
21. BUNRATTY CASTLE, Co. Clare – Castle/Re-erected in Main Hall
22. BURGESBEG [a], Co. Tipperary – Church/National Museum, Dublin
23. BURGESBEG [b], Co. Tipperary – Church/In Storage, Clonmacnoise
24. CAHERELLY CASTLE, Co. Limerick – Castle/Hunt Museum, Limerick
25. CARNE CASTLE, Co. Westmeath – Castle/National Museum Dublin
26. CARRICK CASTLE, Co. Kildare – Castle/Missing
27. CASHEL, Co. Tipperary – Church/*In situ*
28. CASTLEMAGNER, Co. Tipperary – Holy Well/*In situ*
29. CASTLE WIDENHAM, Co. Cork – Holy Well/Private
30. CAVAN, Co. Cavan – Church/National Museum
31. CLENAGH CASTLE, Co. Clare – Castle/*In situ*
32. CLOGHAN CASTLE ,.Co. Offaly – Castle/Missing
33. CLOGHAN CASTLE, Co. Roscommon – Castle/*In situ*
34. CLOMANTAGH, Co. Kilkenny – Castle/*In situ*
35. CLONBULLOGE, Co. Offaly – Original Location Unknown/ In Private Possession
36. CLONLARA, Co. Clare – Castle/Re-erected on Canal Bridge
37. CLONMACNOISE, Co. Offaly – Church/*In situ*
38. CLONMEL, Co. Tipperary – Church/National Museum, Dublin
39. CLONOULTY, Co. Tipperary – Church/GPA Bolton Library, Cashel.
40. COOLIAGH MORE, Co. Kilkenny – Church
41. CORVEEN CASTLE, Co. Donegal – Castle/Missing
42. CULLAHILL CASTLE, Co. Laois – Castle/*In situ*
43. DOON CASTLE, Co. Offaly – Castle/*In situ*
44. DOWTH, Co. Meath – Church/*In situ*
45. DROGHEDA, Co. Louth – Town Wall/Millmount Museum

Drogheda
46. DUNAMAN, Co. Limerick – Castle/*In situ*
47. & 48. ERRIGAL KEEROGE, Co. Tyrone – Church/Ulster Museum, Belfast
49. FETHARD ABBEY, Co. Tipperary – Church/*In situ*
50. FETHARD WALL, Co. Tipperary – Town Wall/*In situ*
51. GARRY CASTLE, Co. Offaly – Castle/*In situ*
52. GLANWORTH CASTLE, Co. Cork – Castle/In Storage
53. HOLYCROSS ABBEY, Co. Tipperary – Church/*In situ*
54. KELLS, Co. Meath – Church/Missing
55. KILDARE CATHEDRAL, Co. Kildare – Church/*In situ*
56. KILLALOE, Co. Clare – Church/Private
57. KILNABOY CHURCH, Co. Clare – Church/*In situ*
58. KILLUA, Co. Westmeath – Original Location Unknown/British Museum
59. KILMACOMMA, Co. Waterford – Original Location Unknown/Missing
60. KILMAINAHAM Co. Meath – Church/Missing
61. KILSARKAN, Co. Kerry – Church/*In situ*
62. KILTINAN CASTLE, Co. Tipperary – Castle/On Well House – Private
63. KILTINAN CHURCH, Co. Tipperary – Church/Missing
64. KNOCKARLEY, Co. Offaly – Original Location Unknown/Private
65. LAVEY, Co. Cavan – Church/National Museum
66. LEMANAGHAN CASTLE, Co. Offaly – Castle/Missing
67. LIATHMOR, Co. Tipperary – Church/*In situ*
68. LIXNAW, Co. Kerry – Castle/National Museum Dublin
69. LUSK, Co. Dublin – Church/Missing
70. LUSTYMORE, Co. Fermanagh – Church/Re-erected in Caldragh Graveyard
71. MAGHERA, Co. Derry – Church/*In situ*
72. MALAHIDE [a] and [b], Co. Dublin – Church/*In situ*
73. MOATE CASTLE, Co. Westmeath – Castle/*In situ*
74. MOYCARKEY CASTLE, Co. Tipperary – Castle/Missing
75. MOYGARA, Co. Sligo – Castle/Missing
76. NEWTOWN LENNAN, Co. Tipperary – Church/National Museum, Dublin
77. PORTNAHINCH, Co. Laois – Castle/Missing

78. RAHAN, Co. Offaly – Church / Castle Museum, Athlone
79. RAHARA, Co. Roscommon – Church / Roscommon County Museum
80. RATH (Rath Blathmac), Co. Clare – Church/*In situ*
81. RATOO, Co. Kerry – Round Tower/*In situ*
82. REDWOOD CASTLE, Co. Tipperary – Castle/*In situ*
83. RINGASKIDDY, Co. Cork – Original Location Unknown / Cork City Museum
84. ROCHESTOWN, Co. Tipperary – Church / Missing
85. ROSENALLIS, Co. Laois – Church / Nat. Museum, Dublin
86. ROSNAREE, Co, Meath – Mill/*In situ*
87. & 88. SCREGG CASTLE, [a] & [b], Co. Roscommon – Castle / On Carriage House
89. SEIR KIERAN, Co. Offaly – Church / Nat. Museum Dublin
90. SHANRAHAN, Co. Tipperary – Church/*In situ*
91. STEPASIDE, Co. Dublin – Holy Well/*In situ*
92. SUMMERHILL, Co. Meath – Original Location Unknown / Missing
93. SWORDS, Co. Dublin – Original Location Unknown / Nat. Museum Dublin
94. TAGHMON, Co. Westmeath – Church/*In situ*
95. TARA, Co. Meath – Pillar Stone/*In situ*
96. THURLES, Co. Tipperary – Town Wall / In situ
97. TIMAHOE, Co. Laois – Castle / Missing
98. TINAKILL, Co. Laois – Castle / Missing
99. TOOMREGAN, Co. Cavan – Round Tower/*In situ*
100. TRACTON ABBEY, Co. Cork – Church / Cork City Museum
101. TULLAVIN, Co. Limerick – Castle/*In situ*

ENGLAND
1. ABSON, Avon – Church/*In situ*
2. AMPNEY SAINT PETER, Gloucestershire – Church/*In situ*
3. AUSTERFIELD, Yorkshire – Church/*In situ*
4. BILTON [a], Yorkshire – Church/*In situ*
5. BILTON [b], Yorkshire – Church/*In situ*
6. BINSTEAD, Isle of Wight, Hampshire – Church/*In situ*
7. BRAY, Berkshire – Church/*In situ*
8. BRIDLINGTON, Yorkshire – Church/*In situ*
9. BRISTOL, Avon – Church/*In situ*

10. BUCKLAND, Buckinghamshire – Church/*In situ*
11. BUNCTON/WISTON, Sussex – Church/*In situ*
12. CHURCH STRETTON, Shropshire – Church/*In situ*
13. COPGROVE, Yorkshire – Church/*In situ*
14. CROFTON-ON-TEES, Durham – Church/*In situ*
15. CROSS CANONBY, Cumberland – Church/Missing
16. DARLEY DALE, Derbyshire – Church/*In situ*
17. & 18. DIDDLEBURY, Hertfordshire – Church/*In situ*
19. EASTHORPE, Essex – Church/Colchester & Essex Museum
20. EGREMONT, Cumbria – Church/Missing
21. FIDDINGTON, Somerset – Church/*In situ*
22. HADDON HALL, Derbyshire – Stable/*In situ*
23. HELLIFIELD, Yorkshire – Original Location Unknown/*In situ*
24. HOLGATE, Shropshire – Church/*In situ*
25. KILPECK, Herefordshire – Church/*In situ*
26. OAKSEY, Wiltshire – Church/*In situ*
27. OXFORD, Oxford – Church/*In situ*
28. PENNINGTON, Cumbria – Church/Kendall Museum
29. ROMSEY, Hampshire – Church/*In situ*
30. ROYSTON, Hertfordshire – Cave/*In situ*
31. ST IVES, Huntingdonshire – Church/Private
32. SOUTH TAUNTON, Devon – Church/*In situ*
33. STUDLAND, Dorset – Church/*In situ*
34. TORKSEY, Lincolnshire – Church/*In situ*
35. TUGFORD [A], Shropshire – Church/*In situ*
36. TUGFORD [B], Shropshire – Church/*In situ*
37. WELLS, Somerset – Church/*In situ*
38. WHITTLESFORD, Cambridgeshire – Church/*In situ*

WALES
39. LLANDRINDOD WELLS, Powys (Radnorshire) – Church/ Radnorshire Museum, Llandrindod Wells
40. PENMON, Anglesey – Church/*In situ*

SCOTLAND
41. IONA, Mull, Strathclyde – Church/*In situ*
42. KILVICKEON, Mull – Church/*In situ*
43. KIRKWALL, Orkney – Church/*In situ*

44.   RODIL, Isle of Harris – Church/*In situ*
45.   TAYNUILT, Strathclyde (Argyllshire) – Church/*In situ*

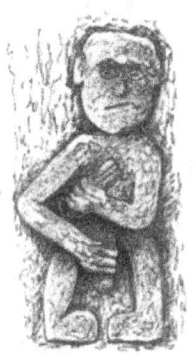

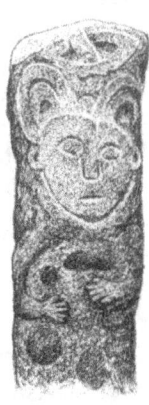

Related Figures

List of figures that were originally classed as Sheela-na-Gigs but which are no longer regarded as falling within this category, although many may still be related to a similar tradition.

Ireland

Armagh: A female figure, once listed as a Sheela-na-Gig, was found in the chapter house of Armagh cathedral. It was said to have been 'dug up many years ago when digging a grave in the cathedral yard'.[1] Andersen did not consider the figure as a Sheela, for she is depicted with a skirt, round breasts, a bow lifted behind her head and a close fitting cap.

Ballycloughduff, County Westmeath: Located 4.5 km east-north-east of Carne Castle, on the gatepost of a former mill a rare example of a male Sheela-na-Gig, or Seán-na-Gig can be found. The right arm is holding an over-large downward pointing penis and the left arm reaches across his chest to rest underneath the armpit. A diamond or chevron is distinctly carved on the middle of the chest and unusually the figure has inward pointing feet.[2]

Carndonagh, County Donegal: When H. C. Lawlor visited the site of this carving nearly seventy years ago the eighth- or ninth-century Carndonagh Cross and its two accompanying stones were buried into the bank opposite Carndonagh church. Since then the cross with its two guardian stones have been removed to a safer place beside the church and the four sides are now visible. A figure carved in low relief on one of these stones is very difficult to interpret due to erosion, but its main features – large head, hands and an indentation where the genitals would be – suggested to Lawlor that it was a Sheela-na-Gig. Although a very interesting carving, it seems doubtful that it is a Sheela and was excluded from Andersen's list.

Cashel, County Tipperary: In the cathedral at Cashel there is a very curious stone which Guest included in her 1936 list but which cannot be truly said to be a Sheela-na-Gig – cat goddess would be a better name.[3] She is carved as a caryatid, intended for a supporting function on a building and is armless with twisted legs, a fat belly.

Clonmacnoise, County Offaly: On the south side of the tenth century north cross at Clonmacnoise is a figure with entwining legs that has been described as Cernunnos-like.[4] Although it is probably from a closely related tradition, the figure is no longer regarded as a Sheela. A similar figure has also been noted on Muirdach's Cross at Monasterboice but was discounted by Guest.[5]

Grey Abbey, County Down: What is dubiously described as a Seánna-Gig or a male Sheela-na-Gig lacking a penis can be found on a Romanesque corbel table.

Kilcarne, County Meath: A supposed Sheela-na-Gig carved on the old font in the church of Kilcarne near Johnstown was recorded by Wakeman in 1879, but does not fall within this category. A photograph published by Andersen shows an erotic theme consisting of 'a remarkable encounter between two or three people'.[6]

Kinsale, County Cork: A figure which is is believed to be a child, rather than a Sheela, can be found on a detached tombstone which is standing against the interior wall of the church of St Multose. Also on the slab are funerary inscriptions dating the stone to the 1700s. Although this may not be classed amongst the Sheela-na-Gigs it is a curious and very unusual carving which owes much to the same tradition.

White Island, County Fermanagh: On White Island there are a number of strange stone figures which probably originate from the early Christian sanctuaries which existed on several of the islands of Lough Erne. One of the figures was formerly listed amongst the Sheelas since its hands are crossed over the abdomen. It is approximately two feet long and is nude apart from a short cloak-like mantle, which was supposed to be 'a rheno, or secular dress'.[7] The legs are crossed but due to a lack of a vulva, it does not fall into the category of Sheela-na-Gigs. However, this tenth-century figure may have acted as an early prototype for it was re-employed horizontally in the same manner as the Sheelas – a supporting stone for the doorway of the twelfth-century church. The large head is typical of many other Sheelas but the broad grinning mouth with its upturned corners is a unique feature. A workman employed to clean up the church site took such a dislike to it he knocked the corner off one side of it.

ENGLAND

Devizes, Somerset: In the museum at Devizes is an unusual figure which derives from the 'rather crazy and disreputable' collection of Joshua Brooke who procured the item around 1905.[8] This well-executed and very naturalistic figure is standing with knees bent and hands resting on the front of the thighs which are widely splayed to reveal the pubic triangle and vulva. A gash running down the stomach area is interpreted as 'an attempt to delineate a phallus' and an analysis by Diane Robinson for the museum revealed traces of a dark, red paint which apparently covered the upper surface of the piece.[9] The carving is only abut 11.5 cm in diameter and is made of rock chalk which being a soft material initially threw doubt on whether it was an authentic Sheela. Although regarded quite conclusively as a fake it still seems odd that somebody would desire to simulate such an artefact, unless Sheela-na-Gigs were commonly known and sold on the black market at that time. Possibly it could also be interpreted as a later cult or ritual object which has its basis in the Sheela tradition.

WALES

Margam: A male figure or a Seán-na-Gig worshipping his large, erect phallus can be found in the Margam Stones museum in West Glamorgan. The figure is carved on a corbel stone and although the exact origin of this carving is not known, it is probably local, and possibly from the ruined abbey.

ADDENDUM TO BRITISH LIST

Weir and Jerman believes the following figures may possibly be Sheelas, but they await further confirmation.

Bugthorpe, East Yorkshire: According to Weir and Jerman, this very 'typical' Sheela with her Herculean shoulders is situated on the south respond of the Norman chancel arch at St Andrews, Bugthorpe, just east of York. Apparently it had passed unnoticed because 'at some time in the past the "offending" parts have been filled in with plaster and then the whole church interior has been covered in thick whitewash.'[10]

Elkstone, Gloucestershire: On a corbel table is a figure which must have been a Sheela. Her lower abdomen is cut away but features are strongly reminiscent of Kilpeck.

Ely Cathedral: Sheela on a corbel but out of sight above an aisle.[11]

SHEELA-NA-GIG ON THE INTERNET

In recent years there has been an increasing interest in the Sheela-na-Gigs on the World Wide Web and several sites have been placed on the Internet which either give information or act as forums for discussion on the subject.

One site that is recommended is that of John Harding in England who is carrying out on-going field research and publishing his findings on the web site. < *www.jharding.demon.co.uk/*>

FOREWORD

1: Patrick Holland in the Foreword to *Sheela na Gig*, James O'Connor, Fethard Historical Society, 1991.

2: *Irish Times*, 9 July 1990. 'Please Can I See the Sheela-na-Gigs', Katie O'Donovan.

1: INTRODUCTION

1: Helicon History of Ireland, *The Catholic Community in the seventeenth and eighteenth centuries*, 1981, as quoted in A. Weir & J. Jerman, *Images of Lust – Sexual Carvings on Medieval Churches*, Batsford, London 1986, pp. 14–15.

2: George R. Lewis, *Illustrations of Kilpeck*, London, 1842, p. 15.

3: *Sheela na Gig*, James O'Connor, Fethard Historical Society, 1991, p. 6–7; John O'Donovan, *Ordnance Survey Letters, Co. Tipperary* (typed copy), Dublin, 1840, p. 152.

4: R. A. S. Macalister, 'Temair Breg: A Study of the Remains and Traditions of Tara', *PRIA*, Vol. 24 C, 1919, p. 231.

5: G. T. Stokes, 'Figures known as Hags of the Castle', *JRSAI*, Vol. XXIV, 1894, pp. 77–81 & pp. 392–394.

6: E. M. Guest, 'Ballyvourney and its Sheela-na-Gig', *Folklore*, Vol. 48, 1937, p. 375.

7: E. M. Guest, 'Some Notes on the Dating of Sheela-na-Gigs' *JRSAI*, Vol. VII, 1937, p. 176.

8: Jorgen Andersen, *The Witch on the Wall: Medieval Erotic Sculpture in the British Isles*, Allen & Unwin, London 1977, p. 113.

9: By Professor A. L. Hutchinson and G. E. Hutchinson, the list, illustrations and a distribution map is contained in their publications of the Binstead Idol in *Proceedings of the Isle of Wight Natural History and Archaeological Society*, Vol. VI part IV, 1970, pp. 240–46 and plates I a-c, II a–g.

10: Jorgen Andersen, *The Witch on the Wall: Medieval Erotic Sculpture in the British Isles*, Allen & Unwin, London 1977.

2: TRADITION, FOLKLORE AND POPULAR BELIEF

1: J. O'Connor, *Sheela na Gig*, Fethard Historical Society 1991, p. 15

2: John O'Donovan, *Ordnance Survey Letters, Co. Tipperary* (typed copy), Dublin, 1840, p. 142.

3: E. M. Guest, 'Some notes on the dating of Sheela-na-Gigs' *JRSAI*, Vol. VII, 1937, p. 127.

4: *Ibid.*, p. 128.

5: J. O'Connor, *Sheela na Gig*, Fethard Historical Society 1991, p. 15 – this instance of its use was related by Nóra Ní Shuilliobháin to the *Irish Times* in 1977.

6: John O'Donovan, *Ordnance Survey Letters, Co. Tipperary* (typed copy), Dublin, 1840, Vol. 1, pp. 152–153. In the report on the Kiltinan figure he used *Sile Ni Ghig* and *Sheela ni Ghig*, whilst in a later letter from Nenagh on 18 October 1840 he used the variation *Sheela Ny Gigg*.

7: Thomas Wright, *The Worship of the Generative Powers During the Middle Ages of Western Europe* (1866), in *Sexual Symbolism, A History of Phallic Worship*, Julian Press, New York, 1957, p. 35.

8: Patrick Dinneen, *Irish Dictionary*, Irish Text Society, 1927; Síle is defined as 'Julia; an effeminate or uxorious man; a boy too fond of girls' society, a girl too fond of being with boys'.

9: *Ibid.*

10: S. Cherry, *A Guide to Sheela-na-Gigs*, National Museum, Dublin 1992, p. 2.

11: Janet and Colin Bord, *Earth Rites*, Granada Publishing, 1982, p. 69.

12: M. Harrison, *The Roots of Witchcraft*, Muller, London 1973 and T. C. Lethbridge, *Gogmagog, The Hidden Gods*, Melrose, London 1957.

13: An interesting instance of the use of *Síle Ní* is given in a poem by Tadhg Ua Súilliobháin called 'Sighile ni Ghadharadh', 'where *Sighile* is an allegory for *Éire* once beautiful, now despoiled but with the inevitable salvation (of her rightful Prince) on the horizon'.

14: Johann Georg Kohl, *Reisen in Irland*, 1–2, Dresden, 1843, Vol. 2, p. 207 in J. Andersen, *The Witch on the Wall: Medieval Erotic Sculpture in the British Isles*, Allen & Unwin, London 1977, p. 23.

15: E. Guest, *JRSAI*, series 7, Vol. 6. 1936, p. 127.

16: A. Weir & J. Jerman, *Images of Lust*, London 1986, p. 15.

17: James O'Connor gives a similar story relating to a travelling-woman and a policeman is also recalled by Pádraig Ó Mathuna of Cashel. James O'Connor, *Sheela na Gig*, 1991, p. 19.

18: John Windele, *Topography of Cork West and Northeast*, manuscript in The Royal Irish Academy, Dublin, p. 710.

19: J. Byrne, 'The Parishes of Templeroan and Wallstown', *Journal of the Cork Historical and Archaeological Society*, Vol. 8, 1902, p. 87.

20: Richard Worsley, *The History of the Isle of Wight*, London 1781, p. 216; Andersen, p. 30.

21: E. Clibborn, 'An Ancient Stone Image called Sheela-na-Gig at Lavey', *PRIA*, Vol. 11, 1840–44, p. 565.

22: E. Rynne, 'A Sheela-na-Gig at Clonlaragh', *Munster Antiquarian Journal*, 1967, p. 221.

23: This is according to information given by a Mr Cooke in F. R. Montgomery Hitchcock, *The Midland Septs and the Pale*, Dublin, 1908, pp. 30–31.

24: E. Guest, *JRSAI*, 1935, p. 114.

25: *Ibid.*

26: J. O'Connor, *Sheela na Gig*, Fethard Historical Society 1991, p. 11.

27: E. Guest, 'Ballyvourney and its Sheela-na-Gig', *Folklore*, Vol. 48, 1937, p. 357.

28: *Ibid.*, p. 376.

29: *Ibid.*

30: *Ibid.*, p. 380.

31: J. Grove White, 'Historical and topographical notes on Buttevant ...' *JCHAS*, 1905.

32: Andersen, p. 88.

33: *Ibid.*, p. 29.

34: *Ibid*, p. 130.

3: THE ROMANESQUE CONNECTION

1: Andersen, p. 53.

2: A. Weir and J. Jerman, p. 4.

3: Andersen, p. 39.

4: A. Weir and J. Jerman, p. 17; pp. 145–150.

5: E. P. Kelly, *Sheela-na-Gigs, Origins and Functions*, National Museum, Dublin, 1996, p. 10.

6: Andersen, p. 129.

7: A. Weir, 'Exhibitionist and related carvings ...', p. 62.

8: Etienne Rynne, 'A Pagan Celtic Backrgound for Sheela-na-Gigs', in *Figures from the Past: Studies of Figurative Art in Christian Ireland in Honour of Helen M. Roe*, ed. E. Rynne, Glendale Press, Ireland, 1987, pp. 198–199.

4: IRISH PROTOTYPES

1: E. Bhreathnach, and C. Newman, *The Discovery Programme*, Tara, 1995, Government Publications, p. 52.

2: Etienne Rynne, 'A Pagan Celtic Backrgound for Sheela-na-Gigs', in *Figures from the Past*, ed. E. Rynne, 1987, pp. 194.

3: A. Weir, 'Exhibitionist and Related Carvings in the Irish Midlands, Their Origin and Function', in H. Murtagh (ed.) *Irish Midland Studies: Essays in Commemoration of N. W. English*, 1980, p. 2.

4: John Feehan, *The Landscape of Slieve Bloom*, Blackwater Press, Dublin 1979.

5: W. F. Wakeman, 'On the church of White Island', *JRSAI*, Vol. 15, 1879–82, p. 283.

6: E. Guest, *Folklore*, Vol. 48, 1937, p. 387. It is possible that the figures may have come from the wooden churches on Lough Erne that were apparently burnt down in 837 AD.

7: O'Connor, p. 20.

8: H. C. Lawlor, 'Grotesque Carvings Improperly called Sheela-na-Gigs', *The Irish Naturalists Journal*, Vol. I, No. 9, 1927, p. 182.

9: The identification of this small figure depicted in a scene as being among the damned in the Last Judgment cannot be incontrovertibly seen as a Sheela or as even belonging to the Sheela class.

10: E. Guest, 1935, p. 115.

11: Etienne Rynne, *A Pagan Celtic Background for Sheela-na-Gigs?* Glendale Press, Ireland, 1987, p. 190.

12: *Ibid.*

13: *Ibid.*, p. 191.

14: *Ibid.*, p. 194.

15: J. Love, 'An Ancient Ivory Carving of Sheela-na-Gig found near Annagh, Co. Tipperary', *JRSAI*, 1874–75, p. 241.

16: Chris Corlett, 'Christian Head Cult?' *Archaeology Ireland*, Winter 1998, Vol. 12, No. 4, Issue No. 46, p. 17.

17: A. Weir and J. Jerman, p. 14.

18: Daragh Smyth, *A Guide to Irish Mythology*, 1988, p. 135.

19: J. Michelle, *Sacred England*, Gothic Image, Glastonbury, 1996, p. 14.

20: Rynne, 1987, pp. 198–199.

5: THE HAG OF THE CASTLE

1: Liam de Paor, *The Peoples of Ireland*, London 1986, p. 103.

2: *Ibid.*, p. 99.

3: P. Harbison, *Guide to the National Monuments of Ireland*, Dublin 1970 edition.

4: The first great love poet in the Gaelic language was a Norman by the name of Fitzgerald, Earl of Desmond (1363–98). E. Kelly, *Sheela-na-Gigs – Origins and Functions*, The National Museum of Ireland, 1996, p. 45.

5: A. Siggins, 'Heads and Tails of Stone', *Journal of the Roscommon Historical Association*, 1990, pp. 45–48.

6: Andersen, pp. 124–125.

7: *Ibid.*, p. 107.

8: John Windele, manuscript in RIA Library, Dublin, p. 710; Andersen, p. 14.

9: M. A. Ashton, 'Sheela na Gig at Fiddington', *Somerset Archaeological and Historical Society*, 1980, p. 113.

10: Andersen, p. 111.

11: Just inside the doorway of Kilnaboy church is a strange, half animal-looking figure which is employed on its side as a later addition to the church.

12: Andersen, p. 108.

13: J. Feehan & G. Cunningham, 'An Undescribed Exhibitionist Figure from Co. Laois', *JRSAI*, Vol. 108, 1978, pp. 117–8.

6: THE MYTHOLOGY OF THE SHEELAS

1: J. O'Connor, p. 21.
2: Anne Ross, *Pagan Celtic Britain*, Routledge, Kegan, Paul, London/ Columbia University Press, New York 1967, p. 146.
3: M. Green, *Celtic Goddesses*, British Museum Press, London 1995, pp. 84–5
4: Etienne Rynne, 1987, p. 194.
5: P. Mac Cana, *Celtic Mythology*, Newnes Books, Middlesex, 1985, p. 86.
6: E. Guest, *Folklore*, Vol. 48, 1937, p. 382.
7: The Clifford Collection, RIA Library, Dublin, *PRIA*, 1840–44.
8: Andersen, p. 95.
9: Cross and Slover, *Ancient Irish Tales*, Harrap, 1937, p. 431.
10: Nuala Ní Dhomhnaill, 'Sheelagh in her Cabin', in *From Beyond the Pale, Art and Artists at the Edge of Consensus*, Irish Museum of Modern Art, Dublin 1994, p. 55.
11: Mac Cana, p. 121.

7: FROM GODDESS TO SAINT

1: Mary Condren, *The Serpent and the Goddess*, Harper and Row, San Francisco, 1989, p. 65.
2: Brigit's clan is the Tuatha Dé Danann yet she is married to their arch enemy, the Fomorian King Bresso.
3: Seamus Ó Catháin, *The Festival of Brigit, Celtic Goddess and Holy Woman*, DBA Publications Ltd, Dublin 1995, p. 57.
4: E. Guest, *Folklore*, Vol. XLVIII, 1937, p. 383.
5: E. Guest, *Folklore*, Vol. 48, 1937, p. 3.
6: E. Guest, *JRSAI*, 7, Vol. 6. 1936 p. 116; The Sheela is carved on a quoin stone, so her original setting would not have been the holy well.
7: S. Ó Catháin, p. 73.
8. Janet and Colin Bord, p. 75.
9: *Ibid.*, p. 75. Professor Geoffrey Webb found a male organ carved in stone inside an altar. This led him to look at other altars of ruined churches that he was surveying with a view to restoration.

8: THE SYMBOLOGY OF THE SHEELA-NA-GIGS

1: Miranda Green, *Symbol and Image in Celtic Religious Art*, Routledge, London 1989, p. 169.
2: Margaret Killip, *The Folklore of the Isle of Man*, Batsford, London 1975, p. 176.
3: H. P. Brewster, 'Saints and Festivals of the Christian Church', 1904, p. 13, in Barbara Walker, *The Women's Encyclopaedia of Myths and Secrets*, Castle Books, New Jersey, USA, 1996, p. 1045.
4: Professor D. Fraser, 'The Heraldic Woman' in *The Many Faces of Primi-*

tive Art, ed. Douglas Fraser, New Jersey, 1966, p. 81; Andersen, p. 137.

5:   Mac Cana, p. 58. Another instance of this is 'Queen Medb [who] turned the six posthumous children of Cailin into witches and warlocks, destroying one arm, one leg and one eye of each. She arranged their training in magic ... and they were instruments of Cúchulainn's death.'

6:   A. Siggins, 'Heads and Tails of Stone', *Journal of the Roscommon Historical Association*, 1990, p. 45.

7:   Green, p. 129.

8:   *Ibid.*, p. 129.

9:   For more details on this see Andersen, fig. 84, p. 123.

10: Andersen, p. 106.

11: Anne Ross, *Pagan Celtic Britain*, 1967, p. 117.

12: John Feehan, *The Landscape of Slieve Bloom*, p. 159.

13: Heritage Guide, No. 4, The Beltany Stone Circle, *Archaeology Ireland*. The head was found in close proximity to the stone circle of Beltany, Co. Donegal.

14: P. Power, *Sex and Marriage in Ancient Ireland*, Mercier Press, reprinted 1993, Cork & Dublin, p. 78.

15: Andersen, p. 125–6.

16: Andersen, p. 126–7.

17: Eamonn Kelly, *Sheela-na-Gigs. Origins and Functions*, 1996, p. 34.

18: Green, p. 163; A recent example of this is the banshee, who is often seen holding a comb or combing her long hair and there are several stories connected to the loss of her principle symbol, the comb.

19: R. Bailey, 'Apotropaic Figures in Milan and North-West England', *Folklore*, Vol. 94, 1983, p. 114. According to this article shears in Medieval England were used as a symbol of woman.

20: Andersen, p. 89.

21: For example in the 'Táin Bó Cuálgne', just before the great encounter, the Goddess Medb requires to urinate and in doing so she forms three great dykes 'so that a mill could find room in each dyke', and the place became known afterwards as *Fual Medbe*, 'Medb's Urine'. That the dykes were so large is no surprise as Medb did have an enormous sexual capacity, on an average going through 'thirty men in a day or Fergus once'.

22: Máire Herbert, 'Transmutations of an Irish Goddess', in *The Concept of the Goddess*, Routledge, 1996, p. 145.

23: *Ibid.*, p. 147.

24: Andersen, p. 77.

9: THE SHEELA-NA-GIG ARCHETYPE

1:   E. Guest, 'Some Notes on the Dating of Sheela-na-Gigs', *JRSAI*, 1937.

2:   Margaret Murray, 'Female Fertility Figures', *Journal of the Royal Anthro-*

pological Institute of Great Britain and Ireland, Vol. 64, 1934, p. 94.

3:   *Ibid.,* p. 95; many Baubo figures were brought from Cairo by German scholars at the turn of the century and are best seen in the museums in Berlin.

4:   A. Weir & J. Jerman, p. 113.

5:   *Ibid.*

6:   *Ibid.,* p. 114.

7:   Leroi-Gourhan, André, *The Art of Prehistoric Man,* Thames and Hudson, London, 1968, p. 296.

8:   Marija Gimbutas, *Language of the Goddess,* Thames and Hudson, London, 1989, p. 106.

9:   *Ibid.,* p. 106.

10: *Ibid.,* p. 101.

11: *Ibid.,* p. 193.

12: *Ibid.,* p. 253.

13: H. Kramer & J. Sprenger, *Malleus Maleficarum,* Dover Publications, New York, 1971, p. 776.

14   Gimbutas, 1989, p. 253

15: *Ibid.*

16: G. Chaloupka, *Burrunguy,* Northart, Australia, p. 8.

17: Andersen, p. 131.

18: *Ibid.,* p. 132.

CATALOGUE – IRELAND

1:   D. Keeling, 'An Unrecorded Exhibitionist Figure (Sheela-na-Gig) from Ardcath, County Meath', *Riocht na Midhe,* Vol. 7 (3), 1984, pp. 102–4.

2:   J. Feehan & G. Cunningham, 'An Undescribed Exhibitionist Figure from Co. Laois', *JRSAI,* Vol. 108, 1978, pp. 117.

3:   John O'Donovan, *Ordnance Survey Letters, Tipperary II,* typed copy.

4:   Andersen, p. 28.

5:   J. Byrne, *Journal of the Cork Historical and Archaeological Society,* Vol. 8, 1902, p. 87.

6:   Windele manuscript, RIA Library, Dublin, Vol. 12 I 10, p. 710.

7:   C. O'Brien and P. D. Sweetman, *Archeological Inventory of Co. Offaly,* 1997, OPW, Dublin, p. 143.

8:   E. Guest, *JRSAI,* Vol. IX,1939, p. 48.

9:   A. Weir, 'Exhibitionist and Related Carvings in the Irish Midlands, Their Origin and Function', in H. Murtagh (ed.) *Irish Midland Studies: Essays in Commemoration of N. W. English,* 1980, p. 71.

10: Andersen, p. 146.

11: E. Guest, *JRSAI,* Vol. 66, 1936, p. 116.

12: F. R. M. Hitchcock, *The Midland Septs and the Pale,* Dublin, 1908, pp. 30–1.

13: Hitchcock, p. 30.

14: Andersen, p. 106.
15. E. Rynne, 1967, p. 221.
16: Guest, 'Irish Sheela-na-Gigs in 1935', *JRSAI*, series 7, VI, 1936, p. 117.
17: Andersen, p. 148.
18: *Ancient Monuments of Northern Ireland*, Vol. I, 1966, p. 99.
19: Andersen, p. 82.
20: O'Connor, p. 13.
21: A. Weir, 'Exhibitionist and Related Carvings in the Irish Midlands, Their Origin and Function', in H. Murtagh (ed.) *Irish Midland Studies: Essays in commemoration of N. W. English*, 1980, p. 65.
22: C. Manning, 'A Sheela-na-Gig from Glanworth Castle, Co. Cork', in *Figures from the Past: Studies of Figurative Art in Christian Ireland in Honour of Helen M. Roe*, ed. E. Rynne, Glendale Press, Ireland, 1987, p. 279.
23: Andersen, p. 119.
24: P. Lyons, *JRSAI*, Vol. LXVII, 1937, p. 127.
25: *Ibid.*, p. 24.
26: Guest, 'Irish Sheela-na-Gigs in 1935', *JRSAI*, series 7, VI, 1936, p. 118.
27: *Journal of the Kerry Archaeological and Historical Society*, Vol. VI, 1973, p. 23.
28: O'Connor, pp. 4–11.
29: Guest, 'Irish Sheela-na-Gigs in 1935', *JRSAI*, series 7, VI, 1936, p. 104.
30: Guest, 'Irish Sheela-na-Gigs in 1935', *JRSAI*, series 7, VI, 1936, p. 110.
31: Guest, 'Irish Sheela-na-Gigs in 1935', *JRSAI*, series 7, VI, 1936, p. 119.
32: Austin Cooper's notes as quoted in Guest, *JRSAI*, Vol. 6, 1936, p. 111.
33: P. J. Hartnett, 'Malahide Abbey', *JRSAI*, Vol. 84, 1954, p. 179, pl. xxvii.
34: Andersen, p. 150.
35: Guest,'Irish Sheela-na-Gigs in 1935', *JRSAI*, series 7, VI, 1936, p. 114
36: Guest, 'Irish Sheela-na-Gigs in 1935', *JRSAI*, series 7, VI, 1936, p. 111.
37: A. Weir, 'Exhibitionist and Related Carvings in the Irish Midlands, Their Origin and Function', in H. Murtagh (ed.) *Irish Midland Studies: Essays in Commemoration of N. W. English*, 1980, p. 67.
38: Guest, 'Irish Sheela-na-Gigs in 1935', *JRSAI*, series 7, VI, 1936, p. 117.
39: Andersen, p. 151; D. N. Johnson, 'Sheela-na-Gig at Rahan', *JRSAI*, Vol. Cl, pt 2, 1972, p. 169.
40: M. Murray, 'Female Fertility Figures' *Journal of the Royal Anthropological Institute*, LXVIV, 1934, plate X, figure 21.
41: Guest, 'Irish Sheela-na-Gigs in 1935', *JRSAI*, series 7, VI, 1936, p. 113.
42: Guest,'Irish Sheela-na-Gigs in 1935', *JRSAI*, series 7, VI, 1936, p. 115.
43: R. P. Colles in an untitled communication in *PRIA* 1840.
44: M. Murray, 'Female Fertility Figures' *Journal of the Royal Anthropological Institute*, Vol. LXVIV, 1934, pl. x, fig. 21.
45: Guest, 'Irish Sheela-na-Gigs in 1935', *JRSAI*, series 7, VI, 1936, p. 114.
46: Andersen, p. 152.

47: *Ibid.*

48: G. T. Stokes, *JRSAI*, Vol. XXIV, 1894, p. 80 and p. 393 – 'a grotesque figure requiring further inquiry'; Andersen, p. 152.

49: Photograph was published in *Man*, Vol. XXX11, 1932, p. 45.

BRITAIN

1: Andersen, p. 140.

2: *Ibid.*

3: *Ibid.*, p. 30; Worsley, *The History of the Isle of Wight*, 1781, p. 216.

4: Andersen, p. 140.

5: *Ibid.*

6: *Ibid.*, p. 141.

7: *Ibid.*

8: J. Harding, Sheela-na-Gig website – www.jharding.co.uk..

9: *Ibid.*

10: *Ibid.*

11: Andersen, p. 141.

12: J. Satchell, 'The Pennington Sheela-na-Gig', *Kendall Parish Magazine*, information booklet. Information supplied by J. Tripos.

13: K. and G. Jones

14: R. Bailey, 'Apotropaic Figures in Milan and North-West England', *Folklore*, Vol. 94: I, 1983, p. 114.

15: *Ibid.*, p. 116.

16: *Ibid.*, p. 113.

17: Andersen, p. 142.

18: S. Jackson, *Celtic and other Stone Heads*, Batsford, London 1973, p. 37, fig. 60.

19: Andersen, p. 11.

20: *Ibid.*

21: J. Satchell, 'The Pennington Sheela-na-Gig', *Kendall Parish Magazine*, p. 20.

22: M. Murray, p. 98.

23: Andersen, p. 129.

24: S. Piggot, *William Stuckley*, Thames and Hudson, London, 1950, p. 121.

25: Andersen, p. 143.

26: M. Murray, p. 98.

27: C. J. P. Cave, *Roof Bosses in Medieval Churches*, CUP, Cambridge, 1948, p. 214.

28: Andersen, p. 144.

29: W. J. Hemp, 'Some unrecorded Sheela-na-Gigs in Wales and the Border', *Archaeologia Cambrensis*, Vol. XCIII, Cardiff, 1938, p. 136.

30: Andersen, p. 142.

31 *Ibid.*, p. 143.

RELATED FIGURES

1: H. C. Lawlor, *Irish Naturalists Journal*, Vol. I, No. 9, 1927, pp. 182–184.
2: A photograph of the figure is published in an article by A. Weir, 'Exhibitionists and related carvings ...', in H. Murtagh (ed.) *Irish Midland Studies: Essays in commemoration of N. W. English*, pl. 18.
3:: Guest, 'Irish Sheela-na-Gigs in 1935', *JRSAI*, series 7, VI, 1936, p. 114.
4: Etienne Rynne, 'A Pagan Celtic Backrgound for Sheela-na-Gigs', in *Figures from the Past: Studies of Figurative Art in Christian Ireland in Honour of Helen M. Roe*, ed. E. Rynne, Glendale Press, Ireland, 1987, p. 196.
5: Guest, 'Irish Sheela-na-Gigs in 1935', p. 115.
6: Andersen, p. 153; Guest, 'Irish Sheela-na-Gigs in 1935', p. 111.
7: W. F. Wakeman, 'On the church of White Island', *JRSAI*, Vol. 15, 1879–82, p. 283.
8: J. A. Jerman, 'Simulation or Dissimulation? A figure from the Brooke Collection', Wiltshire Field Magazine, Vol. 76, 1981, p. 171.
9: *Ibid.*, p. 172.
10: A. Weir and J. Jerman, p. 116.
11: *Ibid.*, p. 39.

BIBLIOGRAPHY

JRSAI *Journal of the Royal Society of Antiquaries of Ireland*
PRIA *Proceedings of the Royal Irish Academy*

Andersen, J. 'Sheela-na-Gig at Clenagh Castle, Co. Clare', *North Munster Antiquarian Journal*, Vol. 19, 1976.
——. *The Witch on the Wall: Medieval Erotic Sculpture in the British Isles*. Allen & Unwin, London 1977
Aston, M. A. 'A Sheila-na-Gig at Fiddington', *Somerset Archaeology and Natural History*, Vol. 123, 1979.
Bailey, R. N. 'Apotropaic Figures in Milan and North-West England', *Folklore*, Vol. 94, No. 1, 1983.
Barrow, G. L. *The Round Towers of Ireland*. Academy Press, Dublin, 1979
Bord, J. & C. *Earth Rites*. Granada, London 1982
Byrne, J. 'The Parishes of Templeroan and Wallstown', *Journal of the Cork Historical and Archeological Society*, Vol. 8, 1902.
Cherry, S. 'Sheela-na-Gigs from County Cork', *Journal of the Cork Historical and Archeological Society*, Vol. 98, 1993.
Cherry, S., *A Guide to Sheela-na-Gigs*, National Museum, Dublin 1992,
Clark, R. 'The Great Queens: Irish Goddesses from the Morrighan to Cathleen Ni Houlihan', *Irish Literary Studies*, No. 34, 1991
Clibborn, E. 'An Ancient Stone Image called Sheela-na-Gig at Lavey', *PRIA*, Vol. 11, 1840–44.
Condren, Mary. *The Serpent and the Goddess: Women, Religion, and Power in Celtic Ireland*. Harper and Row, US 1989
Cross, T. P. & Slover, C. H. *Ancient Irish Tales* [a collection of translations]. Harrap, London 1937.
Dobson, D. 'Primitive Figures on Churches', *Man*, Vol. XXX, No. 8, 1930.
Feehan, J. *The Landscape of Slieve Bloom*. Blackwater Press, Dublin 1979
——. & Cunningham, G. 'An Undescribed Exhibitionist Figure from Co. Laois', *JRSAI*, Vol. 108, 1978.
Gleeson, D. F. 'Sheela-na-Gig at Burgesbeg, Co. Tipperary', *JRSAI*, Vol. IX, 1939.
Goodwin, J. P. 'Sheila-na-Gigs and Christian Saints', *Folklore*, Vol. LXXX, 1969.
Green, M. *Symbol and Image in Celtic Religious Art*. Routledge, London 1989.
——. *Celtic Goddesses, Warriors, Virgins and Mothers*. British Museum Press, London 1995.
Guest, E. M. 'Irish Sheela-na-Gigs in 1935', *JRSAI*, series 7, Vol. VI, 1936.
——. 'Some Notes on the Dating of Sheela-na-Gigs', *JRSAI*, Vol. VII, 1937.

——. 'Ballyvourney and its Sheela-na-Gig', *Folklore*, Vol. XLVIII, 1937.

——. 'A Sheela-na-Gig at Clonmacnoise', *JRSAI*, Vol. IX, 1939.

Hartnett, P. J. 'Sheela-na-Gig at Malahide Abbey, Co. Dublin', *JRSAI*, Vol. 84, 1954.

Hickey, H. *Images of Stone*, Blackstaff, Belfast, 1976.

Hitchcock, F. R. M. *The Midland Septs and the Pale*. Dublin, 1908.

Hutchinson, A. L. & G. E. 'The 'Idol' or Sheela-na-gig at Binstead', *Proceedings of the Isle of Wight Natural History and Archaeological Society*, Vol. VI part IV, 1970.

Jackson, S. *Celtic and Other Stone Heads*, Batsford, London 1973.

Jerman, J. 'The Sheela-na-Gig Carvings of the British Isles; Suggestions for a Reclassification, and Other Notes', *County Louth Archeological Society*, 1981.

Johnson, D. N. 'Sheela-na-Gig at Rahan, Co. Offaly', *JRSAI*, Vol. V, 1972.

Keeling, D. 'An Unrecorded Exhibitionist Figure (Sheela-na-Gig) from Ardcath, County Meath', *Riocht na Midhe*, Vol. 7, No. 3, 1984.

Kelly, E. P. *Sheela-na-Gigs – Origins and Functions*. The National Museum of Ireland, Dublin 1996.

Kohl, J. G. *Reisen in Irland*, 1–2. Vol. 2, Dresden 1843.

Lacy, B., et. al., *Archeological Survey of County Donegal*. Donegal County Council, Lifford 1983.

Lawlor, H. C. 'Grotesque Carvings Improperly called Sheela-na-Gigs', *The Irish Naturalists Journal*, Vol. I, No. 9, 1927.

Lawlor, H. C. 'Two Typical Sheela-na-Gigs', *Man*, Vol. XXXI, No. 4, London 1931.

——. 'Two More Irish Sheela-na-Gigs', *Man*, Vol. XXXII, No. 49, London 1932.

Love, J. 'An Ancient Ivory Carving of Sheela-na-Gig found near Annagh, County Tipperary', *JRSAI*, Vol.XIII, 1874–75.

Lyons, P. 'Sheela-na-Gig at Kilmacommon, Co. Waterford', *JRSAI*, Vol. LXVII, 1937.

Mac Cana, P. *Celtic Mythology*. Newnes Books, London 1985.

Manning, C. 'A Sheela-na-Gig from Glanworth Castle, Co, Cork', in Rynne E. (ed) *Figures from the Past: Studies of Figurative Art in Christian Ireland in Honour of Helen M. Roe*. Glendale Press, Ireland 1987.

Minahane, J. *The Christian Druids*, Dublin [privately published].

Murray, M. 'Female Fertility Figures', *Journal of the Royal Anthropological Institute of Great Britain and Ireland*, Vol. 64, 1934.

Ní Dhomhnaill, N. 'Sheelagh in her Cabin', in *From Beyond the Pale, Art and Artists at the Edge of Consensus*. Irish Museum of Modern Art, Dublin 1994.

Ó Catháin, S. *The Festival of Brigit, Celtic Goddess and Holy Woman*. DBA Publications Ltd., Dublin 1995.

O'Connor, J. *Sheela-na-Gig*. Fethard Historical Society, Co. Tipperary 1991

O'Doherty, S. 'Sheela-na-Gig at Cooliagh', *Old Kilkenny Review*, New Series, Vol. 2, No. 1, 1979.

O'Donovan, J. *Ordnance Survey Letters, County Tipperary* (typed copy), Dublin 1840, Vol. 1.

Piggot, S. 'A primitive carving from Anglesey', *Man*, Vol. XXX, 1930.

Ross, A. *Pagan Celtic Britain*. Routledge, Kegan, Paul, London/Columbia University Press, New York 1967.

Rynne, E. 'A Sheela-na-Gig at Clonlara, Co. Clare', *North Munster Antiquarian Journal*. Vol. 10, 1967.

——. 'A Pagan Celtic Background for Sheela-na-Gigs?' in Rynne E. (ed) *Figures from the Past: Studies of Figurative Art in Christian Ireland in Honour of Helen M. Roe.*, Glendale Press, Ireland 1987.

Siggins, A. 'Heads and Tails of Stone', *Journal of the Roscommon Historical and Archaeological Society*, Vol. 3, 1990.

Smyth, D. *A Guide to Irish Mythology*, Irish Academic Press, Dublin 1988

Stokes, G. T. 'Carved Female found in Early Churches, Castle, etc.' (Supplement List) *JRSAI*, Vol. XXIV, 1894.

——. 'Figures Known as Hags of the Castle, Sheelas or Sheela-na-Gigs', *JRSAI*, Vol. XXIV, 1894.

Wakeman, W. F. 'On the Church of White Island', *JRSAI*, Vol. 15. 1879–82.

Weir, A. 'Exhibitionists and related carvings in the Irish midlands: their origins and functions', in H. Murtagh (ed.) *Irish Midland Studies: Essays in commemoration of N. W. English*, Athlone 1980.

Weir, A. & Jerman J. *Images of Lust – Sexual Carvings on Medieval Churches.* Batsford, London 1986.

Windele, John, 'Topography of Cork West and Northeast', MS in The Royal Irish Academy, Dublin.

Worsley, R. *The History of the Isle of Wight*. London 1781.

Wright, T. 'The Worship of the Generative Powers during the Middle Ages of Western Europe (1866)', in *Sexual Symbolism, A History of Phallic Worship*. (ed. Knight & Wright), Julian Press, New York 1957.